THE VOCATIONAL QUEST

Government attempts in recent years to create a national system of vocational education and training have marked a profound shift both in educational policy and in underlying concepts of the purpose of education. Relations between schools and the working world are changing all the time and the implementation of ideas of vocationalism has forced a blurring of the time-honoured boundaries between education concerned with concepts, and training concerned with skills. The challenge now is to define how schools can give young people the foundations for life in a working world in which they are likely to have to change jobs and where work will fill a smaller proportion of their lives than ever before. Meeting the challenge will require profound changes in the educational and training systems in the direction of a core of fundamental studies for all young people and a more broadly based approach to training. *The Vocational Quest* critically assesses the evolution of vocationalism in Britain in historical terms and examines how the particular forms that have come into being in the last few years compare with developments in other parts of the world, including Continental Europe, Japan, the United States, Australia and New Zealand. It argues for new forms of communication and partnership between formal education and training and the wider community, in which values will be shared and no one partner will win at the expense of the others.

Malcolm Skilbeck is Deputy Director responsible for Education and Training at the OECD, Paris. **Helen Connell** is a freelance educational consultant and researcher. **Nicholas Lowe** is a Policy Analyst for Westminster City Council. **Kirsteen Tait** is London Director of the Open School.

KEY ISSUES IN EDUCATION
Series Editor: Robert Burgess, University of Warwick

THE VOCATIONAL QUEST

New directions in education and training

Malcolm Skilbeck, Helen Connell,
Nicholas Lowe and Kirsteen Tait

London and New York

First published 1994
by Routledge
11 New Fetter Lane, London EC4P 4EE

Simultaneously published in the USA and Canada
by Routledge
29 West 35th Street, New York, NY 10001

© 1994 Malcolm Skilbeck, Helen Connell, Nicholas Lowe and Kirsteen Tait

Typeset in Baskerville by LaserScript, Mitcham, Surrey
Printed and bound in Great Britain by
Mackays of Chatham PLC, Chatham, Kent

British Library Cataloguing in Publication Data
A catalogue record for this book is available from the British Library

Library of Congress Cataloging in Publication Data
The Vocational Quest: new directions in education and training/
Malcolm Skilbeck . . . [*et al.*].
p. cm. – (Key issues in education.)
Includes bibliographical references and index.
1. Vocational education – Great Britain. I. Skilbeck, Malcolm.
II. Series.
LC1047.G7V63   1994
374'.941 – dc20   93-40797
CIP
ISBN 0–415–10915–9

CONTENTS

FOREWORD

Of the many reforms and changes of direction that have marked English educational policy and practice in recent decades, none has been more profound in purpose and effect than endeavours to create a new national system of vocational education and training. The explanation reflects more than a century of concern over Britain's industrial performance and, in more recent decades, economic weakness. More than this, however, the new vocationalism represents a profound challenge to an aristocratic and effete culture that, whatever its past merits, has weakened the country and resulted in educational and training systems that are simply inadequate to meet the challenges of the emerging global order.

As for the term 'new vocationalism', that raises as many questions as it answers. We have used it, consistently we hope, to refer to a complex amalgam of ideas, policies, legal and regulatory structures and practical endeavours whereby the nation's education and training systems have been reformed and restructured through government-led, partnership-type initiatives. These reforms, not all successful, have had as their principal purpose greater partici-pation, especially by young school-leavers who are ill-equipped for either working life or further education, and an improved quality and relevance of the various schemes and arrangements put in place to foster and encourage continued engagement in some kind of employment-focused education and training. It is 'new' not so much because of individual components, such as work-based, broadly defined training, and partnerships between employers, training authorities, government and employment agencies, but because of the concerted drive to bring these and other elements together in highly visible and well-financed schemes. The new vocationalism which focused on work preparation or work-focused training has extended into schools to present a broad orientation and more positive attitudes towards working life. The ancient distinctions between education and training are, as a conse-quence, becoming blurred: skills, for example, often treated as the province of training – concepts perhaps being the counterpart in education – are now as much regarded as a function of education, just as conceptual development is seen as an important part of the generic training needed in the future.

The recency as well as the extent of several of the most significant of these changes in the vocational sphere means that it will be many years before their full impact is felt or their significance can be adequately appraised. This does not, however, absolve us from the responsibility of trying to make sense of the changes occurring in our midst. Nor should we shy away from appraisal and judgement since, lacking these, policy-makers and practitioners have no means of testing the value of their endeavours against alternative perspectives be they comparative or historical. Thus in this book we attempt to map the evolution of ideas about vocational education, compare them with developments in other countries and relate them to the mainstream educational thinking of which training is, after all, but a part.

Our efforts to make sense of the numerous courses and qualifications that have proliferated in Britain in recent years illustrates the scale of strategic moves, at the national level, entailing various kinds of partnership with industry and the educational and training institutions, to build a comprehensive and coherent national system out of the miscellaneous legacy from the nineteenth and much of the twentieth centuries. If governments and their agents can be criticised for the limitations of what they have as yet achieved in this regard, they can be commended for the seriousness and determination, now extending over several decades, with which they have addressed a set of long overdue and most complex tasks. But it is not our objective to praise Caesar any more than to bury him. Many more tasks remain to be accomplished before Britain can feel content that it has in place a robust, healthy system of education and training for all up to and including the years of early adulthood. No less than provision of the highest possible quality of education and training for all will suffice as a target.

Our starting point for this book was modest and our study has far outgrown its beginnings. In 1984 the Manpower Services Commission (MSC) requested the principal author, then at the University of London Institute of Education, to carry out a study of the Core Skills Project of the Youth Training Scheme (YTS) parallel to the development work on core skills and evaluation studies then under way. The MSC was interested in setting its inquiries into core skills in a wider educational context, that of general education on the one hand, and of vocational education and training developments in certain other countries on the other. From these beginnings, our analysis has led us back into what can only be termed the blunders and missed opportunities of the historical record, and outward more recently to the other vocational education and training initiatives, some of them in time eclipsing the Core Skills Project and the YTS itself. We have also reviewed, in brief order, some of the key developments and issues in vocational education in a selected group of other countries in the belief that, while literal transfer is seldom feasible, we have much to learn from the contemporary experiences of others as well as from our own history. Throughout the volume, authoritative national and international sources of education and training statistics have been used. Nevertheless, there is not always agreement among them, which reflects in part different procedures for calculating data and the categories by which they are classified.

Our aim throughout has been to pursue and as far as possible unravel the main threads which together constitute what we and others have termed the new vocationalism. Although we trace some of these threads from their historical origins and others on a comparative basis, our purpose is neither historical scholarship nor systematic comparison. Rather, it is to hold up mirrors, and thereby provide contexts which help to explain the direction taken in some of the major initiatives of recent years. Of these, the YTS, its meteoric rise to a glittering if short-lived spectacle of the firmament, is, in many respects, the centrepiece of the new vocationalism. One of the central ideas or underlying strategies in the YTS is core skills. Like the YTS itself, the idea of core skills was neither original nor able to meet all the hopes and expectations invested in it. Yet, its links with so much else in the new vocationalism and the wider developments in schooling, and its significance as a central organising construct in the overall strategy for youth training provide us with sufficient reason for the attention we give it.

However, the YTS is but one of several major moves taken by government and its agencies to strengthen Britain's endeavours in vocational education and training. Its dilution and perhaps disappearance are indeed already in sight. We need to see these several moves together, in order to understand the scope and the significance of the changes that have occurred. Such is the scale and range of activity, however, that no single study, unless it were to degenerate into a mere catalogue, can hope to encompass all the developments. Inevitably a choice has had to be made. The extensive bibliography not only documents the themes we have taken up, it also serves as a reference, albeit not a complete one, for the new vocationalism as it has emerged in the UK since the 1970s.

What, it will be asked, have the vast efforts and the massive resource inputs that have characterised government involvement in the new vocationalism achieved? Have the problems and deficiencies to which it was directed been sufficiently or adequately addressed? Have the sought-for changes been realised in practice? The issues are altogether too complex and the research base too limited for straightforward answers to be given, although some glib ones have been proffered, not least by official spokespeople. Appraisal is needed, but must be hedged about by qualification. Moreover, the vocationalising of education is a large-scale normative exercise with powerful overtones of state control which means that the assessment is more a matter of social, political and ethical values than it is of judgements about effectiveness and efficiency within some preconceived and uncontroversial normative framework. Indeed it is one of the features of the new vocationalism that a new normative framework for assessing the educational system as a whole has emerged and we are now moving in new worlds. Within the limitations of the new and unfamiliar, we have nevertheless, not confined ourselves to description, synthesis and exploration; but have offered our own judgements and appraisals as a critical reflection on both the goals and the ways of achieving them that have been advanced under the new vocationalism banner.

Notwithstanding the already considerable body of literature on the subject, there is need for more independent analyses of the new vocationalism than it has yet received. We indicate some of the directions that such inquiries might pursue: evaluation of outcomes and impact of individual programmes and schemes; studies of the assumptions and values underlying new structures and strategies; and research to establish teaching–learning processes that might seem best fitted to achieve the basic objectives that are summarily stated in much of the policy literature on the attributes sought for and needed by youth.

What started, in our case, as a limited inquiry into the nature and place of core skills in the YTS has greatly expanded, in recognition of the strategic significance of the concept of core skills in the new vocational movement and also in response to the scale and diversity of policy developments since the YTS was launched. For various reasons, this pace of change may be expected to slow, thus providing opportunity for systematic consolidation and for the kinds of research and analysis that are needed to give the whole movement the depth and quality that have been lacking.

Whilst acknowledging the difficulty of estimating the significance of the numerous policy statements and directions and keeping track of the constantly shifting landscape of practical activities, we believe that the new vocationalism requires the positive interest and vigilant attention of a well-informed public and education profession. The changes are of a scale and a kind that have implications far beyond the traditional domain of vocational training.

SERIES EDITOR'S PREFACE

Each volume in the *Key Issues in Education* series is designed to provide a precise, authoritative guide to a topic of current concern to teachers, researchers and educational policy-makers. The books in the series comprise an introduction to some of the key debates in the contemporary practice of education. In particular, each author demonstrates how the social sciences can help us to analyse, explain and understand educational issues. The books in the series review key debates, and the authors complement this material by making detailed reference to their own and others' research, which helps to illustrate the way research evidence in the social sciences and education can contribute to our understanding of educational policy and practice.

All the contributors to this series have extensive experience in their chosen field and have worked with teachers and other educational personnel. The volumes have been written to appeal to students who are intending to become teachers, working teachers who seek to familiarise themselves with new research and research evidence, social scientists who are engaged in the study of education, and policy-makers whose advice and decisions need to be well grounded both in empirical data and the views of key actors in the field. Each author seeks to make educational research and debate accessible to those engaged in the practice of education at these different levels. A bibliography is provided at the end of the volume for those who wish to pursue the topic in greater depth. The series provides a comprehensive guide to contemporary issues in education and demonstrates the importance of social science research for understanding educational practice.

This volume focuses on a key issue of international discussion, development and debate: vocational education and training. Using both historical and comparative methods and drawing on an extensive volume of recent reports and innovations, the authors focus on core skills as a central organising concept, together with an evaluation of the new vocationalism.

Within the book evidence is assembled from a range of different countries with the result that this is an important volume for a variety of practitioners, policy-makers, researchers and students nationally and internationally.

Robert Burgess
University of Warwick

ACKNOWLEDGEMENTS

The genesis of this book was a grant from the Manpower Services Commission (MSC) to the principal author for a study of the Core Skills Project of the Youth Training Scheme. This grant facilitated participation by the OECD Secretariat and representatives of several member countries, the University of London Institute of Education, and experts from several OECD countries. It was Professor Robert Burgess who initially encouraged the writing of the book and who has offered wise counsel on its progress. Assistance with bibliographical research was provided by Yelena Cockett, Michael Wood and Olivia Ann Lowe, and with the preparation of the manuscript by Lynn Cairns, Diane Read and Valerie Cisse. We are grateful to staff in a number of organisations and ministries who have provided information. They include, in the UK: the MSC (and its successor organisations), the Department of Employment, the Department of Education and Science (and its successor, the Department for Education), the Scottish Education Department (and its successor, the Scottish Office Education Department) the Department of Education for Northern Ireland, the National Council for Vocational Qualifications; numerous education authorities and individuals in Australia, France, Germany, Japan, New Zealand, Sweden and the United States; and colleagues at the OECD. Particular mention should be made of the contributions made in the early stages of the study by Dr Gilbert Jessup, and Ms Margaret Levy. The assistance of all these individuals and organisations is gratefully acknowledged. None of those who have assisted and advised us is, however, responsible for the interpretations and opinions expressed herein.

LIST OF ABBREVIATIONS

ABC	*A Basis for Choice* (FEU report)
AEC	Australian Education Council
ANTA	Australian National Training Authority
ASF	Australian Standards Framework
ATC	Accredited Training Centre
ATO	Approved Training Organisation
AVCTS	Australian Vocational Certificate Training System
BEP	Brevet d'Études Professionelles
BGJ	Berufsgrundbildungsjahr
BIAC	Business and Industry Advisory Committee to the OECD
BT	Brevet de Technicien
BTEC	Business and Technician Education Council
CAP	Certificat d'Aptitudes Professionelles
CBI	Confederation of British Industry
CEDEFOP	Centre Européen pour le développement de la formation professionelle
CEREQ	Centre d'études et de recherche sur les emplois et les qualifications
CERI	Centre for Educational Research and Innovation
CGLI	City and Guilds of London Institute
CPVE	Certificate of Pre-vocational Education
CSE	Certificate of Secondary Education
CTC	City Technology College
DAEs	Dynamic Asian Economies
DENI	Department of Education for Northern Ireland
DES	Department of Education and Science, England and Wales
DfE	Department for Education, England and Wales (established 1992)
DoE	Department of Employment, UK
DVE	Diploma of Vocational Education

EC	European Community
EURYDICE	Education Information Network in the European Community
FE	Further Education
FESC	Further Education Staff College
FEU	Further Education Unit
GCE	General Certificate of Education (O level – Ordinary level; A level – Advanced level)
GCSE	General Certificate of Secondary Education
GNVQ	General National Vocational Qualification
GSVQ	General Scottish Vocational Qualification
HMI	Her Majesty's Inspectorate
ILO	International Labour Office
IMS	Institute of Manpower Studies
ITS	Instituut voor Toegetaste Sociale Wetenschatpen
LEA	Local Education Authority
LEC	Local Enterprise Company, Scotland
MSC	Manpower Services Commission
NAFE	Non-Advanced Further Education
NCC	National Curriculum Council
NCE	National Commission of Education
NCVQ	National Council for Vocational Qualifications
NEDC	National Economic Development Council
NPT	National Proficiency Tests
NRA	National Record of Achievement
NRoVA	National Record of Vocational Achievement
NTB	National Training Board, Australia
NTI	*New Training Initiative*
NVQ	National Vocational Qualification
OECD	Organisation for Economic Co-operation and Development
OTF	Occupational Training Family
RSA	Royal Society of Arts
RVQ	Review of Vocational Qualifications
SCOTVEC	Scottish Vocational Education Council
SEAC	Schools Examination and Assessment Council
SEB	Scottish Examination Board
SFEU	Scottish Further Education Unit
SOED	Scottish Office Education Department
SVQ	Scottish Vocational Qualification
TA	Training Agency
TAFE	Technical and Further Education
TC	Training Commission
TEC	Training and Enterprise Council
TEED	Training, Enterprise and Education Directorate

TUAC	Trades Union Advisory Committee to the OECD
TUC	Trades Union Congress
TVEI	Technical and Vocational Education Initiative
Unesco	United Nations Educational, Scientific and Cultural Organisation
UVP	Unified Vocational Programme
VET	Vocational Education and Training
YOP	Youth Opportunities Programme
YT	Youth Training
YTS	Youth Training Scheme

1

EMERGENCE OF THE NEW VOCATIONALISM

There are . . . two things about man's future of which I think we can be certain. One is that things will not come out all right in the end if we merely sit by and let them happen. The other is that things will most probably turn out well for man if he conscientiously works at the task of making them do so.

(Montagu, 1961, p.27)

INTRODUCTION

In this chapter, we outline the diverse and numerous factors that lie behind the emergence of new – and the reinforcement of some old – forms of vocationalism: what is meant by a vocational orientation in the education of young people, and why it has emerged. We do not, at this stage, differentiate between the settings – school, office, workshop, specialist college or whatever – since these factors are at work in all of them, and there are aspects of the responses which are common to all. Differences of course there are; they are considered in later chapters where a more detailed appraisal is made of the main theme of this chapter.

SETTING THE SCENE

For reasons that are primarily economic, the years since the early 1970s have witnessed a major resurgence of interest in the vocational role of education and training in the personal and social processes of formation which are governed by such purposes as preparation for working life and occupational choice, and the matching of human capabilities to labour market needs and opportunities. This interest is part of the close attention being given to the conditions necessary to sustain growth in the modern economy (Abramovitz, 1988). In the face of massive challenges to reorient and restructure, to achieve greater efficiency, to find new economic

1

opportunities, and, more recently, to alleviate or forestall youth (and adult) unemployment, countries have increasingly turned to education and training as an investment in the future. This has given a strong functional or instrumental tone to a great deal of the contemporary debate about education, whose purposes and procedures have always included vocational preparation, albeit often indirectly, usually in conjunction with other values both personal and social, and seldom in sufficient degree. Changes reflecting the redefinition of the vocational factor, ways of making it a more explicit aim of education and the transformation of the nature and conditions of work are all evident; these are occurring within enterprises, both private and public, in schools and colleges and in public policy (OECD, 1989a, 1991b). Notable, too, are the so-called new growth theories which single out research and development, education and training as crucial factors in economic growth and thereby provide a stimulus to researchers and policy-makers to identify key points for intervention, including a working life orientation in schooling (Eliasson, 1987; Scott, 1989; Eliasson *et al.*, 1990; Romer, 1990; Bishop, 1991).

Education in general has been coloured by the increased attention that has been given to its economic and its wider social utility (Skilbeck, 1990, Chapter 2). Of particular interest, however, is a distinctive movement of ideas, policies and practices which has emerged during the last quarter of the twentieth century. Known variously as the new vocationalism, preparation for working life, transition from school to work or simply as vocational or technical education and training, this movement has, in Britain and many other countries, been the source of significant and frequently controversial innovations in educational structures, content, methods and funding. A major challenge to much that is established in the education system, it has generated a growing volume of analysis and research, public policy initiatives, action in both the public and private spheres of education, training and employment – and sharp divisions among advocates and critics.

The initial focus of the new vocationalism in the 1970s and 1980s was on adolescents aged 14–18 – at the point of transition from compulsory schooling to working life. Increasingly, as a response to demographic change (the ageing population) and to shorter-term employment needs, the focus is widening to include continuing education and training for mature adults including re-entrants to the workforce (OECD, 1991b). The initial stage, however, remains of great importance not least because it directly connects the all too frequently separate domains of schooling and general education with specialised vocational preparation and experience of working life. It is to this initial or transitional stage that the principal arguments of this book are addressed.

The different traditions – of general, school-based education with its roots in a culture of broad-based knowledge and understanding and of technical, vocational training with its origins in specific, employment-related tasks and its preparation for work through work – are converging. The diversity of interests involved, competing purposes and programmes and the pace of change in the working world, are sources of energy but also of uncertainty and confusion.

The very terminology, of 'education', 'vocational', 'training', 'skill', 'competence', 'working life' and so on, has become fluid: definitions need to be operational and provisional, relative to and clarified in the context of particular programmes and inquiries. While consistency is not easy to sustain, we shall, in this spirit, treat 'education' as a comprehensive term for purposive, structured human and social formation, governed by intellectual and ethical principles, directed at knowledge, understanding and their applications and informed by a spirit of critical inquiry. 'Vocational' refers to those educational functions and processes which purport to prepare and equip individuals and groups for working life whether or not in the form of paid employment. 'Training' is task specific but nevertheless, in our usage, a part of education and subject to the values, criteria and principles which govern educational processes generally, even though, as frequently used, its reference is to factual knowledge and unreflective skills. Obviously, those who control education, vocational preparation and training will in both policy and practice colour the interpretation given to these functions and processes. One of the most striking modern developments, affecting the vocational sphere as much as other aspects of education, is the emergence of new forms of control: the growth of parent power, of the influence of industry and commerce and of various partnership and collaborative procedures for decision-making. Less common until recently in school systems, the partnership principles have been long established in technical and vocational education.

As we look back on some two decades of rapid growth and change in vocational education, we can identify both the major landmarks and the tasks that must be addressed if this transformation of ideas and structures is to take effect in soundly conceived practice. Much has been achieved, as a result of immense effort during a period of change unparalleled for the scale and intensity of commitment to reform of vocational education and training. After this extended period of innovation and experimentation it is also necessary, now, that we undertake something of an educational audit. To what extent has this vocationally oriented drive contributed to our broader educational practice and values? What have we learnt about the problems in vocational education and training and how best to overcome them? Why is there a continuing sense of unease about the direction of reform, a questioning of assumptions, values and of what has been achieved? These questions have acquired a fresh significance in light of the immense changes now under way in the general secondary and higher education sectors – changes which should be informed by the experiences of reform in vocational education and training as much as they will, in turn, impact upon it.

3

The rationale for the national vocational drive in Britain since the 1970s is multifaceted, but its main purposes have been clear and stark: to create and consolidate a comprehensive system of vocationally oriented education and training for all young people; and to bring education and training at the mid-adolescent stage into line with perceived requirements of the work environment. In turn these purposes reflect concern – concern about the state of the economy, its competitiveness, adaptability and potential for growth, concern about the capacity, unaided, of schools, colleges and training bodies to meet these requirements as the nature of work itself undergoes substantial changes, and an overriding concern about the inadequacy of an education system which, for all the changes, remains unduly stratified and exclusive.

Education and training are, it has been proposed, to be perceived instrumentally and from a particular standpoint. Notwithstanding the efforts made, the resulting achievements, and the clear and valuable corrective provided by this national vocational drive, there is still risk of a cramped vision and an inadequate understanding of the place of the vocational dimension in a wider philosophy and system of universal, life-long education. It is in the nature of a reform which, its full potential yet to be realised, runs the risk of over-determination by its narrower rather than its broader purposes and values. In Britain, at least, this is the contention of the critics who have been quick to seize upon the values underlying major government initiatives even more than the change strategies that have been adopted (Finn, 1987; Holt, 1987; Jonathan, 1990).

Major central governmental initiatives both within and outside the formal schooling and further education sectors have been the key factors in the new vocational drive. Industry and commerce have in varying degrees co-operated and there have been a number of joint ventures, but there is no doubt about the prime mover. A considerable diversity of patterns is evident in Britain as among the other industrialised countries and the British experience both contributes to and can be better understood – and perhaps better directed – when seen in this international context. Key elements in the newer British approaches are also more clearly seen and appreciated when set against a background of national history. The new vocationalism is unintelligible unless it is situated or contextualised in this way.

VOCATIONALISM AND THE RESTRUCTURING OF EMPLOYMENT

Vocationalisation of education includes, but goes beyond, training for a job or paid employment. On the one hand, it is a dimension of education for life, for living, of which work in some form is an all but universal attribute: 'vocationalism' is a process or activity, the imparting and the acquisition of broadly defined skills and knowledge believed to have a discernible relationship with the capabilities needed for productive work and required or expected of workers, now and in the future. This aligns 'vocationalism' with a philosophy of purposive activity designed to accomplish results and render service (Dewey, 1916, Chapter XXIII). On the other hand, vocationalism is a function, whereby the education system services the workings of the economy, deriving its purpose and rationale from some assessment of economic need and requirement, such as trained manpower for the labour market (Ashton *et al.*, 1990, Chapter 9). Both dimensions draw attention to the fundamental importance of vocational education in any society. In doing so they remind us that a critical problem for Western societies has been the persistence of dualism – a disunity rather than a unity of relationships: mind and body, head and hand, leisure and work, theoretical culture and utility, superior and inferior occupations.

From its foundation, systematic, popular or public education has always had a vocational content and function, even if it has not been recognised as such. The new vocationalism is a critical movement – radical in the sense that new foundations are being put in place and new structures erected on them. The issue is not whether education should be vocational, but what vocationalism means in contemporary terms, what could count as adequacy or quality of vocationalism, and how well the vocational orientation is balanced with other purposes and values of education.

Even though some industrialised countries seem reasonably satisfied with their provision of vocational education and its orientation, the new vocationalism as an educational force has not been an isolated trend, limited to economies in trouble or those moving into what is now frequently, if rather loosely, described as the post-industrial era. Societies throughout the world are aware of a lack of synchrony between, on the one hand, human, societal and economic needs and, on the other, the processes of production and distribution of wealth. A classic example is the unresolved environmentalist debate between conservation and exploitation of natural resources. Another is the apparent inability of many governments, in both the industrialised and developing countries, to solve the chronic problems of large-scale youth and adult unemployment. Every central government and educational planner is, to at least some degree, concerned with the matching of manpower, or, rather educated and trained people, to the drive for economic growth (Hughes, 1991). This is a drive which entails structural adjustment – that is, a restructuring, not only of jobs but also of industrial and social relations and organisation (OECD, 1991b).

Such restructuring necessitates an overview of the whole territory of vocational education and is perforce resulting in several different kinds of fusion. The number of fields of vocational and professional life has been reduced through job restructuring; professional associations and unions

5

have amalgamated; the number of training 'lines' has been reduced through regrouping (Mathews, 1989a, b; Rojot and Tergeist, 1992). As work itself becomes more highly organised globally and not only locally and nationally, more dependent on research and on advanced knowledge and refined sensibilities in workers, more interactive in terms of both structures and relations, so do the domains of 'work' and 'education for work' become interactive. The corollary to the 'vocationalising of education' is the 'educating of work' – its transformation into an educative culture. We are still at an early stage in this revolution, practice falling far short of what is technically and organisationally possible, let alone of advanced ideas.

Significant long-term, rather than short-term cyclical, changes in the nature and structure of jobs in industrialised countries have occurred over the last two decades. These long-term structural changes, as exemplified in the case of Britain, are acting to decrease the number of unskilled jobs available for young school-leavers, especially males, reduce full-time jobs generally, make greater use of sub-contracting, increase part-time temporary jobs, demand multi-skilling of the existing labour force, and provide jobs requiring higher-level skills – that is, a more educated workforce (Ashton *et al.*, 1990, Chapters 6 and 9). These structural changes in recent years have worked in the same direction as the cyclical downturn of the economy, exacerbating unemployment, especially among youth. Such long-term changes indicate that even the smaller youth cohorts of the next few years, allied with any significant upturn in general economic activity, will not fundamentally ameliorate employment prospects for the young unskilled.

The widespread development of global markets, especially, has changed the terms of competition in many product markets, notably those of large-scale manufacturing industry. Companies with strong national bases from which they export to other national product markets are being transformed into transnational companies with the world as their market and no particular national allegiance or single base. As a consequence, production can be transferred between or cascaded across countries, weakening the link between the level of product demand in a national economy and established levels of demand for labour. This trend has led to the loss of many unskilled and semi-skilled jobs in manufacturing in Britain as in other industrialised countries. Technology and economic globalisation pose a profound challenge to established national practices in allocating and organising work (OECD, 1992i, 1994).

In parts of the service sector in Britain, particularly in the distribution, hotel and catering areas, increasing industrial concentration has occurred, with the consequent larger national and international companies adopting different systems of labour management and utilisation from those of the older family firms displaced in the process. A drop in full-time and increase in temporary part-time jobs (especially for mature women rather than

6

youth) has been quite marked in this sector in Britain. Employers have sought recruits with good interpersonal skills, as quality of client contact has become of key competitive concern.

In commerce the introduction of information technology, and in manufacturing information technology and advances in machine design to produce computer numerically controlled (CNC) machines, robots and flexible manufacturing systems, have worked to enable a smaller number of more highly skilled individuals to achieve a given output. From its retrospective review of member country labour markets in the 1980s, the Organisation for Economic Co-operation and Development (OECD) drew one basic conclusion: 'that more training and retraining will be required' (OECD, 1991a, p.59). The issue is, however, not only a quantitative one, important as that is for an under-educated country like Britain, but one of form, content, relevance and quality.

VOCATIONALISM: A WORLDWIDE TREND

A broadly defined vocationalisation has been a common thread which runs across the education and, increasingly, the employment policies of every country, whatever its level of development, political system or geographical location. In the post-war era, it has been advanced under many shapes and forms depending on the ideology and economic system of each country, through such concepts as unity and diversity in the curriculum, career guidance and education, polytechnic and polyvalent education, work experience, multiskilling and pre-vocational and further education and training. Since the early 1970s there has been a powerful impetus as well in most, if not all, OECD countries towards vocationalisation of the curricula of basic and post-compulsory schooling and towards a multiplication of vocational training measures designed to bridge perceived gaps between educational provision and social and economic needs (OECD, 1985b; Levin and Rumberger, 1989; Papadopoulos, 1991).

Such developments are not confined to the major industrialised economies. Many less industrialised countries have long been concerned with enlarging and updating the vocational dimension of the education systems they inherited from the colonial past (Coombe, 1988). Strenuous efforts continue to be made to orient primary and secondary education towards meeting the perceived needs of adult working life and to adapt them to local and national development requirements, both economic and social, nowadays usually under the rubric of 'human capital formation' or 'human resource development policies' (Rawkins, 1993). At higher levels, the aim has been functional education within the framework of established development plans, again with the goal of raising the competence of the citizenry to the highest possible levels (Foster, 1965; Lauglo, 1983; King, 1984; World Bank, 1991). Surveys and consultation meetings carried out under the auspices of the Commonwealth Secretariat, and under the Commonwealth of Learning, which has been established to foster and strengthen international collaboration in distance education among the 40-plus members of the Commonwealth of Nations, confirm the very strong interest in reshaping the education of the 14–16-plus age group to bring it into line with national development needs (Commonwealth Secretariat, 1987). Unesco, too, has sought to give a fresh impetus to its long-standing involvement in technical and vocational education by launching a project for the creation of an International Centre for Technical and Vocational Education (Unesco, 1991, 1992). The language of 'enterprise culture' and the competence required of effective workers in such a culture has, too, emerged in the Asia–Pacific region of Unesco (Unesco, 1990).

In the era of planned economies of the former COMECON countries, a commitment to the principle that labour is the fundamental source of human value was part of the declared ideology. The human capital theory in some form or other has indeed long had widespread support across political and ideological boundaries: Adam Smith and Karl Marx had much in common. The theme of education and training for productive work has for long played a significant part in the Central European countries as it has in other parts of the world (ILO, 1979; Ailes and Rushing, 1980; Lauglo and Lillis, 1988; O'Dell, 1988). How far this will remain a focus following the recent and continuing political changes in these countries remains to be seen. Given the necessity and the widely declared aim of restructuring their economies, it is to be expected that the development of education and training in these countries will retain a very strong vocational flavour, albeit on somewhat different ideological premises.

The new vocationalism in several of the Western industrialised countries belonging to the OECD may be said to be rapidly following a direction which some other countries, from a variety of value positions, began to pursue many years earlier. Put in simpler terms, this may be expressed as a recognition of the fundamental importance in educational provision during the compulsory years of schooling of an explicit element of 'preparation for working life' and of the necessity for all youth, beyond the compulsory years, to have the opportunity of systematic training and of continuing general education.

It is important to realise that we are not witnessing an isolated phenomenon, one that has the fragility of a particular, transitory set of politico-economic circumstances. Dissatisfaction by certain employers and employer groups with the performance of the education system in some of its basic functional tasks may seem to be the immediate cause of this change, but to treat the trend as a mere reaction to what are often conflicting and somewhat superficial criticisms is to misconceive the fundamental transformations that are taking place.

The distinctively late twentieth-century global combination of economic growth (and the attempted reduction of barriers thereto), technological change, structural transformation of the workplace, democratisation and the universal quest for material betterment are among the factors of over-riding importance (OECD, 1992h,1992i). How these factors are perceived – whether as deterministic of or interactive with educational values and processes – and the extent to which their importance is assessed by the different actors, both nationally and internationally, provide the dynamic for action, or, just as frequently, inaction or confusion. Thus whether or not employers perceive a skill shortage or inadequacy may be as much a function of work organisation and of other structural features such as financial management and industrial relations (demand side) as of the outcomes of schooling (supply side) (Cassels, 1990; Commission on the Skills of the American Workforce, 1990; Finegold, 1992). Moreover, there are wide differences in the employment sector with respect to technological applications and hence in the perceived need for 'technological literacy' and other skills (Rumberger, 1987). There is also the question of whether policy for vocational education is best directed – as much of it has been in Britain – at the lower skills echelon, the early school-leavers, or at the middle and higher skill levels. A greatly improved dialogue between the actors and more refinement of the categories of analysis used in research, interpretative literature and policy-making are necessary conditions for achieving more coherent and effective policies (OECD 1991b, 1992c).

During the immediate post-war period, continuous economic expansion and full employment came to be considered normal in OECD countries, allowing for the cyclical fluctuations of the business cycle. In recent years they have remained stated objectives of national policy if muted by the determination to maintain a balance at the macro-level between potentially contradictory and destabilising trends. There is a growing recognition that countries do not merely trade their way out of difficulties or 'fix' their economies at the level of macro-policy; they must increasingly assure themselves of highly trained, flexible workforces. Moreover, these trained work-forces need outlets for their talents, competences and energies: they need jobs. This is indeed a key element in the move towards the complementary micro-economic policies of structural adjustment. 'Structural adjustment' means, in effect, the reform of the socio-economic structures which inhibit or reduce the capacity of countries to pursue longer-term development goals and to relate to one another in mutually beneficial ways in the international environment of trade and exchange. Education and training are central to any programme of structural adjustment for the very obvious, if sometimes neglected, reason that it is upon the educated and trained capacity of the actors – the people – that the ability to restructure and to gain from its benefits depends.

We have, belatedly, entered the era where, as Bruce Raup and his co-workers long ago put it, 'the improvement of practical intelligence' is coming to be recognised as a primary policy goal (Raup *et al.*, 1943). In this respect, we have indeed entered a new era. Whether conventional, full-time, paid employment for all or practically all youth and young adults will continue to be delivered by the advanced economies is a moot point. It does not, however, vitiate the claims being made for ever higher levels of education and training, with preparation for work as one of the primary policy objectives.

This new 'education era' is characterised not only by a recognition of the need for what the OECD Ministers of Education referred to as a high quality of education and training for all (OECD, 1992c). Comparability and transparency of credentialled knowledge and skills across national boundaries assume greater importance than ever before in the new Europe (Commission of the European Communities, 1991b; Bertrand, 1992); globally the spread and transferability of technology, of industrial and commercial organisations and the moves to establish agreed 'rules of the game' in international markets and trade are among the factors that are leading to a reappraisal of the vocational content and structures of education. Moves towards mutual recognition of qualifications throughout Europe are bringing additional pressure for both breadth and a restructuring of vocational qualifications in Britain. The age of self-contained national systems of vocational education and the attendant qualifications and certification processes – however adequate they may have been in their own terms – has passed. While these propositions may receive assent in principle, their practical consequences are, however, far from clear.

RISING EXPECTATIONS OF BASIC SCHOOLING

The forces for change – scientific, technological, economic, social, cultural – call for a renewal of policies for education and training, yet there is far too little understanding of the actual dynamics of these forces and agreement over just what changes in education are most needed. Nevertheless, in pursuit of long-established goals relating to universal literacy, social participation and equity, Western countries, Japan and many developing countries have invested massively in education, throughout the whole of the post-Second-World-War era. This expenditure has assumed that economic benefit and other social goods would accrue in the short and the long term, although not necessarily directly (Hughes, 1994).

From the inception of public education systems, the economic argument has been clearly reflected in investment in vocational education and training, however impoverished provision may have been in practice. Other predominant notions, dating back to the Enlightenment, have been that education is crucial in the formation of culture and the maintenance of social order and that it can contribute significantly to equity, social justice and material advancement. Nowhere is this doctrine more tellingly advanced than in the writings and actions of the eighteenth-century

10

polymath, Benjamin Franklin (Best, 1962). For Franklin, as for many who have followed him, the quest is for betterment of the human condition, and this includes the economic condition. But, in the particular rendition of the concept that Franklin gave, betterment has of necessity a component of universal, practical education whose utility was no less social than individual, no less material in its effect than intellectual and moral. Franklin's own life experiences and his benevolent utilitarianism naturally led him to incorporate preparation for gainful and socially useful employment in his educational schemes.

The new vocational thrust in Britain may seem a far cry from the reform schemes of Franklin and other philosophical minds of the Enlightenment. Of all the major, system-wide trends in contemporary education, it is potentially, if not actually, the most revealing in its contemporaneity and its messages for the future development of policies and programmes for the education system as a whole. Yet it is part of a living tradition in education which extends back, beyond the doctrines of the eighteenth century, to antiquity. The debate about vocationalism is a debate about the nature of education and the directions of the culture. Thus it is of far wider significance to all parts of the education system and for the future of British society than may seem the case at first glance. This is evident if we consider what has often been regarded an unduly narrow educational concern: job preparation.

One of the most serious problems in many countries is matching people to jobs, and jobs to people: positive labour market policies which address not only aggregate skill levels but identify targets for employment growth and ways of achieving those targets which include but cannot be confined to comprehensive education and training policies. Measures are needed to stimulate both demand and supply (OECD, 1994). The ability in industrially advanced countries to place young people in jobs, in the years up to the first oil crisis in 1973, meant that, on the quantitative side, there was no glaring mismatch between educational provision and social and economic needs. Inefficiencies in enterprises including poor selection and training policies and deficiencies in the quantity and quality of education were widely, if unwisely, tolerated. From the point of view of the individual and the state, failure at school was not necessarily the end of the line, because a person could always get an unskilled job and hope, maybe, to progress from there. This is not to say that there was great public or professional satisfaction with education systems, but the job placement function of schooling, always a latent consideration, has become increasingly problematic.

In some parts of the community and in many countries, even in times of high youth employment, there was a justifiable concern that schools and colleges did not offer the type and quality of education which was relevant to the concerns of everyday life and working people. This may be a quantitative problem – insufficient numbers of candidates qualified for particular

11

jobs, as has been the case in Germany – or a qualitative one – inadequately trained or prepared people for whatever jobs are available. In the United States, for example, as early as the late 1940s, advocates of 'life adjustment' education were critical of schooling for its failure to prepare young people for jobs and social participation (their programmes in turn were criticised for lack of substance and intellectual challenge) (Ravitch, 1983). While this dissatisfaction and related concerns about schooling have not been ubiquitous, they have become powerful enough to generate major changes – of which the modern vocational movement is itself an example. The critique has extended with labour or employment ministries adding their assessments of schooling to those made by the educators and the employers (Confederation of British Industry, 1989, 1993; SCANS, 1991).

How have schools and educational policy responded to these critiques and to the challenge to reform? Among the OECD countries, educational reform has become a constant theme, not, to be sure, just as a consequence of economic concerns. In secondary education, for example, reforms have included extending the period of compulsory attendance, school structure and organisation (for example, comprehensive schools, non-selective entry, mixed ability grouping), curriculum restructuring and renewal, improvements in teacher education and the monitoring and assessment of performance. Issues of social justice, equity, efficiency and a refined sensitivity towards children's needs have featured in these reforms. But so, too, has a quite definite understanding of the changing needs of the world of work.

In some countries, new structures of secondary education have been erected, with proposed vocational streams and qualifications that have equal status with the established academic stream. France provides a striking example, at least of the intention of equality. In other countries, previously separate vocational schools or streams have been integrated into mainstream schooling in the junior high school years, if not beyond. This move has, however, had the unintended consequence of disadvantaging students in the new practical and vocational stream at schools because of a tendency to assimilate that stream to the general, academic model of the traditional secondary school rather than to rethink the whole basis of secondary education.

In the face of these concerns, universal secondary education, charged with educating the entire population, has been challenged to excise traditions based on progressively weeding out those identified as unsuitable, rather than nurturing them; it has been expected to make itself attractive to all of its clients and to excite their interest. The consequence has been demand for a more effective curriculum, for learning more closely in tune with patterns of growth and the world in which the children live (Skilbeck, 1990). Dissatisfaction with the perceived results of the attempts made to respond to this requirement was the first stage in the development of the current drive for relevance, of which the new vocationalism is a part. It was thus the move, first, towards a mass and then a universal system of secondary education which radically changed preconceptions about what this level of education was for. Thus was provided a dynamic for change internal to the education system whose effects are now strongly felt. This historic move, therefore, may be regarded as satisfying several of the conditions necessary for the emergence of the new vocationalism. It cannot be said, however, that secondary education in Britain, or indeed in other industrialised countries, has reformed itself to the extent needed.

Thus, not only exogenous factors in the wider society and economy but also factors internal to the school system at the secondary level have played a significant, if generally overlooked, part in the emergence of the new vocationalism. For a fuller account, however, we must consider the *interaction* of factors external and internal to the school. Several of these have already been noted, but to be reminded of the heterogeneous nature of these factors, in a country whose reform policies and strategies have had a worldwide impact, it is instructive to look back to events following 1957 when the Soviet Union launched the first Sputnik and triggered a wave of alarm in the United States, where the comprehensive secondary school had been the norm for decades.

'Life adjustment' education had been tried, as a way of making the comprehensive secondary school more relevant to its universal membership but had not produced the quality of performance expected. Many Americans felt threatened technologically, economically, militarily and even ideologically by the then Soviet Union – much as increasingly throughout the 1980s they felt a Japanese threat (National Commission on Excellence in Education, 1983; Ravitch, 1983). In both instances, education was seen as having much of the responsibility and, as a result, became the object of substantial, external pressure for change.

It had seemed axiomatic that the best system would produce the best technology and Americans tended to assume that educational reform was a key to both. The role and quality of mathematics and science teaching in particular were targeted for attention (National Commission on Excellence in Education, 1983; Kliebard, 1986; Bennett, 1987, 1988; American Association for the Advancement of Science, 1989). While international studies of school performance did not conclusively demonstrate that the American systems of education and training were inferior to those of the then Soviet Union, they did, in addition to showing the extreme difficulty of comparing the objectives and performance of different education systems (Husen, 1982), give rise to considerable anxiety. It became evident, also, that while large-scale public education is financially onerous, it is extremely difficult to tell how cost-effective it may be (Ailes and Rushing, 1980). Whatever may be the conclusion on this point, criticism of the performance of American schooling has continued; reform has been set as a major goal of national policy (Bush, 1991) and a vast industry of comparative educational analysis is developing (OECD, 1992b). The American reform agenda extends to reversing the decline of the always marginal territory of vocational education.

Other factors in some Western countries, Britain included, led to the effectiveness of educational provision being questioned. That mass education systems were unable to eradicate inequality significantly in a short space of time was of particular concern in countries with large disadvantaged minorities and/or strong social democratic governments. There was and is consternation about rising levels of violence among young people. Should – or could – the mass education systems have prevented this from happening? With the expansion of secondary education to cover all age groups in most industrialised countries, numbers of youngsters appeared to derive very little advantage from it. When the world economy slipped into recession in the early 1970s, the incapacity of cash-hungry education systems to pay off in economic terms appeared to be completely confirmed, at least to the satisfaction of crusading interest groups and political parties. Economic recovery in the 1980s and the sustained growth cycle of that decade brought about not so much a restoration of confidence in education as a growing sense of the need for qualitative improvement and greater relevance to socio-economic demands. Anxieties previously in the background now came to the fore in the public mind. What was significant, however, was a vastly increased weight of public feeling and emphasis on accountability and tangible, measurable outcomes (Jencks, 1973; Coleman, 1979; Ravitch, 1983; OECD, 1989b).

Effective preparation for the labour market came to rank high among such outcomes but, ironically, this occurred during a period when the youth labour market in many of the industrialised countries entered what is now widely believed to be terminal decline. It was not the mainly American concern about technological slippage but unemployment consequent on recession in the early 1970s, and now chronic in many countries, that intensified the demand for relevance and through this led to the demand for more and better vocational training, among other developments. The dream of full employment was shattered and this had much greater meaning to the average voter than the relative strength of the techno-economic systems of West and East. Though the shortage of jobs relative to demand was only indirectly, if at all, attributable to education systems, failure at school now meant losing the chance of participating in the labour market, a real factor in everyday life. Monetary inflation was accompanied by qualifications inflation. The value of the currency slipped, not uniformly to be sure since business cycle and market fluctuations have at some times benefited engineers or builders, at other times the tourist and finance sectors; but even the university degree steadily lost its commanding position (OECD, 1993b).

In many sectors, employers pick and choose and, with increasing frequency, a basic standard of 'relevant' education is a necessary, if not a sufficient, condition for any kind of employment. At the same time, a constant refrain from employers is the need for a high level of skills (BIAC and TUAC, 1991).

Even though, in many occupations, there is no close link between the content of qualifications and the tasks to be performed in the workplace, the screening function of the qualifications process remains active.

Socio-economic systems have come to be perceived as having failed youngsters, as much as the other way around. Such failure was one symptom of a growing malaise compounded of crime, violence, poverty, family break-up and urban decay. What could education do? The mismatch between youth expectation, wants and demands fuelled, if not generated, by material plenty in high growth economies and the readiness and ability of youth to be gainfully employed was reduced to a 'skills gap'. Close the gap, and by a feat of astonishing simplification, many of the social ills would evaporate. From another perspective, it was necessary to make substantial changes to the education systems so that they became attractive to young people. Not least for political reasons, youth needed to be kept off the labour market but in a constructive way, through a form of tutelage which would be redesigned to prepare them realistically for new adult working roles and a generalised social responsibility. Educational institutions, therefore, have felt obliged to rethink their mission, strategies, organisation and curricula.

A SKILLED WORKFORCE FOR THE FUTURE

Future economic prosperity and social 'health' and stability have thus come to be seen, as never before, to depend on a putative labour force that in its entirety is educated, skilled, motivated and aware. Upon the foundations of a strengthened basic education, a superstructure of vocationally oriented, work-preparatory education and training needed to be erected. The debates on technological change, on international competitiveness and social order, have moved from the fear of job losses to the new kinds of employment opportunities that are being or need to be opened up – to the educated and trained, not the unskilled. The structure of everyday life, being transformed mainly as a consequence of the impact of new technologies in information, communication, production and distribution, is being seen as a kind of lodestone. The emergence of new industries, notably in the service and high knowledge-base sectors, together with the growing acceptance that conventional, full-time, paid employment of youth will not form part of the future employment pattern of industrial (and post-industrial) countries, indicate that education and training need a new direction. Training for a specific occupation or even clusters of occupations is being supplanted by strategies for 'generalisable skills' or general transferable education, a theme on which there has been a great volume of discourse (IMS, 1982; Jones, 1982; Benson and Lloyd, 1983; Gill, 1985; OECD, 1986a; Mathews, 1989b; Confederation of British Industry, 1989, 1993; Raizen, 1991).

Changing levels of expertise and work organisation in industry, commerce and the public services call for a dynamic and competent population (Raven, 1984). Yet, in most of the industrialised countries there is a necessity – not always acknowledged – to face up to the harsh realities of competing from a base which is underdeveloped in relation to the new technologies and to the capacity of some trading partners. Disenchantment with economic theories of full employment and optimum growth has accompanied a questioning of the modern mechanism to maintain satisfactory levels of wealth and distributive welfare. Education and training, among other areas, naturally have come under scrutiny. Both old-fashioned and futuristic ideas have been readily examined for seams of sense. The results have not always borne witness to either common sense or a depth of understanding. Interpretations of the classical thinkers have at times been extremely one-sided: Adam Smith's economics, for example, has been grossly decontextualised with a resulting '[im]balance between the sacred and the secular' (Davie, 1981).

In the most general sense and in an age when the sacred is co-opted, compartmentalised and packaged, a highly secularised education has come to be regarded somehow as able to help overcome unemployment and pull the economy out of recession. In other words, education has to show what it is 'good' for in purely instrumental terms. But it is reasonable to ask whether the 'remedies' satisfy even the instrumental and secular requirements, let alone the need human beings and societies have for the moral, intellectual and spiritual riches of the 'sacred'. In seeking greater relevance and utility, more precision and applicability, educators must confront the charge of reducing the complex processes of human growth and development to instruments in the service of limited and ephemeral ends, or of powerful socio-economic interest groups.

This risk is perhaps most apparent in educational responses to technological change. These often appear as adaptations to inexorable forces rather than intelligent and creative use of a resource. Technological advances are a consequence of the 'push' from the progress of science and the 'pull' from growth-based economies (OECD, 1992h, 1992i). The consequences are manifold if very uneven as between countries, regions and different sectors of the population. The 'pull' becomes ever more salient as 'policy' concerns dominate the funding of scientific research and economic globalisation proceeds. 'Technological innovation has been a key weapon of international competition' (O'Connor, 1987, p.30). Among the most significant of these implications for a system of universal education has been that fewer people are required in the manufacturing process and of those fewer people, the need for the unskilled – a traditional resource for manufacturers – is evaporating as micro-electronics-based technologies become ever more pervasive. Robots are replacing the unskilled on automobile assembly lines, while the skilled minds and hands of specialist print workers are being bypassed as wholly new technologies are brought on stream. Innumerable school-leavers find themselves unemployed, not only because of fewer jobs, but also because they are not adequately prepared for the work that is being done on the shop floors and in those service and knowledge-based industries where some expansion is taking place. The quasi-permanent surplus of labour which rapidly emerged in most countries during the world recession of the early 1970s has been thus aggravated by technical progress including the globalisation of business (Ashton *et al.*, 1990). This has given yet more force to the vocationalist thrust, fuelling a perception in some quarters that education systems are failed or inadequate instruments which do not meet their clients' essential needs. The felt need for highly trained people has grown concurrently.

In recent years, the effect of demographic change, to which we have already alluded, has brought a new element into the situation. Smaller age cohorts in most industrialised countries are now moving through the secondary schools; and the late 1980s witnessed an important shift from concerns about youth unemployment as such, a 'manageable cost', to greater competition by employers for the skilled worker, hence greater interest in the skills that are required and in the skills–jobs matching process. Demography is a dynamic major factor in the new alignment – of education, training and employment – not only with respect to the fluctuating proportion of school age students but with reference also to an ageing population.

Uncertainty about national economies and institutions in the region of the Pacific basin has been, since the 1960s, a growing source of concern in Western societies (IMS, 1985; Ernst and O'Connor, 1989). Japan constitutes a serious challenge to all the other industrialised countries: its economic growth scarcely checked by recession in the 1970s, having ridden, seemingly with ease, the new technological tide, and in the 1980s amassed enormous trade surpluses which in the 1990s are, while still growing, placed in investment projects around the world. The rapid economic progress of the group of newly industrialising countries (so-called 'dynamic economies') of Singapore, Malaysia, Korea, Taiwan, Hong Kong and Thailand, is further evidence of the vitality of this major world region. Many countries, not least Britain, are fearful of sliding into a state of relative, long-term underdevelopment, from which it would be difficult to climb back (Cassels, 1990). There is no doubt that, even as the Japanese economy seems to falter, this sentiment of losing the race – much more powerful, but similar to that felt in the United States after Sputnik was launched, in the late 1950s – will continue to spur nations to seek reform of their education and training systems, to set goals for them and to pursue these energetically. Although the challenge of the new politics and economics of Eastern and Central Europe is still in the form of a massive dependency relationship with the Western economies, in time they, too, will become a significant part of the internationally competitive environment. With strong – if historically distorted – education and training systems, these countries will, in the future, be part of the international process of standard-setting, the outcome of which no country will be able to ignore.

A reconstructed system of work-oriented education and training, broadly defined, forward-looking, relevant to perceived social and economic needs and grounded in international as well as national socio-cultural realities, means greater emphasis on things operational or perceived as such: the technical, the scientific, the productive, the instrumental, the relevant and the practical. Education of this kind is expected to 'produce the goods', to be accountable, many of its outcomes measurable and its particularities confirmed in the experiential domain of the everyday world. Concrete and effective, with specific stress on employable skills and the work ethos, such a form of education might seem to have an easy passage to the heartland of national policy-making and finance. This has indeed been the case in Britain since the 1970s. It is reasonable, however, to ask just what it means to be 'relevant' and 'practical' in an age of increasing scientific, technological and more generally intellectual sophistication. Moreover, it is an age of ever closer ties between nations where the context of 'application' and 'relevance' is the product of a vast interplay of dynamic forces. High levels of cognitive development, of social knowledge and competence and the ability to function effectively in complex, changing life environments will better serve the demands of 'relevance' and 'practicality' than traditional notions of technical skill.

PRACTICAL RELEVANCE IN SCHOOLING

The new vocationalism in the developed world has some of its deepest roots in this ideal of practical relevance: applicable knowledge and skills. 'Applicable', however, is ambiguous and it is frequently unclear as to whether this is intended to mean 'here and now' or general applicability in a fluid situation whose future is scarcely predictable. 'Practical' has innumerable connotations and is always relative to ends and purposes and to the state of material development. Since educational ends and purposes relate the performance of specific tasks to such criteria as the testability of knowledge, critical reflection and the growth of understanding, the 'practical' and the 'relevant' are neither self-evident nor uncontestable.

In a generic sense, however, to be practical is to be capable of performing the task at hand – whether that task is designing a microchip, planning a scheme of urban transport or carving a scroll to replace a decayed capital in a medieval cathedral. Whether such capabilities are 'relevant' is a question whose answer takes us beyond an analysis of the immediately presented end to a consideration of the significance and value of the enterprise being undertaken. From an educational standpoint, 'practical relevance' refers *both* to quite specific capabilities and to principles of procedure, concepts, ideas and skills that are generalisable, capable of application in varied and changing circumstances and able to be built upon, developed and extended through acquired knowledge, experience and further systematic studies.

Standard academic education usually claims the latter, more general qualities. Historically, it has, in considerable measure and for particular groups of students, lived up to the claim. As an instrument of universal education, let alone specific training in the first sense of 'practical relevance', it is, nevertheless, from this perspective seen to be founded on disciplines and methods which are adapted neither to the needs of large numbers of individual children, nor to the general requirements of society and the economy. This is not surprising; the academic is part of a foundation of universal education and makes no claim to address all of the elements of a comprehensive system of education and training. Traditional academic schooling, structured according to theoretical disciplines of knowledge and regulated by a narrow regimen of tests and examinations, is, however, overly geared to developing only that slice of the pupil population which happens to respond in the right way at the appropriate time. Mass primary and secondary education are frequently accused of not stretching children enough. On the one hand, academic elitism and its social–cultural correlates are too exclusive; on the other, attempts to produce a truly universal system of basic schooling have been only partially successful. Schooling is on the march: it is not yet clear about its new destinations.

These changes reflect a variety of pressures for curricula and approaches to teaching and learning which, at one and the same time, prepare effectively for adult and working life and are reasonably demanding forms of well-structured general education for every individual child. Most British teachers and educators, harking back to the 1944 Education Act, would probably argue that these objectives have long been intended to be an integral part of provision. We can agree that they are, but the debate is – and for a long time has been – about the extent to which they have been, and how best they can be, achieved (Central Advisory Council for Education (England), 1963). What kind of person is it who is well prepared for active adult and working life, how are the necessary qualities to be developed and who is to be in control of the process? The language of the debate may be new, but these are perennial questions. It would be a mistake to suppose that educators have avoided them. It is, more than anything else, the rapid change in the wider socio-economic and cultural environment that accounts for the tensions and the difficulties in finding new solutions. Addressing these tensions and the attendant difficulties, educators and other analysts have identified competences – such as a broad range of 'entrepreneurial' qualities which set new targets for curricula, pedagogy, assessment and certification. We discuss these in greater detail in subsequent chapters.

Much of the emphasis on practical relevance is directed towards improving basic competence (OECD, 1989b). 'Competence', like 'practical relevance', is a term that lends itself to an excessive preoccupation with the immediacies of the work environment. The competence we have in mind is of a more strategic nature: an ability to meet the immediate requirements of the working world, coupled with flexibility, openness, creativity and the capacity to identify and solve problems, to manage change and to continue learning.

Can we infer that society in its demands for a more practical and relevant education is well informed or that the media accurately reflect considered public perceptions? We are doubtful and point to a divergence of opinion about just what kinds of competence are of most value. Movements in most countries aim to identify the skills that are deemed to be essential to master and to ensure that these are learned at school. But 'skill', in splendid isolation – or compounded with 'multi', 'flexible formation', 'transferable', 'generic', 'high level', etc. – is yet another of those ambiguous, question-begging terms which abound in the policy statements, programme plans, innovative projects, conferences and the literature of vocational and, increasingly, the whole of education. It has the seductive quality of appearing logical – an outcome of precise analysis of, for example, the relationship between preparation and manufacture and the roles of designer and operator in precision engineering (Merchier, 1991). 'Skill' is, therefore, 'practical', 'relevant', a means of linking schooling/training tasks with real work, with life, of focusing action on the attainable and the measurable. But, apart from the dysfunctions that occur in the manufacturing process, new technologies must be integrated, work organisation changes are needed, industrial relations issues affect task definition. 'Skill' needs to be contextualised and analysed with relation to other qualities both active and dispositional, such as 'knowing', 'valuing', 'intending', 'willing'. Attempts to enumerate skills, to describe and articulate (for example, into hierarchies) and to teach and acquire them independently of content, context and relations represent a chimera, the pursuit of which is costly and frustrating (Jonathan, 1987).

More mature and informed assessments of the needs of youth and society are needed to replace the shrill and often naive advocacy of 'skills' in vocational education and 'the basics' in the earlier years of schooling. They call for a reformulation of the curriculum of primary and secondary schools around a well-constructed 'core' of fundamental and essential learnings, with the aim of making school attractive and stimulating to the intelligence and aptitudes of its primary clients, the children (Skilbeck, 1985). We shall argue, also, that the continuance of a framework of broadly defined core learnings into the years of late adolescence is more appropriate than the quest for either specific or generic vocational skills.

Young people are not, of course, oblivious to these debates and discussions. Closer attention needs to be paid to their views and aspirations. Educators accustomed to expression, find it difficult to listen, to inform themselves. Youth tends to feel that education is not preparing them for their future, whether in the narrower or the broader sense just defined (Commission of the European Communities, 1982). An influential OECD publication reported as follows:

> Young people are especially critical of the relationship between school and work. They believe that the schools are divorced from 'life' and 'life's occupations', and that they are mostly concerned with the next level of education. Secondary school-leavers, therefore, get short shrift.
>
> (OECD, 1983b, p.24)

Being divorced from 'life', of course, is not the same as 'failing to prepare for work'. Preparation for work is indeed a function of schooling, but it is not the only one and nor is it reducible to narrow, task-specific training whether work- or school-based. While many studies indicate an alienation of youth from the prevailing mores and values of society, it is not sensible to pigeon-hole youth as a disaffected generation which will, ultimately, 'settle down'. There is a gap between the perceptions and values of youth and those of society at large which should be a source of concern. Employers' views vary more from enterprise to enterprise than from country to country. In areas where they have few links with the education system, many tend to complain that young people are inadequately prepared either to step into jobs or into induction programmes. A majority of employers across the world seek to take on personnel with ever higher educational qualifications. In its forward-looking 1989 report, the Confederation of British Industry's taskforce on vocational education and training, for example, set 'world class targets' for Britain's skills revolution:

> The practice of employing 16–18 year olds without training leading to nationally recognised qualifications must stop. These national attainment targets . . . would make qualifications at craftsman, technician and their equivalent levels in service industries the norm.
>
> (Confederation of British Industry, 1989, p.9)

This call for improving foundation skills and qualifications of young people was maintained in the CBI's 1993 *Routes for Success* (Confederation of British Industry, 1993). An OECD report on education and work noted, however, that:

> The tendency to prefer the more schooled concords, of course, with observations that the educational qualifications of those holding jobs seem to be influenced more by the supply of qualifications than by the needs of jobs. Taking the uncertain link between jobs and qualifications along with the informal preferences for the universally increasing supply of the more schooled yields an expectation that the formal minimum qualifications for jobs will inexorably rise, independently of changes in

the nature of jobs. As so it has been found in virtually every country examined, industrialised or developing.

(OECD, 1983b)

These assertions are, nevertheless, debatable. That they are being made at all indicates that there are indeed problems of both content and form in newer vocational educational initiatives which have their repercussions in the multiplication of credentials. The very fact that universal basic education in the developed world is now taken for granted has raised expectations about the 'raw material' of the labour market and set new requirements for the next stage: upper secondary, apprenticeship, on-the-job training, and so on. It is, of course, entirely reasonable that the huge expenditure on compulsory education and the many hours spent in the classroom should be justified by satisfactory levels of skill, ability and understanding among the vast majority of young people. It is also obvious that public authorities must develop policies, deploy resources and otherwise foster action to strengthen and improve the quality of education at this next stage. However, there are still far too many employers who resist the idea that they, too, have a responsibility for the training and education of their workforce, thereby reinforcing the all too prevalent belief that education and training are a cost but not an investment.

The demand for a relevant school curriculum, with an established central body or core of learning, cannot of course be illegitimate. Nor can there be objections, in principle, to the building of a superstructure of qualifications and credentials. What is contentious is what is to be deemed relevant, what that core should be, how and where it should be taught, how it should be encoded for purposes of assessment and validation, who should decide and who should pay, and what pathways into further and higher education, work and adulthood should follow. These questions have set a large part of the agenda of change in education in recent years. High up among the answers is a set of theses about vocational education and training, both within and beyond the school.

SUMMARY

There has been a resurgence of interest in the world's industrialised countries in the vocational dimension of education. This has not been confined to specified vocational training or preparation courses, to specialist vocational institutions or to work-based programmes, but includes a reappraisal of the nature and function of basic education at the school level.

No single characteristic defines this new vocationalism. It is marked by variety of policies and programmes and diversity of action and actors. But it is guided, if not propelled, by a determination to establish closer and better interrelationships between the experience of both formative education and preparatory training and the working world.

Countries facing major economic challenges – to restructure, to re-energise, to achieve greater competitive strength, of which Britain is a notable example – have turned to education and training as instruments of social and economic reform. The extent to which education is vocationalised becomes a new measure of economic and social performance.

All countries experiencing rapid change due to scientific and technological evolution, demography, industrial reorganisation and an interplay of social forces, are challenged to rethink their strategies for education. Vocationalism looms large among these strategies of adaptation and social learning, as a significant element in the quest for structural adjustment, improved quality and enhanced competitiveness. The demands made of schools are more numerous, the criticisms sharper and the challenge all the greater to perform in accordance with socio-economic objectives, as a result of these pressures. There are dangers and risks in the prevalence of instrumentalist and utilitarian strategies. Granted the pressure resulting from technological transformation, economic globalisation and the expectation of electorates, appropriate responses through education and training are not self-evidently a matter of practical, applicable, relevant skills.

2

EDUCATIONAL FOUNDATIONS
FOR WORKING LIFE

The antithesis between a technical and a liberal education is falla-
cious. There can be no adequate technical education which is not
liberal, and no liberal education which is not technical: that is, no
education which does not impart both technique and intellectual
vision . . . education should turn out the pupil with something he
knows well and something he can do well.

(Whitehead, 1950, p.74)

INTRODUCTION

Principal among the foundations for productive working life in both individual and social terms is a country's national educational and training
system. That system typically embraces large and complex sub-systems for
policy-making, financing, resourcing and operating schools, training
centres, colleges and higher education institutions in both the public and
private sectors. The personnel complements are large and varied; in one
way or another, practically the whole of society is involved or connected
with some form of institutionalised education.

Our emphasis in this chapter is on those educational experiences, at the
level of basic schooling, intended to prepare young people for their initial
experience of working life and likely to be effective in doing so. At the same
time, we envisage a progressive strengthening of provision for further
education and training within the framework of a policy of lifelong learning. Thus we must think of 'foundations' in a dual sense: what is a sound
basis for initial entry into work and/or continuing formal education; what
are the fundamental concepts, forms of knowledge, competences and
learning habits that seem best fitted to equip young people for a life that
will include education and further training as the norm? For such a life is
nothing less than we can contemplate for the future of any society which
claims the epithets of modern, effective and democratic.

24

What is required of these foundations is a broad, general education which is both attractive to the learner and formative in the sense of a systematic introduction to and an initial experience of the main fields and forms of human activity of which work is one. Not to provide such foundations or to do so in a weak and ineffectual manner is to bring into question subsequent education for both individuals and society. An appraisal of vocational education and training, at whatever stage, necessarily raises questions about the quality and adequacy of these foundations.

We begin by reviewing the directions of change in the relationship between the contemporary school and the external working environment. For the compulsory or the basic years of schooling, the question of a common core of learnings for all students remains problematic, and we explore the outlines of the current debate as it relates to vocational preparation. Certain trends in schooling have become particular vehicles for a greater vocational emphasis, and we review these briefly.

THE CHANGING SCHOOL–WORK ENVIRONMENT

Periods of compulsory or basic schooling generally range in length from eight to ten years in the Organisation for Economic Co-operation and Development (OECD) countries and many others. Increasingly high retention rates beyond the compulsory years mean the extension of schooling for many or most young people to ages 17, 18 and older. Schooling in many countries is now preceded by extensive provision of early childhood care and pre-school facilities, France being perhaps the most notable of OECD countries in this respect. Countries generally look upon the compulsory years as a minimum period in which to provide, for all young people, foundations for personal and social life, hence the universal tendency to state broad aims and to require a wide range of studies (OECD, 1983a, 1985a; Skilbeck, 1990).

Young people from the ages of 14 to 16 and onwards are confronted, after the close tutelage of compulsory schooling, with the need to make what are often decisive choices, both for themselves and, indeed, taking a longer-term view, for the future of society. Students by this age are in many countries at very different stages in their formation, notwithstanding the many ostensibly common elements in their education to that point. Their interests vary, naturally; they are not all equally competent, and disturbingly large numbers are performing at unsatisfactorily low levels; their perceptions of (and interest in) the world of work vary quite markedly, within as well as between countries (Walker, 1987). The personal and social cost of mediocre levels of achievement on a large scale is too high, the risks for our collective future too great. The diversity that is apparent in the middle years of secondary schooling is all too often negatively charged, from the standpoint of the students (frustrated and disappointed) and from that of society (inadequate performance).

25

Differences in levels and types of achievement in learning do indeed have an important bearing on the range of educational and training choices open to any young person. Below a certain level, (and notwithstanding some countervailing pressures towards a deskilling of parts of the labour force), there are few occupational choices left and practically none that would seem to us worthwhile, unless combined with other significant interests which themselves generally require a good standard of education. That is the stark message of the economic, technical, industrial and commercial changes discussed in Chapter 1.

Transition to working life or courses of study preparatory to it for the first time become a significant concern for many young people from the ages of 14 to 16 and onwards. That is undoubtedly a factor in their motivation and interest. By then, it is too late for schools to embark upon substantial 're-education' and 're-training' programmes which, unavoidably, will be largely a reproduction of the school climate and school values already experienced. Something different is needed; it is unsatisfactory on many counts to say either 'more of the same' or 'specific job training'. That 'something different' brings into question the adequacy of the kinds of general education provided in secondary schools. By 'different' we mean a reappraisal of what schools offer. However, the pressures and constraints we have already discussed challenge many previous assumptions about transition: for many young people there is no prospect of paid, continuous work; nor can we confidently predict future trends in the form and content of work. If vocationalising education means giving it a work orientation, these considerations must be taken into account. At the 14–16 stage, the prospect of work is increasingly distant and obscure, even if student choices are influenced by career interests.

It cannot be assumed that efforts to maintain some kind of broad and common educational experience for all youth should be abandoned at this stage of their development simply because young people themselves often declare a lack of interest in them. Of course, the organisation and content, both of general educational and specific training programmes need to take into account individual interests and differences. Equally, as we have argued, they must be concerned with the claims of a wider, shared culture, participation in a democratic society and certain fundamental needs and values which define a common humanity. A critical reappraisal of the curriculum and organisation of learning in secondary schools is required. Such criticism has not been wanting, whether it be from the standpoint of 'human capital' theorists seeking greater internal and external efficiencies for schooling or from social theorists who view the school curriculum as an initiating context for the production function of work and a device whereby socio-economic inequalities and cultural hegemony are reproduced (Bowles and Gintis, 1976; Bourdieu and Passeron, 1977). It is clearly insufficient to adopt the approach of either 'compensating' at ages 14–16 and beyond for what has been inadequately done before then or dismissing it as wasted and irrelevant and putting in place a wholly new educational regime, a kind of 'let's start all over again' approach.

Whether we regard school curricula as, potentially at least, usefully formative or unfairly reproductive, an orientation of education and training towards working life (in further and higher education) requires curricula and learning situations which engage the interest and motivation of youth. This turns out to be a formidable challenge as has been found in many education systems where, for one reason or another, school retention rates are rising and the years of schooling are thereby increasing for youth who, until very recently, gladly shook the dust of the classrooms from their heels as soon as the legal minimum age of leaving was reached. For reasons of student motivation, social justice, employment opportunities, and economic needs, among others, a vocationally oriented appraisal of secondary schooling indicates that changes are necessary.

It is during the period of mid adolescence that, since the Second World War, young people have been faced with a crucial decision, whether to stay in the formal education system, pursuing one or other of the separate routes or tracks which by then have opened up, or to seek some kind of paid employment. Now, in Continental Europe, the United States, Canada, Japan and Australasia, the prospect of staying in the formal education system, willingly or not, is already a reality or is rapidly becoming so for practically all youth (OECD, 1993a, p.117).

In Britain, as in some other countries, too many of them have in recent years opted for neither continuing education nor work, but for a combination of supported or partially supported unemployment and a life at the margins of the social order. This is a course which is extremely hazardous for individuals and society alike. The employment–unemployment crisis constitutes a fundamental worldwide problem, personally and socially. The collapse of the youth employment market has been swift and massive. The consequent traumatisation of youth's hopes and expectations which had been, for decades, fed on the prospect of paid work perhaps in harness with specific, job-related training, was sufficient reason for major policy changes. The curriculum of basic schooling – whatever weaknesses and deficiencies may be laid at its door – has for long been the foundation as well as the entry point for the world of work. But delayed entry into the workforce has become an increasingly established pattern and is now, in Britain as in many other OECD countries, an explicit object of policy. New curricula, new institutions, new teaching and learning strategies, new forms of assessment and accreditation are all needed and to a greater and lesser degree are being introduced in many systems. Greater emphasis is being given to conceptualisation, a problem-solving approach, reasoning in the context of real-life situations, 'learning to think and thinking to learn' in a quest for that elusive balance between abstract, disciplined knowledge and manipulative skills and applied techniques (Maclure and Davies, 1991; Araujo e Oliveira, 1992, Chapter 2).

There is a convergence, at least on this point, between the more enlightened theories of the workplace and its needs and the reformers of the education system. Hence there is a common interest in the concept of a changing work culture, and a changing education culture. The end of 'Taylorism' or 'Fordism', with its presupposition of lowly educated workers, atomised, rigid and routinised tasks, and the emergence of high-skill, flexible, collaborative 'Toyotism' in the production process is also the beginning of the reformation of work and the reconstruction of education (Piore and Sabel, 1984; Mathews, 1989a; OECD, 1992i). Symbolically, at any rate, that is the direction of change in the interaction between school and work environments.

The theme of transition to working life and the attendant emphasis on work-based and work-related training from adolescence until early adulthood has taken on a particular character and is of great importance in the United Kingdom, given the significantly high proportion of young people who still do not complete secondary education. It is not so everywhere, as we see in more detail in Chapter 4. Some countries have chosen to prolong the period of general education through formal schooling to the point where, for example in Scandinavia, the USA and Japan, the norm is continued full-time education up to the age of 17, or indeed beyond. In the German-speaking countries, where education and training for substantial numbers are shared between the formal education institutions and the workplace (dual system), there is a comparable recognition that the years of adolescence are vital for the educational formation of all. The theme of partnership is of universal interest and takes a variety of forms of which the dual system of apprenticeship is but one (HMI, 1991b; Sako, 1991; OECD, 1992g).

While the choices being made at this stage are imposed, to an extent not fully understood, by labour market conditions, the positive holding power of the school and the value accorded to a continuing broad general education must not be underestimated as forces in their own right. This is evident in an overview of curriculum trends in member countries published by OECD (Skilbeck, 1990). Indeed, so strong is this feeling that in some quarters it is considered to be the only realistic solution (Deasy and Penn, 1985).

In one form or another, education rather than full-time paid employment and including specific training, whether in schools, colleges, the workplace, or other settings, is set to become the norm for adolescents in the years ahead where it is not already so. From an employment perspective, this means that this education will necessarily have a vocational dimension but one which reflects the anticipated, longer-term future rather than reproduces the assumptions and practices of the past for immediate application. Our discussion of this in the preceding chapter points towards a broad and deep general education incorporating work experience and studies of working life. From the student perspective, such an education must be liberated from the rigidities of the past, and become truly engaging and formative, abandoning its numerous restrictive and illiberal practices.

The 'transition' is, therefore, towards a continuing education, with employment a more distant goal (and not necessarily for all). We observe in the industrialised democracies a definite trend towards some form of continued education and training, perhaps lifelong, for all youth beyond that stage where, only a few years ago, a majority were entering the workforce aged between 14 and 16. There is, at present, considerable diversity of policy, opinion and practice regarding such questions as to whether work experience and preparation for work, for example through vocational and career guidance, should play a larger role, who should direct and organise the programmes and whether a 'schooling' or a 'working life' model should prevail. These divergences embody differences of culture and tradition; they leave open the question of whether efforts should continue to be made to extend a common core of education and training to all youth beyond the age of 14 (or 15/16) or whether, as had been the UK trend, a range of cores (or no core at all) should progressively be introduced from age 14 onwards. The 1988 Education Act and the new curriculum and assessment frameworks which have followed it indicate that that age will henceforth be raised and that the school will be the provider of one kind of core curriculum (the 'national' curriculum) for all students to age 16. Ministerial moves also suggest a possible interest in a post-16 core in the years to come. That and the extremely ambitious attempts to produce a national system of 'levels of competence' – within the national curriculum (attainment levels) and through the activities of the National Council for Vocational Qualifications (NCVQ), is a direction which, if really pursued, could ultimately bring together for the first time ever, the divergent streams of work, training and education (NCVQ, 1987, 1992a). We return to this topic in Chapter 5.

The option of full-time paid employment is unlikely ever again to become genuinely open to significant numbers of young people at 16. But this is not to say that links with working life or its impact on schooling will or should weaken. What is meant here by 'working life' and its impact on schooling encompasses quite a range of considerations: direct work experience and various forms of work preparation, including career education as part of the school curriculum; evaluations that are increasingly being made of the quality of schooling and consequent modifications according to work values; introduction of systematic schemes of general or specific vocational guidance and training, special schemes for employing personnel from industry and commerce in the school sector, and the development of school–employer programmes for school–work transition. What is needed is a more systematic approach based on a considered educational rationale, well-designed and properly evaluated programmes and an end to the lingering social and academic snobbery that divides schooling into 'academic' and 'non-academic', with work experience and vocational education for the latter not the former.

Such values of working life as personal responsibility for tasks, competence in handling production processes, tools and instruments, information-processing capability, resourcefulness and flexibility, team work and time management are increasingly affirmed as relevant for pedagogical practice and for long have been advocated by educational progressives (Connell, 1980, Part 1). Changing technical and organisational requirements of the workplace can inform curriculum design and set targets for the performance of students (and teachers). Provided the best practice and highest standards are chosen and not worst cases, it is perfectly reasonable to assess selected aspects of schooling against relevant criteria of working life. Moreover, the changing organisation of work in society challenges formal educational institutions to rethink their structure and the organisation and content of studies. Is this a capitulation of educational values to those of the marketplace, a mere co-option of schooling and of children's development? Critics who hold this view demean the value and significance of productive work in human and social development, often confusing 'work' with 'employment under capitalism'. They also fail to distinguish qualities in work that are educative and liberating from those that are habitual or even harmful to the worker.

The traditional academic bias of the school, notably the long-established subject structure of the secondary school curriculum, is profoundly challenged by reflections and developments such as these, which, from the standpoint of a contemporary view of needed competence, represent a fundamental critique of schooling (Raven, 1991). There have been numerous responses, but not many that have been thought out and planned right through to the point of agreed long-term new directions. As a result, it would not be misleading to suggest that, in most societies, there are uneasy relationships and unresolved tensions in the school–workplace nexus. The value of continued general education as a basis for training is affirmed; as a consequence, it is right to press the school to change its ways, just as the organisation and content of work needs to change both to provide fulfilment of workers and to sustain economic well-being. The pressure cannot be one way, only on the schools, a point to make in relation to school–industry partnerships (OECD, 1992g).

For such reasons as these, it is now necessary in discussions of employment and the economy to question alike the level and quality of demand from the employment sector and the quality and relevance of the education and training of the young to mid adolescent students. In debates over the nature and role of working life in the training of youth, we must bring under review the objectives, content, organisation and presentation of what the school typically offers as the core curriculum. Such a move has been under way, for example, in Australia through the Australian Education Council (AEC), a body comprising the federal education minister and the education ministers of the states and territories (Australian Education Council, 1992). Notwithstanding the scale of change in the development of the national curriculum in Britain, and the large investments in work-related education and special training programmes, it is not at all evident that the issue of the working life dimension has been sufficiently worked through. The national curriculum is essentially bounded by the traditions of academic disciplines.

A revitalised, broadly defined core curriculum of the compulsory years of schooling, which we discuss below, might be considered as a foundation for either a new kind of core in the post-compulsory years or for an array of differentiated programmes for that period. In either case, linkages between the culture of 'schooling' and that of 'working life' must be forged. Unless we take this broader view, moves to improve the situation through new, post-school or college special purpose training schemes now and in the future will lack an adequate foundation. Conversely, there is a danger of redundancy, if work-based training replicates what schools could and should have achieved at an earlier stage. Innovations cannot exist or grow in isolation from the 'cultivated fields' in which they are being implanted.

THE EDUCATION OF THE ADOLESCENT: COMMON OR DIVIDED LEARNING?

Adolescence is a turning point in a social as well as a personal sense. How should we organise education and training at this stage? There are several possibilities. One direction is to abandon the idea of the common school and hence a common core curriculum, and to divide the educational and training programmes into a series of institutionally separate tracks or routes. Hence the tradition of stratified or differentiated secondary schooling, including the division between academic/general and technical/vocational, against which advocates of comprehensive schools have resolutely set themselves. In this tradition, still strong in many countries including Germany, individual students usually join different groups or age cohorts passing along these tracks. Conventionally, and in many school systems, these tracks roughly correspond to three forms or ways of organising knowledge: declarative knowledge of the form *that* so and so is the case, organised in complex systems with a strong cognitive base; procedural knowledge of the form, this is *how* to do or perform *x* and *y*, organised in sets of tasks with a high replicative component; and both of these two forms of knowledge organised into life tasks, problem-solving exercises and interest-based projects. To each of these three knowledge structures, corresponding school types or streams have been attached,

31

particularly in the countries of Europe: the grammar school or *Gymnasium*, and academic *lycée*, the technical or specialist vocational school; and the 'secondary modern' school.

These conventional distinctions are, however, breaking down in many countries as a result of the preferences of students and their parents (in Germany, for instance, the flight from the *Hauptschule*) or of the changing employment demands and rapidly increasing participation rates (in France, for instance, the multiplication of the vocational baccalaureates). Nor can the distinction between declarative and performative knowledge provide an adequate basis for distinguishing types of school/tracks and types of curricula. The cognitive requirements for performance in an age of high technology have increased; performance is becoming more a matter of operationalising concepts, cognitive maps and principles than of deploying discrete skills drawn from a pool of established practice.

Whilst there are arguments favouring the classical forms of differentiation into separate school (and knowledge) 'types', from age 15 onwards, the case against is much stronger. Differentiation is a goal within the structures of knowledge, performance and institutions; it does not preclude common elements and can be a spur to creative forms of integration. The challenge for curriculum designers is to construct common frameworks which are characterised by fundamental concepts, bodies of knowledge and operative strategies and a wide variety of differentiated interpretations and applications.

One practical question arising from the carving out of separate tracks, new as well as old, is their appropriateness to individual and social needs which may be much more diverse and fine-grained than these broadly defined tracks allow. Another relates to the ease of switching from one track to another, should the need arise. Separate tracks can become institutionalised ruts. Above all, we want to affirm the personal and social value of continuing the quest for some common, foundational studies throughout the years of adolescence.

Thus a second approach to the problem is the attempt, within the general or common high school, or in the education and training/school and work nexus, to maintain elements of a common core of education for everyone (Skilbeck, 1985). There are arguments for this over and above the forms and uses of knowledge pertinent to the rising levels of demand generated by changes in work content and organisation. These have long since been powerfully expressed in John Dewey's educational philosophy (Dewey, 1916) of a shared democratic ethic in an age of science and technology on the one hand, or, on the other, of liberal general education focused on cultural achievements and fundamental human qualities whose development and training is held to be essential for the humanity of all people. More recently, Jürgen Habermas has drawn attention to the importance of communicative competence in social bonding – a common discourse (Habermas, 1989).

If we look beneath the surface of the stated aims and values of the educational systems of all the countries that espouse the Western liberal, democratic tradition we discover that there are requirements for social, cultural, political and economic life and for personal development that could not possibly be met if we were to draw a line at ages 14 or 15, concluding that by that stage general education, citizenship education, values education and personal development education have finished, to be displaced by specialised work preparation and differentiation of the age group into quite separate streams and institutions. That such differentiation occurs is testimony to the capacity an educational system has to sustain massive contradictions and discontinuities.

Historically, what we have witnessed is a vicious divide: little or no continuing education and training of any sort for substantial numbers leaving formal school at 14–16; a rich if still restricted provision for a minority staying on to enjoy the rewards of advanced qualifications.

Now, the question is, by what means and with what kind of orientation can we best achieve a regime of stimulating, motivating general education for all youth? The answer we propose is universal schooling throughout adolescence, based on a common core of varied learnings, with an admixture of work experience and, over and above the common experiences, various kinds of differentiation in recognition of distinct individual and social needs.

The approach through a common core does not result in an undifferentiated curriculum mass. Choices of specialisation are available, in the form of electives, including general or specific vocational training and work experience and individualised study or work/study programmes.

Within the common core itself, differentiation can and indeed must occur, in respect of levels of study, exemplary materials for teaching and learning and assessment procedures (Gorter, 1986).

Both the American and the Japanese, as well as some of the European systems, have adopted or are moving towards this pattern. The dual system of the German-speaking countries appears to stand out by contrast. Even so, there is, at least in Germany, a substantial common component in the form of required subjects and all youth are in education or training, part or full time, to age 18.

In practice, the concept of common core learnings is greatly vitiated since opportunities and pressures for student choice and the provision of separate tracks and levels increase with age, as we see in more detail in Chapter 4. It is not necessarily a matter of a sharp bifurcation between a core of general education and distinctly differentiated programmes, however much institutional (and financial) arrangements may tend that way. In specialised training programmes, for example, elements of general education can be retained; in the common school, the core curriculum can be progressively reduced as a proportion of students' learning and, within the

33

schooling model, not all schools are 'common' – there is a continuing if, numerically speaking minority, strand of technical–vocational secondary schools. In all cases, school and workplace can collaborate. Institutions and programmes of study can be located along two continua: common core and differentiated learnings; school- or institution-based and work- or enterprise-based.

The issues hinge on the need for, and the nature of, a core curriculum for all adolescents and the most appropriate setting for particular learning experiences – school or work. We introduce these issues here, in the context of the debate over common and differentiated learnings. The specific issue of a core curriculum is discussed in more detail in Chapter 3.

Significant differences exist in organisational arrangements, which to a large extent reflect different national traditions, perceptions and values. The research evidence on the learning effects is slight – but it is rare to find that a significant change of policy is based upon or accompanied by a comprehensive research programme. Among educationalists, arguments have been advanced about the need to strengthen relationships between the common school and a common or core curriculum, the social and cultural value of shared experience within a common core, and the necessity to continue developing, in all youth, a common core of basic and fundamental skills, knowledge and understanding in any educational programme (Skilbeck, 1985). On the other hand, these arguments are vigorously challenged, also by educators, on such grounds as the difficulty of reaching agreement in democratic societies about what the core is to comprise, the necessity of acknowledging cultural pluralism, and the supposed arbitrariness of imposing a common set of requirements on young people who are diverse in intellectual attainments, interests and so forth (Crittenden, 1982). It is often difficult to arrive at any consensus between interest groups, especially now that multi-ethnicity is an accepted feature of many societies. It becomes necessary to introduce that perspective into the core curriculum debate, not as a reason for not proceeding, but for precisely the opposite reason: that the reality of cultural diversity obliges education to pay greater attention to the meaning of shared values, citizenship, social cohesion and ways of combining them with the development of cultural pluralism (Lynch *et al.*, 1992, Part 1).

Evidently, most OECD countries – up to the end of the compulsory years of schooling, but not beyond – retain some kind of visible common core, albeit often quite attentuated, in the curriculum. However minimal its scope, and notwithstanding a generous interpretation of what is or can be 'common' in learnings pitched at different levels and organised in separate tracks or streams, the curriculum normally includes common, compulsory elements (OECD, 1983a, 1989b; Gorter, 1986; Skilbeck 1990).

The normative belief in a common or shared minimum of learnings for all citizens continues to make its claims heard, despite the difficulties, the criticism and the impetus towards differentiation. But, just as the common structures of schooling in many societies begin to break down between student ages 14 and 16, so is the idea of the common curriculum increasingly difficult to relate to the reality of policy and practice – in curriculum, pedagogy or institutional organisation. This is true within the formal education system. When, alongside that system, an attempt is made, as in the United Kingdom through the Youth Training Scheme (YTS) and, up to a point, through the centrally funded Technical and Vocational Education Initiative (TVEI) in secondary schools (see Chapter 5), to introduce a parallel sphere of training with strong links to the workplace, the whole issue of a core curriculum becomes problematic. It is timely to rethink the core curriculum on a wider plane than vocationalism, but it is as a result of the vocational thrust that many of the questions are surfacing.

VOCATIONALISING TRENDS IN SCHOOLING

The vocational thrust in schools does not result from nor is it embodied only in policy imperatives, sets of prescriptive legislation or other such authority sources; rather it is a derivative of diverse trends and movements, ideas and practices which have evolved over many years in different national and cultural settings. We review several of these distinctive national settings in Chapter 4. In all of them, school systems have for a very long time been alert to the need for a variety of vocational roles to be carried out.

All countries have, in the years since the Second World War, shown a considerable expansion of *career guidance*. Great efforts have been made to inform pupils, while still at school, of the options that lie before them in terms of employment and training, frequently with special support for low achievers and girls. In Britain, career education and guidance was set as a cross-curricular theme for all students during compulsory schooling in the National Curriculum (DES, 1989), and the Confederation of British Industry sees reinvigorating the Careers Service as a key element in its programme for improving the skill levels of Britain's youth (Confederation of British Industry, 1993). Individual teachers may have career guidance responsibilities; or a specially trained corps might go into the schools and talk with students (OECD, 1985b; Vorbeck, 1985). Teacher or career officer guidance is a facility which can be developed in addition to or, better still, within the curriculum. It is not a substitute for vocational curriculum content or for the meaningful activities by students themselves which should form the target or outcome of guidance.

Attempts that are now commonly made to *increase awareness of the world of work* from primary school onwards are a kind of structured guidance with general relevance to all students and thus a contribution to the idea of a common core curriculum. This may take the form of a few hours a week, for example in a cross-curriculum theme, actually studying the environment of work and the organisation of the economy with concomitant efforts to improve learning of what are perceived as practical skills.

That it is now generally recognised that *science and technology* should be a part of the curriculum from very early on in primary school has much to do with the public perception of them as, or having the potential to be, practical and work-related fields of study. Again, we see in this the concept of a common foundation of knowledge and understanding which, with its practical orientation, gives students a feeling for objects and their relations in the physical and material worlds. Certainly, the methods used to teach scientific subjects at the primary and secondary stages are increasingly based on guided and structured experimentation and discovery. Similarly, technology, which is now compulsory in the lower secondary schools of many countries and features increasingly in primary schools, is part of a general core of studies with a very definite relevance to working life. It is in technology as a school subject that the shift in work content from craft to design is more clearly visible than in any other subject of the curriculum. Computer studies have similar characteristics and their spread at both primary and secondary stages is indicative of a more practical approach to the curriculum. Recognition, however, is not the same as achievement. 'Scientific literacy – which embraces sciences, mathematics and technology – has emerged as a central goal of education. Yet the fact is that scientific literacy eludes us in the United States' (American Association for the Advancement of Science, 1989, p.3). This is a potent reminder of the need to achieve success not at the level, merely, of national goals, policy statements and programmes, but in every classroom. Too little emphasis has been given, in the general drive towards 'practical', 'relevant', 'work-oriented' studies, to the actual needs of teachers in the classroom, to the resource requirements and the structures needed to support long-term innovations (Layton, n.d.).

If classroom realities are given insufficient attention in much of the high-level policy reporting and debate, the need for new *partnerships between the school and the world of work* has been increasingly recognised both by commerce and industry on the one hand and education authorities on the other. Many of the innovations in vocational education and training discussed in later chapters result from and demonstrate such partnerships.

There has been a growing trend, developing links between compulsory/post-compulsory provision and employers in general whether from industry, commerce or administration. Twinning schools and colleges with firms, asking their representatives to sit on governing bodies, inviting guests to address or mix with students, introducing material on work and working life into the curriculum, well-planned visits by schools to industrial and commercial sites and schemes for teachers to spend periods in the workplace to improve their understanding and skills are just some of the many means being used in different countries (Noah and Eckstein, 1988; OECD, 1992g).

36

Perhaps the most attractive method of creating links with the outside world has been *work experience programmes*, which have mushroomed in all countries since the 1970s. Education systems have increasingly given credit for skills, knowledge and aptitudes acquired through work experience. University entrance requirements in some countries allow experience in lieu of paper qualifications. There is a general trend towards development of what may be described as a new credential currency, that is, a framework that makes interchangeable, when appropriate, educational qualifications, work experience and training. Perhaps the clearest example of this on a national scale, is the framework being erected in Britain by the NCVQ.

In an effort to break the barriers of narrow occupational preparation, to strengthen the case for vocational education at the school level, to provide a genuine alternative to the prevailing academic models and to develop organic links between the curriculum of schools and that of work-based education and training, a great deal of interest has been expressed with regard to the idea of *general vocational skills*. Mostly in North America and the UK, various lists have been developed of 'transferable' or 'generic' skills using such categories as 'problem-solving', 'communication', 'process', 'interpersonal' or 'practical' (OECD, 1982b). These lists are intended both as a basis for vocational education programmes and as a means of evaluating the skills acquired by individual trainees. Such lists do not and cannot constitute a vocational educational curriculum. They do, however, provide a focus and may serve as a helpful check to be applied in preparing curriculum objectives and reviewing assessment schedules for the lower and upper secondary cycles. In this way, learning objectives derived from analysing cross-vocational needs can be brought into general education, where various lists of aims and desirable outcomes have already been aired.

The foregoing overview of trends is intended to be indicative of directions; it is in no sense exhaustive. The multiplicity of programmes and activities over the past two to three decades has, on the one hand, demonstrated a concern to meet new challenges in the education–work relationship and, on the other, led to the realisation that transition from school to working life can no longer be the object of limited, stop-gap measures for particular groups. Overall provision, dialogue and co-ordination have to be developed. As we see further in Chapter 4, in all countries courses are offered to young people of post-compulsory school age either in separate, usually employer-led training programmes or in upper secondary or further education. In some countries, such as Sweden or the United States, vocational programmes have been incorporated into the upper secondary cycle; naturally this means that special provision has to be available for drop-outs and low performers. Some countries have also set up pre-vocational courses to improve the general education and vocational skills of school-leavers. These broad measures do not, of course, serve only to address a social and economic need; they also reduce the number of registered unemployed (OECD, 1985c).

If we are to succeed in developing and enhancing competences needed for the labour market, they need to be clearly identified, not in the abstract but in reference to working life. This is more difficult than it sounds since these competences must also incorporate skills and other qualities or learnt attributes which are 'general' and 'transferable' in a rapidly changing world.

Research continues on enumerating the qualities, aptitudes and dispositions that are thought to be desirable in school-leavers, trainees and new employees. These attempts necessarily draw on predictions about labour-market needs in the future and generally foresee the arrival of a new technological culture in which Taylorist or Fordist task divisions will be relegated to social studies textbooks. Teachers need a greater consciousness of the world of work if they are to exercise their professional skills and judgement in educating students towards understanding, knowing about and performing vocational roles. Changes in work are highly suggestive, an invitation to educators to exercise creativity and imagination in both curriculum design and pedagogy.

Machines throughout industry and commerce are either taking charge of standard tasks or being integrated into new processes whose human operatives require a capacity to think and act in systems terms as well as competence in specific, machine-related skills. Human beings will design, programme, direct, work alongside and if necessary fix and adapt machines which are themselves part of an intelligent system. The new technologies increasingly enable firms and contractors to offer customisation, services and goods catering specifically for the individual client, complementing existing mass-produced items. The marketplace society as a whole is undergoing rapid and unpredictable movements; specialised techniques are evolving at a fast rate. As we saw in Chapter 1, management and employees are alike required to show flexibility, adaptability and initiative in order to stay up to date and to compete successfully. But competition is not all. Co-operation, co-ordination and teamwork are essential. Individuals will not be able to continue performing the same specific tasks for long periods of time as the work functions that they will fulfil will not remain the same. They will not be able simply to respond to the demands of the systems with which they work; they will have to interact with them, with their colleagues and outsiders. They will be expected to solve problems as they arise, to improvise, make decisions, devise good procedures and improve the quality of the services and products that are dispensed by their group. Manifestations of this type of relationship and behaviour may already be found in Japanese practices such as job rotation, quality circles and the variable production line. Such changes in the labour force and production organisation are seen by some commentators as a step towards greater democratisation and individual responsibility and participation (Pratzner and Russell, 1984; Mathews, 1989b). They see the future work environment as potentially humanist, in direct contrast with the mechanisation of human

38

beings which characterised the first assembly lines and automated systems. These, however, are values or attributes of the work environment which are not inevitable but will be the fruits of broadly based education and training.

Pratzner and Russell place interpersonal, group-process, problem-solving, decision-making and planning skills under the general heading of group problem-solving, a term that is at once more embracing and indicative of higher-order human activity. It sums up quite neatly the general nature of abilities and aptitudes which forward-looking societies will, in the future, expect of labour-market entrants. Compulsory education and vocational schemes will need to develop and foster these in children and young adults. Here vocationalism can find itself very much in line with liberal educational theory which advocates precisely these humanistic qualities as being essential to the healthy development of individuals and society.

Thus, in orientating education and training towards 'working life' we must be particularly careful to avoid imposing narrow occupational prescriptions, dated images and stereotypes of work culture and organisation. The directions of change at work that are singled out by analysts call for qualities that, we have argued, are best developed by means of a high-quality, broad, general education throughout the compulsory years and beyond, which combines continuing study of a wide range of subject matter with, *inter alia*, themes and orientations that progressively draw students into the changing world of work.

SUMMARY

The foundations of working life and preparation for it are laid down in the compulsory years of schooling. On a basis of a system of universal primary or elementary education, widely established in industrialised countries by the end of the nineteenth century, we have witnessed, in the twentieth century, the universalisation of secondary education, extending steadily through the years of early, through mid, and now into late adolescence. Vast changes in the provision, organisation, content and methods of schooling have been necessary; many countries are still in the midst of these development and reform processes.

The relatively recent collapse of the youth labour market has added momentum to these changes and the prospect of schooling for all up to the end of adolescence becomes ever closer. Such schooling may be full time or part time in combination with enterprise-based occupational training.

For a variety of reasons, most systems of education seek to maintain elements of a common core curriculum notwithstanding the increasing diversity of student populations in the upper years. Increasingly, a vocational orientation is complementing traditional academic curricula. A wide range of vocationalising trends is apparent. Their educative potential is considerable and, properly articulated into systematic programmes of study and work experience, can be a means of bringing the worlds of education and work closer together. New designs for schooling, including a restructured common core curriculum and forward-looking pedagogical activities relevant to the changing realities of working life, are needed.

3

THE CORE LEARNINGS
CHALLENGE

[T]here must be a complete rethinking of the domains of human experience to be encountered commonly by children and youth in their progress through school toward effective, satisfying lives as citizens, parents, workers, and thoughtful participants in their culture.

(Goodlad, 1986, p.27)

INTRODUCTION

It is necessary to transcend the fruitless debates about which discrete subjects or topics to include in or exclude from the core curriculum, such debates leading inevitably towards a hardening of established academic positions and the politics of pressure groups and lobbies, while generally bypassing the wide range of curricular and pedagogical issues facing educational systems (Gorter, 1986; Skilbeck, 1990). A more strategic and creative approach is required, in order to address the relationship of the curriculum to educational goals, objectives and values, to account for the perspective of the learner and to ensure that there is a considered response to changes and issues in the broad social–cultural–economic context of education. Certain dimensions and aspects of the core curriculum are particularly salient in the vocational debate. These include core competences and skills, giving rise to a set of issues bridging the 'schooling' and 'working life' models of education and training.

DEVELOPING THE MEANING OF CORE CURRICULUM

There is a long history of core curriculum discussion and debate and, as a result, several ways in which we can think about 'core curriculum' (Skilbeck, 1985). All have their place, but they should not be confused with one another.

First, core can be analysed administratively, with explicit reference to the institutional or system-wide setting in or through which the contents and

41

structures of required learning, whatever they may be, are determined, whether local school or workplace, or regional/state/national education system, or a national curriculum or training authority. In this sense, the core refers to *whatever all students in that institution or system are required in common to study as part of the curriculum* (compulsory). Thus, all school systems specify study of basic subjects – for example, mother tongue and mathematics – as a common requirement of all schools and all students. From this perspective, the core is usually defined as what the state requires to be taught and expects to be learnt (compulsory, again) in all relevant institutions. In France, this is a national responsibility; in the United States it may be a state or even a district one, although the federal government and various national bodies have made strenuous efforts to achieve a national *de facto* core through a series of reviews and reports on the nation's schools, with recommendations on desirable or essential learnings for all students (Adler, 1982; National Commission on Excellence in Education (USA), 1983; Bennett, 1987; Bush, 1991; SCANS, 1991). Regional accreditation and college entrance requirements in the United States can produce a *de facto* core. A *de facto* core can also be established by the requirements of public examinations and accreditation systems (conditional compulsory). The 1988 Education Act for England and Wales aims to ensure that a legally required core curriculum is taught in schools, defined as so many compulsory subjects, with a nationwide age-based and graded testing apparatus added on to the existing system of public examinations for secondary school students. As the Dearing Report shows, years after its introduction the new systemic process was still evolving (Dearing, 1993).

From this administrative definition various inferences can be drawn, and there are certain consequences. The core is determined according to established authority; its content and structure may have any number of forms according to the authority in question; its delivery may be monitored and assessed by these same authorities. Who controls the core is often an issue of greater moment than what it contains. Pursuing such control becomes a target of those who seek change.

Second, the core may be thought of as *a comprehensive set of essential learning contents* defined according to subjects, topics, themes, areas and types of experience and ways of learning and teaching, and justified with reference to theories and views about their importance on educational, social or cultural, economic or other grounds, rather than a legally constituted authority. Within this view, subject specialists may refer to core (central, basic) learnings in their subject, without thereby implying that the subject itself should be part of core (compulsory) learnings for all students. However, a content core normally comprises a set of required subjects or subject content either loosely coupled or integrated to a greater or lesser extent. The questions to ask, here, are what *should* or might be included in the core and what are the grounds for such decisions. Thus the issue for exponents of new approaches to vocational education is what kind of case is likely to be most successful in any attempt to modify or change the existing core which, in schools, is traditionally grounded in academically defined subjects: English, history, science, mathematics and so on.

Third, the core may be viewed as *a set of learning processes or procedures* including strategies of teaching and learning, and the settings for such learning. This is to emphasise the processes of teaching and learning, a reminder that a static list of subjects, themes, topics, etc., gives us little understanding of the practicalities of what is taught and learnt. Thus a particularly crucial point in relation to vocational education and training is that the 'how' and the 'where' are just as important as the 'what'.

As part of the new vocationalism, interest has grown in the application of the core curriculum concept through attempts to define *a core of skills* common both to academic subject matter and to a very wide range of occupations or fields of employment (basic occupational competences) and to do this, not only in schools or colleges, but in workplaces as well. The importance of this development is not confined to vocational policy and practice: the core skills idea is a way of rethinking academic content, of relating structures of content to processes of and settings for learning, of systematically relating theory to practice and of bringing together new sets of players in decision-making both nationally and locally.

Many schemes have been advanced to give a more vocational flavour to the core curriculum in schools and beyond schooling. The US Secretary of Labor's Commission on Achieving Necessary Skills referring to 'workplace know how' argued for 'five competencies and a three-part foundation of skills and personal qualities that are needed for solid job performance' (SCANS, 1991, p.vii). The five competencies consist of productive use of: *resources* (allocating time, money, materials, space, staff); *interpersonal skills* (teamwork, leading, negotiating); *information* (acquiring, using, communicating data); *systems* (social, organisational and technological); and *technology* (selection, application, maintenance). For the effective, productive use of these competencies, it is proposed that all workers need *basic skills* (reading, writing, arithmetic and mathematics, speaking and listening); *thinking skills* (creative thinking, decision-making, problem-solving, imagining, reasoning, knowing how to learn); *personal qualities* (responsibility, self-esteem, sociability, self-management, integrity).

Similar examples of core learnings for working life for development in schools and training programmes have now become commonplace in the literature. They give rise to as many questions as they answer, not least in ambiguities of meaning and uncertainties of application. Nevertheless, they point a direction which policy-makers are increasingly ready to follow.

Experimental programmes for the Youth Training Scheme (YTS) in Britain in the 1980s adopted a core curriculum approach focused on competences and skills thought to be relevant to working life. This, the

Core Skills Project, identified a set of core or generic skills which, derived from analysing activities in work, were also recognisably basic schooling skills. It was argued that if effectively learnt by trainees, these skills might be applied or transferred to a very diverse set of occupational settings. This approach to core curriculum is examined further later in this chapter, and in more detail in Chapters 5 and 7.

In the history of curriculum theory, the term 'core' has had a specialised meaning, grounded in the idea that there could (and should) be a small, tightly integrated set of organising principles, values and concepts capable of being applied to any subject matter. These principles, values and concepts were derived from psychological theory and social analysis. They include a problem-solving, constructivist approach jointly by teachers and students towards resolving significant social issues (Alberty, 1947; Smith *et al.*, 1957). In some respects the Core Skills Project of the YTS had this as an aim, demonstrated in attempts to distil a large number of skills into a small, tightly integrated set which would permeate all subject-specific learning.

Taking into account each of the above ways of thinking about core curriculum, we view core curriculum as *a map or chart of planned, interrelated and organised learning experiences which is predicated on a view that there are basic or fundamental learnings which all students should acquire.* Who is responsible for drawing up this map, and on what authority? How are decisions reached about which are the 'basic and fundamental' learning experiences? What rationale is developed for these decisions? What is implied or stated about the sites or settings in which the core curriculum is to be delivered and experienced? How is the implementation of the core curriculum monitored and evaluated? Which learnings are assessed, by whom and against what criteria? How much of the students' time is to be devoted to core as distinct from freely chosen or supplementary learnings? When countries change, extend or decide to adopt a core curriculum strategy – for example, for the 14-plus age group – these are the kinds of questions that arise and inevitably will be answered – for better or worse.

MAPPING A CORE CURRICULUM FOR GENERAL EDUCATION

The question of extending an educationally defined and school-based core curriculum into the adolescent years and beyond is, we have pointed out, controversial. The task of mapping a core curriculum raises issues which are undeniably complex. Arguments used in relation to the education of younger children may no longer be valid, and in many countries (but not all) the relatively simple structure of the common elementary or primary school gives way, during the adolescent years, to a bewilderingly complex array of diverse institutions, qualifications and credentials, many of them highly specialised. Yet curriculum balance and breadth and opportunities for continuing a set of common learnings are just as important at this stage as in the earlier years of schooling. One-sided specialisation is a poor preparation for adult roles including employment; democratic citizenship entails some common values, understandings and capabilities. Continued development during adolescence built on the foundations of primary and lower secondary schooling is preferable to a sudden, sharp divergence of educational experience (Schools Council for Curriculum and Examinations, 1972; FEU, 1984; OECD, 1985b).

But does not the achievement of quality in education and training entail recognition of differences and diversity? There are many who will suppose that what may be required beyond basic schooling is less a commonality of aims and overall curriculum structures than a diversity of approaches and delivery systems. Diversity, however, may be sought and attained not by separation, but within a common framework, thus achieving the benefits of shared knowledge, values and experience. A common core is part, not the whole, of the student's learning; individual differences will be reflected in both the optional, specialised parts of the curriculum and in different rates of progression and levels of attainment.

Earlier learnings need reinforcing; impending adulthood sets new learning tasks common to all youth in the post-compulsory years. These are issues that cannot be brushed aside, yet there remains the question of how they are to be tackled. Core skills and other strategies for vocational preparation could be a platform from which to advance towards a more comprehensive and general programme, or they could be submerged in a drive towards ever greater differentiation and immediate practicality in the work situation. Behind this set of alternatives is nothing less than a permanent crisis in educational and social philosophy: the emancipation and the wider culture of the individual in both personal and social terms contrasted with the individual's subordination to the economic or other needs of the nation and to highly particularised interests. Educational theorists and practitioners have struggled to establish a *modus operandi* between the two. There are some linking terms and concepts which recur in the debate. As we have seen, they include the much abused 'relevance'.

The term 'relevance' features in many discussions of quality in the curriculum of education and training for the 14–18 age group. While it may be conceded, for example by critics of the performance of schools, that the quality and efficiency of a particular type of learning or teaching is high in terms of criteria internal to the subject or area of experience, the relevance of that learning or teaching to social conditions or social policy goals or to longer-term individual needs of learners may be questioned (as, indeed, may be the 'relevance' of policy goals and the assessment of learner needs, since they, too, rest upon assumptions and values). Academic disciplines are often challenged in this way and it is on the basis of this criticism that the alternatives to extended schooling, such as, in Britain, the YTS, have often been advanced. Critics of schooling have, however, usually questioned the level or standard of attainment as well as its suitability. By inference the alternatives they propose are presented as both qualitatively superior to, and more relevant than, what can be achieved through extended schooling. It is important to treat this as a claim to be tested.

According to the criteria used, the core curriculum of a school – or any other institution, or a national system – may be of a high standard, for example intellectually or aesthetically, and yet, of course, be open to criticism or in need of modification because of a partial mismatch with other social requirements. Conversely, a core of vocationally or occupationally defined skills may be appropriate as an element within a more broadly defined core of general education, yet, by itself, be exclusively narrow or utilitarian. As Lantier (1985) says, school and working life participate in the same educative function: the former teaches to know; the latter provides a distinctive experience. This attempt to relate different and often disparate agencies and processes through an analysis of a multiple, shared function is of the utmost importance in considering new national frameworks for education and training.

We need to be clear about the full range of educational and training goals and values that are being pursued or may be available to us and about the strengths of diverse institutional arrangements including the vocational school, in order to make a balanced and judicious appraisal, to define the core curriculum and to determine the roles and relations of the partners responsible for its design and delivery. The broad approach we are advocating acknowledges social and personal aims, values and needs and locates educational and training goals in relation to the kind of society we wish to see develop and the qualities in people that are to be fostered and nourished. While we do not deny the crisis alluded to above, we believe that in both policy and practice there must be a constant quest for defensible action, and that means action that can withstand scrutiny from multiple standpoints.

For the obvious reason of cultural disparity, no two nations will come to the same conclusions about the means for realising their education and training objectives. The dual system of the German-speaking countries is a case in point:

> It is . . . the common conviction of German vocational training circles that 'capability' as the primary aim of training and general skills such as communication, ability to work as a team, logical thinking, problem-solving ability etc. are most easily acquired in the professional and work context.
>
> (Benner et al., 1985, p.290)

This implies a strong distinction between general and vocational, theoretical and applied, education and training and well-developed administrative procedures for assigning roles and responsibilities according to 'school' and 'work' criteria. Apart from the last point the bifurcations of the dual system would be unacceptable or extremely difficult to orchestrate in some other countries (Papadopoulos, 1991).

A system does not repose on abstract concepts or even on rational arguments so much as on social and political attitudes, customs, traditions and behaviour. When the structure of training, for example, is negotiated by employers, unions and the education authorities, it is what is mutually acceptable to them that counts, provided, that is, the voice of the student is also heard. That does not, of course, insulate the decisions reached from critical scrutiny. Such negotiations may exclude important clients – neither the public nor the trainees are normally as well represented as they should be. Moreover, negotiation among interested parties may not take political and macro-economic considerations fully into account. Each country would do well to seek to approach the problem of core learning through wide-ranging socio-cultural analysis as well as the technologies of negotiation. It is in this way that national requirements can be identified and a framework for relevant and sensitive curricular responses developed.

The challenge of the core is not only a matter of content models, of established practice and national cultural settings. Of central importance is the learner and learning itself. As much among vocational educators as in the broader field of schooling, interest has been shown in what are variously called study skills, learning to learn, understanding or self-directed learning (FEU, 1981; OECD, 1991b). There is no point in designing what appears to be a core curriculum if in fact many learners are more or less shunted aside and left behind. All young people need to know how to use and control the knowledge and experience which is constantly pouring in from television, from school, from the workplace or from the people around them. A basic objective for all education must be to foster effective learning, the ability to evaluate information and experience, the capacity to go on learning: learning how to learn. It is encouraging that educators are indicating new ways of doing this, through the development of new cognitive strategies (FEU, 1981; Biggs, 1985; Maclure and Davies, 1991). Practical guides, such as those of the Further Education Unit's *Principles for the Development of Core Skills Across the Curriculum* are another manifestation of this trend (FEU, 1993).

A further desirable core goal and outcome is positive attitudes to life and work or motivation. Leaving school and going to work has traditionally been seen as beneficial in these respects for many young people but, where work is simply not available for many, considerations of self-esteem and a work orientation assume an even greater importance in school. Thus, participatory – including interpersonal and group – skills are a target; individualised, self-motivated attitudes have to be complemented by an understanding of the need for teamwork. Both contribute to self-enhancement and a sense of personal capability and well-being. As for the delivery of these core objectives, pedagogical innovation, training and re-training of teachers on a much enlarged scale will be necessary before real progress can be made. Many educational authorities find it difficult to be optimistic about the possibilities, given the size of the problem and the resources required. The more comprehensive the map, the more detailed the mapping, the greater the number of issues to address. That, indeed, is part of what we mean by the core learnings *challenge*.

DIMENSIONS OF CORE LEARNINGS FOR WORKING LIFE

The call for reformulating the curriculum of primary and secondary schools around an established 'core' of necessary learnings can be seen to have a vocationalist aspiration insofar as the 'core' of necessary learning is intended to include the attitudes, knowledge and skills needed for a successful life, which ought reasonably to cover the ability to provide for oneself, and one's dependants. Beyond this, work is fundamental to fulfilment and a sense of personal worth. If it is a curse to be sent forth from the Garden of Eden with a sweating face to till the ground, enduring thorns and thistles, work is also a necessary element in the commonly perceived life of value and the personal sense of worth. So far from it being undignified and anti-intellectual for schools to prepare all students for work, for them not to do so is a dereliction of a quite basic responsibility. That work, however, as Hannah Arendt argues, is to be thought of as a productive, value-laden human activity, not mere labour (Arendt, 1959, Chapters III and IV). The concept of work includes but extends beyond paid employment; indeed much paid employment fails miserably in providing scope for purposive, creative, productive human activity, activity in which process and product are seen as a continuum and valued for their contribution to the individual and to those who use the products of the activity.

The approach we advocate sets high goals and standards for further education for work, by contrast with a long history of demeaning attitudes and procedures associated with work and the worker. The elimination of so much unskilled toil is perhaps the beginning of the long-awaited 'transformation'. Whitehead, too, exalted work which, he said, 'should be transfused with intellectual and moral vision and thereby turned into a joy, triumphing over its weariness and its pain'. Moreover, he argued it was in the hands of teachers to invest work with these qualities (Whitehead, 1950, pp.67–68). Of course, it is useless for schools to take up these challenges if work itself remains unreconstructed. The challenge is as much to employers and enterprises as it is to the school.

We need no longer ask whether or not a core curriculum for general education should include some kind of work orientation and the foundation of eventual participation in the working world. The question is, what kind of working world do we envisage and how can education, at all stages, assist children and youth to develop the competences appropriate to this working world and the ability to create work in accordance with exalted not debased standards? We have argued that it is for a future vision of the world, not a recapitulation of the elements of a vanishing world, that education must prepare the learner.

A worthwhile curriculum must contain vocational elements; it must inform about the world of work, as a domain for a worthwhile, productive life, encourage effective work habits, teach basic technology and practical skills, develop special interests and aptitudes. But what is necessary is not sufficient. The curriculum must develop the whole range of human abilities, artistic, physical, intellectual and manual, if it is to make sense in a socio-cultural world which provides a context fully comparable in its demands to the exigencies of the workplace. Only thus can we begin to realise the value of work, as both an individual and a social value. Allowing for this, let us turn now to consider in more detail those elements of a core curriculum that relate most specifically to vocational learnings.

The advent of the new vocationalism provides us with the opportunity to reassess the role and nature of vocational learning in the education of our adolescents and to redefine it in the new emerging context. Several *dimensions* are important in answering the question of what constitutes core learnings for working life.

First, we must have ways of identifying those *areas of knowledge and understanding* which are basic and fundamental for a well-developed personal and social life as well as for further, work-related learning in our industrialised society and economy. Work has many and complex relations with life in the wider sense, and core learnings must set preparation for work in a context of education for life. The core of the curriculum cannot be reduced to a thin sliver of reality; it draws its content from the major domains of social, cultural, intellectual, economic and practical life (Skilbeck, 1985). This broad map of learning, in its working life focus, should include both an appreciation of the local, national and international contexts and settings of contemporary working life, and basic awareness and understanding of the key, emerging processes involved in the major productive ventures of our age and their interrelations. It must engage the learner in encounters and experiences from which grows a realisation of the personal significance of work. The complexity of these learnings and the difficulty of determining them on some agreed basis cannot be too strongly stressed. It is, however, clear that the foundations must be broad and general if the working life focus is to be an effective preparation for adult roles and to generate worthwhile experiences for the learner.

A second dimension of the problem of defining the core relates to the need for all youth to develop *shared values* within our democratic social heritage – values which encourage responsible attitudes towards work and working life as much by individuals as by small groups and large organisations. It was Max Weber who gave special emphasis to the concept of 'work ethic' in his historical analysis of the rise of modern industrial society

49

(Gerth and Mills, 1948). Work and its organisation are of as great significance for the so-called post-industrial society as for the industrial society.
No longer fortified by puritanical religion and structured by more hori-
zontal and equal relationships, a modern work ethic must be articulated
with the changing character of work as with the foundations of modern
ethical theory. Much effort is needed to analyse and develop a modern
concept of 'work ethic', a topic which has received far too little attention by
contrast with the excessive preoccupation with decontextualised 'skills'.
Such an ethic is not achieved by misguided attempts to inculcate specific
virtues and habits; rather it grows out of an understanding of why productive work is a fundamental condition of human life, society and culture
and direct experience of the fulfilment that productive work can bring.

A third dimension is that of *transferable* core learnings which are
intended to enable youth to become flexible members of a productive
working community, whether paid or unpaid. This notion of transferability
has a long history in education (for example, the 'transfer of training'
debates in late nineteenth- and early twentieth-century educational psychology) (Connell, 1980, pp.109–116). There has been a renewed interest in
transfer of learning in the context of industrial training, and among
researchers and theoreticians a reasonable consensus has emerged, with
the proviso that the principles and generalisations are indicative not prescriptive (Duncan and Kelly, 1983; Annett and Sparrow, 1986; Evans and
Poole, n.d.; Hesketh *et al.*, n.d.). Considerable variation exists in relation to
the transfer potential of different teaching–learning strategies, between
males and females, between different fields of knowledge and practical
activity and among individuals. Nevertheless, a knowledge of principles,
general knowledge structures, illustrative examples and practical demonstrations and discovery learning are widely attested common elements
favouring transfer. The general trend of findings underlines the importance of higher-order abstractions and schema in education and training
programmes, regardless of whether these programmes are of a more
theoretical or more practical kind.

Transfer is never guaranteed, however; the personal dispositions and
feelings of the actor and the variability of the situations of application are
major conditioning factors. What does not guarantee outcomes may still be
confidently pursued: greater attention to understanding, to principles and
common usable elements, to reinforcement in a variety of typical situations
of application, and to strategies for learning and problem-solving that are
built upon the student's interest and curiosity as distinct from mindless
repetition and recall are directions to follow.

The fourth dimension of the problem, as we see it, is the mapping of
commonly experienced problem or learning task situations, in both formal educational settings and workplaces, real or simulated. Besides providing individuals with breadth, these help foster a common appreciation of the life

experiences of others – an important basis for an integrated, efficient and caring work community.

To summarise, these four dimensions indicate that core learnings are not reducible to a precise set of decontextualised measurable skills, articulated according to preconceived notions of 'levels of difficulty' ('core skills', 'multiskills', etc.); their definition is inevitably an educational project in a socio-cultural, economic and political setting.

Views differ about the substantive domains or fields of knowledge and understanding from which a core curriculum plan can be drawn. We have argued that breadth and balance remain key considerations and that the best foundations of education for working life are to be found in the continuation of general education throughout adolescence, with an explicit orientation towards working life, which will vary in depth and intensity in accordance with the proximity of the student to paid employment. Much detailed, job-specific training is best done in the workplace and through work-based programmes. They should be, however, accompanied by, indeed part of, continued general education.

We do not advocate a core comprising traditional academic disciplines although our core will contain some elements of these. In the belief that the detailed work of curriculum design and construction is the responsibility of the institution and its members – and not of centralised authorities whose role in this respect should be confined to broad goals, frameworks and monitoring – we suggest areas of knowledge and experience which, in combination, introduce students in a systematic way to the main domains of human culture and experience, to ways of analysing and understanding them and to procedures and tools for the application of their knowledge in typical life situations. Such domains can be variously described, for example as follows:

- Arts and crafts
- Environmental studies
- Mathematical skills and reasoning and their applications
- Social, cultural and civic studies
- Health education
- Scientific and technological ways of knowing and their social applications
- Communication
- Moral reasoning and action, values and belief systems
- Work, leisure and life style.

(Skilbeck, 1984b, Chapter 7)

This, by contrast with many of the policy statements on key or core competences, is a broadly defined, open framework: the core curriculum is to be constructed, we suggest, drawing on this framework. There have been attempts to infuse a framework of general education such as this one with a distinctively vocational set of competences; for example, the Australian report *Putting General Education to Work*, presented to a joint meeting in 1992 of the Australian Education Council (State and Commonwealth Ministers of Education) and the Ministers for Vocational Education, Employment and Training (Australian Education Council and Ministers for Vocational Education, Employment and Training, 1992). The Australian Committee, in common with the National Council for Vocational Qualifications (NCVQ) in Britain, saw the strategic task in terms of defining performance levels and determining means of assessing and reporting performance, a concern with measurable outcomes whose importance should not blind us to the need for a more fundamental appraisal of curriculum planning, teaching and learning.

To return to the idea of core areas of knowledge and experience, in the case of Britain there is a considerable degree of overlap between these core areas and the prescribed national curriculum – an unduly detailed prescription, as we see it. But there are also differences, mainly as a consequence of the structure of subject disciplines adopted in the national curriculum and the weakness of the cross-curriculum themes which were intended to provide a degree of coherence and interdisciplinarity. Any nationally prescribed curriculum must be adapted and interpreted, not only with reference, for example, to attainment test requirements, but, of greater importance, to the educational goals and the conditions of individual schools. The 'national curriculum' is not merely to be delivered; it is to be used as a resource by schools in carrying out their overall educational roles and responsibilities. One of these responsibilities is to keep open the growth prospects of the 'ideal' curriculum of the future, a task which respects teachers' professionalism and fosters their creativity.

Since the 1970s there has been a lively debate on the question of who should determine the substance of core curriculum – that is, the content of those common learnings required of all students. It appears to have been answered, in Britain, by the 1988 Education Act and subsequent administrative and legislative action by central government. That is not, however, the whole story. In the vocational as in other areas of the core curriculum, we should continue the search for an agreed and not an imposed national framework, locally interpreted and implemented in such a way as to relate to the specific student and teacher experience, needs and opportunities existing in the individual myriad learning situations.

SKILLS IN QUESTION

'Britain is facing a skills challenge greater than any since the Industrial Revolution' (Trades Union Congress, 1989, p.2). So said leaders of the British trade union movement, who have played a crucial if undervalued role in charting a new course in which education and training achieve a parity with conditions of employment in the new industrial agenda.

The greatest effort to date in defining core learnings within the new vocationalism has been within the dimension of 'core skills' and for those who have left school. Appraisal of the idea of a fundamental strategy of learning through mastery and possession of a set of broadly defined and contextualised core skills is of central importance to this book. What is meant by 'skill' and how skills do or might relate to the core curriculum of the school system is a key issue. What is a skilled workforce? There is much room for debate on this point despite the confident tone of many utterances on the future workforce and the qualities it should display.

In common with many other authorities, the Trades Union Congress (TUC) laments the inadequate quantity and mediocre level of training in Britain by comparison with its major trading partners. Although the key word in the TUC report of 1989 is 'skills', this is shorthand for a complex array of attributes which have as their focus the nature of capability and the conditions needed to exercise that capability, at an internationally high standard, in order to perform the productive tasks required of a modern, rapidly changing economy. The TUC programme envisages the following components: 'a sound foundation of broad-based educational and vocational preparation' (ibid., p.6); training that is industry-led and relevant to employment; opportunities for the progressive development of competences and skills throughout working life; a partnership of individuals, enterprises, education and training authorities; and a national qualification system 'based on a matrix of qualifications, encompassing vocational and academic awards, and the full range of occupations at every level of skill' (ibid., p.7). The model adopted by the TUC but not fully analysed in its paper, is core skills, 'such as communication, health and safety, numeracy and literacy' (ibid., p.7). Later in the text, these rudimentary skills are elaborated to include 'educationally based skills – abilities to reason, analyse and apply knowledge' (ibid., p.8). The primary purpose of the TUC statement is to affirm in general terms the value and necessity of greater attention to and investment in a comprehensive, broadly based programme of initial and continuing education and training; the statement does not, however, so much illuminate the difficult questions of determining a common core of skills, relating them to the diverse character of the employment market, as indicate a broad reorientation for schooling and post-school training.

Kenneth Baker, as Secretary of State for Education and Science, in a speech delivered to the Annual Conference of the Association of Colleges of Further and Higher Education in London in February 1989, gave a more precise, albeit in some respects still tentative, formulation of the aspirations, also voiced by the TUC, towards a broad conception of skill and skill development for all:

Perhaps the time has come at last when we ought to take steps to ensure that at least everyone [sic] up to age 19 is receiving some systematic education or training. . . . Higher numbers in education and training are the means towards an end. That end is to increase the level of skills that are attained. I had better define this term 'skill', which is so freely used and misused. . . . By 'skill' I mean competence, built on knowledge and understanding. Attainment of skills in this wider sense is not just the capacity to perform a particular task, nor is it the empty acquisition of factual knowledge. It is the coming together of competence, knowledge and understanding, and as such it is a proper goal for both educators and trainers.

(Baker, 1989, paras 23–24)

In his post-Fordist endeavour to break the connection between highly specific skills and particular occupations, Baker so conflated 'skill' as to seem to make it indistinguishable from the very wide and diverse range of capabilities for action which are the outcome (or the goals) of the whole of education and training. However, he did, later in the speech, list ('illustrative, not prescriptive'): communication, numeracy, personal relations, familiarity with technology, familiarity with [workplace] systems and familiarity with changing working and social contexts' (ibid., para 42). His audience was further education, not schools. However, in his 1988 Education Act, Baker answered, in a very different way, the core question for schools: as forms of knowledge and understanding expressed in conventional subject disciplines – which should constitute the core of the curriculum for all students in schools.

The government's curriculum agency, the National Curriculum Council (NCC), also took up the issue of skills in the formal education system in response to the Secretary of State (then John McGregor) who in a remit letter of 28 November 1989 asked 'what further needs to be done, by NCC itself or other agencies, to ensure that the curriculum as a whole for Advanced level students, and the teaching and learning strategies associated with it, promote the development and assessment of such (core) skills' (NCC, 1990b, p.2). The NCC further elaborated the charge given to it by referring to a subsequent initiative from the Secretary of State to explain the issue of 'easier transfer between A level and vocational courses' (ibid., p.2). In preparing this paper, the NCC consulted widely and attempted to produce a synthesis – justified, it said, by 'an overwhelming consensus' on the need for a whole-curriculum, sequential, integrated approach to education and training from ages 5 to 19. A deal of confusion is evident in the Council's attempt to unravel the consitutent parts of this complex whole and their interrelationships. The NCC adopted the broad definition of skill – as competence (meaning 'effective performance') which 'implies an interdependence of knowledge, understanding, skills and attitudes' (ibid., p.4). This muddled analysis nevertheless makes it clear that core skills would not be defined without bringing into consideration the forms of knowledge and understanding, the values and the practical capabilities which are held to constitute the core of the curriculum. 'Core skills' seemed, in this document, to be a shorthand for core curriculum and the claims made for these skills are the same as those for the core curriculum, namely a foundation for life and learning, for employment and employment mobility.

However, as it proceeds through the analysis, the Council abandons its earlier all-embracing stance with its confusions and ambiguities and adopts as its set of core skills 'which should be incorporated into the study programmes of all 16–19 year olds: communication; problem-solving; personal skills; numeracy; information technology; modern [foreign] language competence' (ibid., p.8).

Apart from the treatment of a domain (information technology) as a skill ('competence'), objections can be made to this list. First, it is arbitrary, reflecting a tendency common in much of the policy literature to promulgate conventional schemes and lists rather than to provide a rationale, well grounded in either social or pedagogical analysis, together with a coherent framework for action. Second, it is reductionist; and neglects what was earlier posited about interrelationships between skills, knowledge and so on. Third, it has nothing to say about the interrelationships between the skill areas and the curriculum structures and pedagogical practices that might be put in place to develop these interrelationships and thereby assist in strengthening the sought-for links between formal learning and practical action in typical life – and work – situations. Instead, the NCC turned its inquiry towards policy requirement, of the attainment of 'levels' within the separate subjects of the school curriculum.

The second of the agency responses that we consider, to requests from the Secretary of State for Education and Science for advice on how the core skills are to be developed, is that of the NCVQ. The NCVQ was invited to 'consider in greater depth the application of the NCC's full list of core skills to vocational qualifications and the practicability of at least [sic] building communication, problem solving and personal skills into all NVQs [National Vocational Qualifications]' (NCVQ, 1990, p.1). The NCVQ started by elaborating an odd distinction, drawn in part by the NCC, between two categories of core skills: those which are 'most fundamental' and which underpin 'almost all employment functions and are present in all A/AS level subjects and NVQs'; and those which 'are not necessarily inherent in all subjects and occupational areas' but are nevertheless of equal importance. As expressed, these notions of 'most fundamental' and 'equal importance' serve to further confuse rather than clarify the concept of core (ibid., p.1). However, the NCVQ saw as its task not the clarification of such matters but the drawing of distinctions between the schooling model (A/AS examinations and the national curriculum) and the working life model of workplace-based or related training. Moreover, its focus in this as in other documents is operationalisation with a bias towards credentialism. Hence core skills are translated into 'units of competence' attracting 'unit credits within the national system of credit accumulation and transfer' (ibid., p.3). But trainees may not be aware that these occupational competence units in fact embody core skills, so one task – in order to foster transferability – will be to make trainees aware: the core skills, already incorporated in a work-study programme, are to become more visible in the context and the processes of the occupational unit. The NCVQ wished also to emphasise the need for a partnership of responsible education and training agencies to

> create a progressive structure of core skill outcomes (in the form of statements of attainment/elements of competence) for the six core skills, giving priority to the areas of problem solving, communication and personal skills.
>
> (ibid., p.4)

However, somewhat inconsistently with its declaration that the core skills shall not be taught separately from occupational units, it also proposed the design and piloting of 'core skill units'. Although at odds with the claim for the indissolubility of the occupational units and the core skills, the proposal for the design and piloting of core skill units picks up on the recommendation in the NCVQ research and development report No. 6, *Common Learning Outcomes: Core Skills in A/AS Levels and NVQs*, April 1990, that 'a conceptual framework needs to be developed which specifies the core skill areas to be included and their division into components and levels' (ibid., Appendix A, p.2). The NCVQ, however, in common with the NCC, has given far more attention to the division into components and levels – and to linkages with industry on the one hand and the national curriculum on the other – than to the construction of a robust conceptual framework.

There are grounds for scepticism about the emphasis given to skill in much of the official thinking and writing about vocational education which tends on the one hand to over-generalisation and lack of rigour and, on the other, to the isolation and atomisation of human attributes and functions to the point where the *raison d'être* of skill analysis, namely understanding to effect change and make a difference, is lost. Only by viewing skill as an element in a process of action which occurs in contexts can we recover that understanding. Employment is one such context, but the task of occupation mapping in a period of rapid technological and structural change is formidable. Nevertheless, this is the enterprise on which NCVQ embarked, guided by a set of key concepts such as outcomes, competence units, performance levels, standards and assessment criteria, which owe more to the assessment and measurement tradition than to the analysis of technological change, industrial organisation or culture and personality.

While it is a mistake, then, to regard skills as quite separate and distinct from either personality or culture, to attempt to embody them in theories of culture and personality is a daunting undertaking of curriculum design and pedagogy, nowhere satisfactorily undertaken. Skills, which we define as *practical competence or the ability to carry out tasks and solve problems*, can be expressed with a quite deceptive simplicity, and that is part of the problem that faces thoughtful vocational educators. We talk, for example, about the skills of 'reading', 'horse riding', 'word processing' or 'designing' and then proceed to atomise and isolate them or to design systems of progression and levels for which it would take many years of field testing to provide an adequate empirical basis. The acquisition of such skills, their enhancement through structured experience and their expression and application involve a wide range of human and social functions. These include perception, awareness, motivation, values, interpersonal relations and complex forms of human disposition and social organisation. Useful as it may be to isolate skills for analytical purposes and in identifying programme priorities, the matter must not be allowed to rest there. Competences or skills can be and are defined independently of the individuals in whom they are embodied, the socio-cultural setting for individual and group action, and the occupational activities for which they are a preparation. But this is a quite abstract analytical process; interpretation of these abstractions must be conditioned by the constraints of such decontextualising. For policy and operational purposes these constraints are much more salient and their significance brings into question the value of such an approach by comparison with other styles of curriculum making and assessment which are grounded in a situational analysis and proceed, not through the analysis of abstract competences ('outcomes') but through learning content and processes (Skilbeck, 1984b). These and other difficulties associated with the sought-for linkages between competence and occupational requirement are of considerable interest in the European theatre where countries, Britain included, are searching for common elements in different national systems of vocational education (Bertrand, 1992).

Regardless of the chosen setting – workplace, home life, training centre, school or college – the structuring and organising of learning experiences including skill formation is tantamount to curriculum designing and making and should draw upon the substantial experience of curriculum research and development. A core curriculum incorporating defined competences can be grounded in school life, working life, or any other setting, according to choice. As we have seen, a curriculum is a map or chart of planned, structured and organised learning experiences and it may be self-initiated, negotiated or required by others. A core curriculum is one such map or chart predicated on a view about basic or essential learnings which is then elaborated through a series of decisions about content that relate the design to major domains of human expression and experience (for example, occupations; subject disciplines). It is by such curriculum making that we define competences that are to be taught and learnt;

57

curriculum is the translation into learning tasks of whatever framework or categories inform our purposes and goals as educators.

Curriculum making can proceed at many different levels from the individual classroom, school or workplace to national curriculum agencies or government departments. In Britain, with the advent of the national curriculum and the system of national vocational qualifications, curriculum design for young people has become very largely a centralised undertaking dominated by government, by the Departments of Education and Employment and by a small number of national level statutory authorities. The design of a curriculum of core skills, or with core skills as its central theme, has through these means become an object of national policy in Britain.

YOUTH TRAINING AND CORE SKILLS

The idea of transferable core skills was brought into prominence by the YTS, first established in the days of the former Manpower Services Commission (MSC). The evolution and development of the YTS since its inception in 1983 is discussed in some detail in later chapters. Competence in a range of transferable core skills has been one of the four central aims of the YTS, as in other national and regional training schemes in other countries.

Experience from the YTS provides a crucial case study for understanding the concept of transferable core skills and what happens in attempting to operationalise such skills nationally in different and varied regional and local situations. There is much to be learnt about possibilities and problems in the new vocationalism by studying such a case. It provides the foundation for much of the work of the NCVQ and, its serious weaknesses as a national training scheme notwithstanding, has been a turning point in policy for vocational education and training.

The Core Skills Project of the YTS, discussed earlier in this chapter, identified 103 discrete, decontextualised core skills within the five broad areas of: number; communication; problem-solving; practical skills; and computer and information technology (MSC, 1984a, 1985a). These clusters of core skills, recognisably the basis for the ideas and proposals emanating from the NCC and the NCVQ discussed above, were intended as common, basic learnings in a wide variety of workplace settings and ultimately in schools. That is, the project designers envisaged a foundation programme for the YTS in which elements would be common to all students and trainees regardless of their ultimate occupational destination. No comparably detailed analyses of contemporary British culture and society, in particular the rapidly changing and, in many senses, deteriorating work environment, was undertaken then, nor has it been since. Studies there were, and these were drawn upon, but the principal thrust of the enterprise was the creation of an abstract skill model and plans for its rapid introduction including training programmes. This extraordinarily ambitious and radical notion, of a common and universal set of skills that was so distinctive of this aspect of the YTS, raises many questions, not only about the analytical model adopted but also about the continuum of a core curriculum into the later years of adolescence. Thus, although there is much of technical interest in the quest – which ultimately foundered – for a single, simple unitary set of core skills for working life, its greater interest lies in the wide range of educational issues and questions to which it gave rise. These issues and questions provide a link between the general education provided by the schools and the various endeavours both in and out of schools to introduce a working life focus, between the themes raised in the first three chapters of this book and those that follow.

In the theory of vocational education advanced through the Core Skills Project, core skills are posited as elements within a work-based curriculum which are in some sense basic, fundamental or essential for the learners exposed to them (and, by extension, to all students). 'Generic', 'transferable', 'instrumental' were seen as qualities of this set of skills; in this sense, they could be thought of as, to a degree, broadly defined competences, not very specific techniques, to be gained and held by students. The core skills were seen as having utility in designing syllabuses, study programmes and tasks and, when suitably 'worked up', capable of being assessed and scaled, and their acquisition and mastery used as an index of performance, including predicted performance. These attributes of core skills were noticeable in claims made for the core skills as outlined in the manual *Core Skills in YTS* (MSC, 1984a) and promulgated through the Core Skills Project and later incorporated into the mainstream thinking of NCVQ and NCC.

It must not be forgotten that the same skills as those put into a work-based curriculum within the YTS were an element, then as now, in school education – but in a significantly different setting. Core skills, for example literacy and numeracy skills, the conduct of projects, experiments and other small-group tasks, are an established part of formal education and, by age 16, most young people have already experienced them over many years in school. This gives them a measure of authority even if only that of custom and habit.

The concept of core skills, as developed in Britain during the 1980s in the framework of the YTS, provides a way into many of the central issues in the continuing unresolved debate about vocational education. Is the current emphasis on competence, on assessed outcomes and on transcendent frameworks which aim to unify the fields of education, training and working life likely to raise vocational education and training from the low intellectual and social status it has long endured and to strengthen its role in national life? Is vocational education best seen as a distinct field of activity, mainly work-based and always work-related, with its own distinct purposes, language, institutional and organisational prerogatives, and culture of values and practices? If there is a continuity to be established between vocational and general education, what is the role of the concept of a continuing common core curriculum, with a shifting balance of vocationally relevant content and pedagogy? What are the central, organising ideas for designing and developing a curriculum which, as a minimum, provides for an effective transition or set of pathways for young people proceeding through the years of adolescence in some form of institutionalised education and training? The Core Skills Project of the YTS provided, at least potentially, a new way into these and other questions, at a critical stage in the evolution of thinking and policy-making in British vocational education.

SUMMARY

The idea of a core of common, fundamental learnings for working life, and their definition, organisation and delivery to students in appropriate settings, provides a means of interrelating the traditionally – and dysfunctionally – separated domains of general and vocational education. What is needed is to free the core idea from its older academic, subject-based connections and to treat it afresh in a redefined context. The resurgence of interest in vocational education since the 1970s, particularly in the industrialised countries, provides a means – perhaps the best available means – of doing this. The scale and variety of social and economic changes leading to a more conscious drive towards active labour market policies on the part of governments and a critical reassessment of both general and vocational education point up new educational possibilities. Dissatisfaction with the performance of existing educational systems is seen as the immediate but not the only cause of the emergence of the new vocationalism. A considerable range of vocationally oriented learning opportunities is focused most strongly on the 14–18 age group – at the point of transition from compulsory schooling to working life or to further education. Among them, the British YTS has been, its limitations notwithstanding, a significant source of new thinking and policy-making in practice.

While many of the innovations and new learning opportunities tend towards differentiation and specialisation, we should, on balance, be seeking to strengthen those tendencies which lead us towards a core of learnings for all youth for working life. These learnings are not usefully to be conceived as a highly specialised and narrowly defined set of skills. On the contrary, they comprise: areas of common knowledge and understanding which are basic and fundamental for further work-related learning in our industrial society and economy; shared values related to our democratic social heritage and which encourage responsible and positive attitudes towards work and working life; transferable learnings which are intended to enable youth to become flexible members of a productive working community; and commonly experienced learning situations, in both formal educational settings and workplaces, real or simulated. The concept of core skills merits further critical and reflective analysis as it gains currency in national education and training policy. In this as in other respects, the Core Skills Project, developed within the YTS, is of considerable significance. The scope and scale, the fresh approach to curriculum design and assessment of performance, the initial (if unrealised) objective of relating to all British youth and the questions it poses about ways of achieving greater coherence, consistency and effectiveness in the divided and still confused field of adolescent education, mark the YTS out as a major educational innovation, one of several pillars of the new vocationalism in Britain.

4

THE 'SCHOOLING' AND 'WORKING LIFE' MODELS

The traditional methods of teaching had their justification as long as their main function was to create the spirit of basic conformity and that readiness for reproductive adjustment which goes with a static society. But the very same methods become an impediment to the understanding of the world in transition if they hamper the spirit of adventure and of creative adjustment to unforeseen experience.

(Mannheim, 1943, pp.42–43)

INTRODUCTION

What Karl Mannheim said of teaching in 1943 holds true today of the stubbornness with which established structures and organisational arrangements persist. Structures are not readily changed, especially when they are reified into models expressing cultural norms and expectations. The dichotomy between 'school' and 'work' is not adequately bridged by improved transition arrangements. There needs to be a fresh interpretation of the models themselves.

Thus far, we have drawn attention to several of the dominant, over-arching themes in efforts that are being made to give to British education, its goals, values, structure, content and methods, a more definitive vocational character. The emphasis has been on what is to be taught and learnt and the skills or competences that are supposed to develop through this teaching and learning. These learning outcomes are a function not only of the purposes that inform the teaching and the learning and the content of what is presented; no less they reflect also the interests of the controlling authorities and the pedagogical settings or situations and the structures of which they are a part.

In the efforts countries are making to adapt policies and programmes directed at more practical, work-related learning for young people, two often-opposed orientations towards control, setting, content and pedagogy recur: the 'schooling' and the 'working life' models. So far from being in opposition or unavoidable conflict, however, these orientations represent the extremes of a continuum or perhaps directions which need to converge at certain points. The same questions arise for both and the answers show an interesting variability. Which aims and objectives are the best to pursue? Whose values and interests dominate the process? What should be taught and learnt, where, by whom and with what resources? What are the best ways of assessing this learning and communicating it to those who need to know? In reviewing some examples of practice in several national systems, we can see that both the school or educational institution and the workplace are, or may be, appropriate sites for teaching and learning. The choice will reflect national traditions, structures and values. Often it will be a matter of practical convenience being weighed against theoretical formulations and the findings of research. Ideally, the loci of the school and that of the workplace should intersect since each offers something of value that the other cannot. Through selected examples, we suggest a range of organisational responses available to contemporary industrialised countries in addressing the challenge of vocational education among 14–19-year-olds, and illustrate the contexts in which they are situated.

Attempts are being made to co-ordinate activities and policy between countries within regional blocs. Within the European Community, where co-ordination is furthest developed, this process began with seeking comparability for and recognition of qualifications between countries prior to the introduction of the 1992 single market, and has now broadened, for example to include programmes to address within-region disparity of access and provision and to effect qualitative improvements (Commission of the European Communities, 1991b, 1992; Bertrand, 1992; Figueiredo and Steele, 1992). While these developments do not entail structural convergence they provide opportunities for mutual learning.

A number of authors discuss the organisation and setting of vocational education and training using various typologies (OECD, 1985b; Papadopoulos, 1991; Woolhouse, 1991). We find placement at any one of numerous points on the single schooling–working life continuum both more informative of practical options than efforts to construct more complex models and of most relevance to our theme of core learnings for working life. This is because each national pattern shows a different and distinctive balance between the two, and following from this is a greater connection with the culture, traditions, values and authority systems of work or of education.

THE 'SCHOOLING' AND 'WORKING LIFE' MODELS

Patterns of initial vocational education, whether within school, the general system, in specialised training institutions or in the workplace, reflect different answers to two related questions:

1 How far should the education system of schools and like institutions be involved in preliminary preparations for working life? How much and what sorts of vocational education should this system provide? How generalised, foundational or specific should such educational provision be?

2 To what extent should the component of formal and direct educational preparation for working life be in schools and like institutions or in the workplace? Where and under whose authority should that provision be located? Where is such learning best achieved?

When we talk of the 'schooling' model, we essentially refer to systems where the primary responsibility for vocational education lies with the school authorities and the main proportion of students' time is in the school or other formal educational institution rather than the work setting. The distinction is, even so, not altogether clearcut since many large enterprises incorporate training centres or divisions that display features usually thought of as 'schooling'. Moreover, the growth of school–industry partnerships is blurring the lines of control. What distinguishes the enterprise-based centres or divisions from schools and colleges is not so much the curricula, teaching methods or learning tasks as the context of the activity and the bilateral nature of the students' relationships – to the authority structures and organisational patterns of 'work' and of 'education' or 'training'. As we shall see from the examples in this chapter, on the 'schooling' model there are many different ways of organising such vocational programmes. In some countries, such as the United States, a pattern of broad general education for all within a common high school, with vocational learning at an essentially broad, basic and non-specific level, is the norm. In other countries, such as France, vocational education is primarily based in *lycées professionels*, separate institutions from the academically and technically oriented *lycées*, and with quite specialised programmes. We look briefly at the organisation of vocational education in these and some other countries to illustrate both common and variable features of the 'schooling' model.

When we talk of the 'working life' model, primary responsibility for vocational education lies with employers or in a shared arrangement with school authorities, and the major locus of vocational learning is in the workplace, albeit with some off-the-job formal educational provision. This approach is exemplified by the 'dual' system of Germany, Austria, Switzerland and Denmark. Of the four, in this chapter we look briefly at the organisation of vocational education in the Federal Republic of Germany.

In each of the approaches there is in fact a mix of on- and off-the-job learning and formal educational provision, with authority and responsibility for policy and provision variably shared by several parties. Debates about national policies are active in most countries, so it is a field in which change and movement is constant, and responsive to policy in several arenas, including education, economy and industry, all of vital public interest and concern in modern industrial nations. It should be noted, however, that the very use of the term 'dual' indicates a joint responsibility of work-type agencies and school-type agencies. Control is a crucial consideration; thus, in Germany it is the chambers of commerce, not the school authorities, that exercise primary control (Achtenhagen, 1992).

It is not our pupose in this chapter to attempt a detailed or strictly comparative overview of different national approaches. (Others provide this; for example, Cantor, 1989, and EURYDICE and CEDEFOP, 1991.) Rather, in a highly selective way, we aim to indicate in broad terms the range of approaches taken in a number of industrialised countries, among which Britain sees itself, and demonstrate the admixture, in all systems, of elements of 'work' and 'education'. These general models are identified to enable us better to contextualise and situate the discussion of core learnings for working life.

LOCATIONS ON THE SCHOOLING–WORKING LIFE CONTINUUM

The United States

The recent history of vocationalism in the United States has been essentially within the context of, and to some extent bounded by, a deep attachment to the institution of the high school. Since the time of the Smith–Hughes Act (1917) and before, determined efforts have been made to set up distinctive systems of vocational education, but these have been as resolutely opposed. Their development has been bedevilled by unresolved tensions between 'academic' and 'practical', 'general education' and 'specific preparation' and by the generally low status of vocational tracks and programmes compared with those for college/university-bound students (Benson and Silver, 1991).

The United States has long-standing concerns with equality of access to education and cultural unity. The different states, each responsible for its own education system, have created a universal system of common (comprehensive) schools, and it is a common if not always fulfilled expectation that all American youngsters will obtain a High School Diploma generally at age 18. To do so, they must obtain a certain number of credits, only some of which are compulsory. As vocational courses are usually available in upper secondary education, a certain number of vocational credits may be used towards this final school-leaving diploma. State policies are firmly behind this system. The vocational courses provided at school are in general not job-specific but are designed to prepare for broad areas of activity. There are also, in some of the largest cities, 'career-oriented' secondary schools which provide students with a considerable range of post-school options including four-year and community colleges and immediate access to a job (Stern *et al.*, 1992). Commentators often draw attention to the considerable diversity and experimentation across the country (HMI, 1990a; Benson and Silver, 1991; Education Writers Association, 1992).

The entry of vocational education into the United States secondary school came with the 1917 Smith–Hughes Act, establishing the structure and content of vocational education to the present. Despite the fact that only a small proportion of school students have ever enrolled in named vocational courses, this federal legislation enshrined the principle of differentiated curricula for students of different characteristics. This was a thorn in the flesh of those who saw the common school as the chief force for American nationhood. Concern about the consequent social segregation, among other harmful outcomes, has been a persistent strand of criticism ever since, despite the fact that the legislation was introduced ostensibly to increase the life opportunities for the disadvantaged (Benson and Silver, 1991, pp.10–12). Focus on 'at risk' populations has been the key to subsequent periodic reviews of vocational education, especially at federal level, as we discuss further below.

As a consequence of the Smith–Hughes Act, a divergence has developed within the high schools: to put the matter in extreme terms, teachers of the academic subjects are more theoretical ('chalk and talk') and vocational teachers more practical ('hands on') in their approaches. In such a caricature, there is little place for the kind of balance and interplay between theoretical and practical learning by students which Dewey, Kilpatrick and other progressive educators had advocated before and as these divergences occurred (Dewey, 1913; Kilpatrick, 1929; Chion-Kenney, 1992). Critics have not been slow in pointing to a lack of a well thought out, solid foundation of vocationally oriented education (SCANS, 1991; Achtenhagen, 1992).

In 1991, some 75 per cent of American 17-year-olds were enrolled in full-time secondary school (OECD, 1993a). Apart from the small number of mostly large city vocational–technical high schools, the vast majority of secondary schools are general public high schools offering a comprehensive programme from which students choose courses to suit their own interests and abilities. As we have seen, there are variations: between states and regions, and city centre, suburban and rural settings; and there are many specialised programmes including those with explicit vocational preparation targets. These demonstrate that selection, zoning, wide divergences of standards of performance and other forces of stratification exist within the ostensibly common school. Of the three broad tracks within high schools – academic, vocational–technical and general – an increasing proportion of students has, since the 1970s, opted for general track studies, which have the largest enrolments. Specific vocational training, with the exceptions noted above, has been considered by those concerned to be not part of formal education, but the later responsibility of employers.

The major decision point for most students comes at 18–19 years, where post-secondary education offers a very great diversity of possibilities, both private and public, in each of the fifty states. While some go directly into the workforce, the majority proceed to further study: for example, to two-year technical and community colleges, where most short-term certificate and diploma programme awards are in vocational areas, to four-year colleges and universities, where the majority of baccalaureate awards are now in professional and applied fields, or to non-collegiate private proprietary or 'career' schools (Stacey, 1988; Warnat, 1992). Thus, in the United States most of those graduating from high school continue their formal education, commonly at their own expense and, increasingly, combining work, part or full time, and study.

Only a very small proportion of 16–19-year-olds are engaged in work-based education, although this number has increased substantially in recent years. Apprenticeships account for only a small amount of the total training in this age group, but are important for craft workers (Stacey, 1988).

While not part of the vocational education provision, there is a long-standing tradition in the United States – and also in neighbouring Canada – that youngsters should work part-time during the course of their studies. In 1985 over one-third of American students in the last year of high school worked on average nineteen hours a week, mainly in services and retail areas, and the figures are increasing. This ad hoc work experience, however, has not in the main been co-ordinated with the school curriculum, and authorities have on occasion expressed concern, rather, at the possible (though not empirically established) detrimental effect of part-time work on school studies (especially where it stands at more than twenty hours per week) (Stacey, 1988; Conseil Supérieur de l'Education (Quebec), 1992).

There is a widespread, but not unchallenged, assumption in the United States that the best way of preparing young people for adult and working life is through the general and academic education provided by the high school, combined with one or another set of specialised options that may include explicit work preparation. Policy statements at both federal and state levels have affirmed the value of a sound general education as a basis for later specialisation (Bennett, 1987; National Education Goals Panel (USA), 1992).

Since the 1970s, the United States has been the theatre of action for the powerful 'Back to Basics' and 'Minimum Competency-Testing' movements. As we have seen, these grew from anxiety about relevant and effective curriculum, and the call for school accountability, so that functional illiteracy and low levels of competency in essential areas may be eradicated. Following publication of *A Nation At Risk* (National Commission on Excellence in Education (USA), 1983), which criticised the poor performance of American students, there has been a perceptible shift of policy towards a common core of studies for all students which, if put into practice, would entail a reinterpretation of academic and vocational studies in the high school. *A Nation At Risk* made several policy recommendations in favour of reinforcing the learning of English, mathematics, science, social studies, computer sciences and a foreign language. It further recommended that:

> The high school curriculum should also provide students with programs requiring rigorous effort in subjects that advance students' personal educational and occupational goals, such as the fine and performing arts and vocational education. These areas complement the New Basics and they should demand the same level of performance as the Basics.
>
> (National Commission on Excellence in Education (USA), 1983, p.26)

But the United States is a pluralistic society; alongside this shift there are many targeted programmes which seek to foster a stronger vocational ethos. By the mid-1980s, a wide range of design and delivery systems had been put into place:

> institutional-based vocational education in high school, technical institutes, community schools and area vocational schools. Other delivery systems include apprenticeship training, on-the-job training sponsored by industry, the Job Training Partnership Act, and private occupational schools, to name but a few.
>
> (Taylor *et al.*, 1985, p.1)

There has indeed been a perennial quest for improvement in the United States (Cremin, 1961). Concern with the failings in the system and belief in the saving grace of work led in 1969 to a federally inspired initiative known as Career Education to provide a specifically vocational strand to students' study in each year of schooling from 1 to 12. While this model has been implemented to only a limited degree, with some states offering courses on the world of work, there is a considerable diversity of programmes on career awareness, integrated academic and career studies, employer–community–school partnerships and so on. Four of the regionally based educational laboratories, for example, in association with schools developed strategies for experience-based career education (National Institute of Education, n.d.). Among the more searching and imaginative of current proposals to revitalise 'vocational tracks' within the high schools is one that would lead to a restructuring of the high school to enable students and teachers alike to share the roles of learner–instructor and worker in problem-solving rather than didactic approaches to knowledge (Raizen, quoted in Benson and Silver, 1991, pp.16–17). Other innovations spotlight entrepreneurship education, school-based Academies and high quality co-operative education programmes (Ashmore, 1987; GAO, 1991; Education Writers Association, 1992; Stern *et al.*, 1992).

Some 17 per cent of young people do not obtain the High School Diploma; others do so at an extremely modest level of attainment (National Center for Educational Statistics (USA), 1992, p.59). There is a large 'underbelly' of poor motivation and achievement, drop-out and school failures, despite an improving trend among blacks, particularly, and a tide of concern over the performance of American students in comparison with those of its trading partners and economic competitors (Commission on the Skills of the American Workforce, 1990; SCANS, 1991).

In response to these problems, federal government programmes have, as mentioned, targeted so-called 'at risk' groups among 16–19-year-olds seeking to generate skills and motivation, and reduce school drop-out. Various job training programmes to provide the young unemployed and drop-outs with marketable skills have been established, such as those under the Job Training Partnership Act 1982 and Carl D. Perkins Vocational Education Act 1984. The gulf between those who 'have' and who experience school success and the 'have-nots', however, seems to have widened, notwithstanding the long-held belief that in part the school exists to perform a socially ameliorative role and the determined efforts since the early 1980s to improve the overall quality of schooling. National education and health authorities have recently joined in a major initiative, *Together We Can*, to co-ordinate their support services to families of children at 'high risk of failing in school and later in life' (Melaville and Blank, 1993, p.1).

During the 1980s, there began to be demand from business for entry-level workers who could think abstractly and who had analytical skills – and therefore more than the traditional kinds of job-specific skills. This demand has underlain a significant new orientation of vocational education – and, to some extent, general education thinking – which has emerged during the last decade in the United States at the federal level. It showed first with the Carl D. Perkins Vocational Education Act, which aimed through Federal intervention to enrol at-risk populations in vocational programmes of high quality (that is, there was no longer a focus on low-order vocational training).

A second step came with the 1988 House of Representatives bill HR7 and subsequent Carl D. Perkins Vocational and Applied Technology Education Act 1990, which mandated federal funds for the integration of academic and vocational studies, and with the moves to articulate secondary school and community college curricula in the shape of 'tech prep'. Four-year 'tech prep' programmes are designed to provide for technical–vocational education what existing 'college prep' programmes provide for academically oriented students. Essentially 'tech prep' comprises specially designed technical–vocational programmes for the last two years of high school, followed by a two-year associate degree course at community college level –

referred to as '2 + 2' (Hull and Parnell, 1991). In this way, clearer differentiation of programmes is beginning to emerge in the United States at the upper secondary level, but within (for the most part) the single institution of the comprehensive high school.

The purpose of the Perkins Act 1990 was to:

> make the United States more competitive in the world economy by developing more fully the academic and occupational skills of all segments of the population. This purpose will principally be achieved through concentrating resources on improving educational programs leading to academic and occupational skill competencies needed to work in a technologically advanced society.
>
> (Public Law 101 (USA), 1990, Section 2)

Warnat (1992) sees in the Perkins Act 1990 the official start in the United States of the standards movement in vocational and technical education. The Act requires that all states receiving federal funds must develop and implement an accountability system of core performance standards and measures:

> (1) measures of learning and competency gains, including student progress in the achievement of basic and more advanced academic skills;
> (2) 1 or more measures of performance, which shall include only –
> (A) competency attainment;(B) job or work skill attainment . . .;(C) retention in school or completion of secondary school or its equivalent; and (D) placement into additional training or education, military service, or employment . . .
>
> (Public Law 101 (USA), 1990, Section 115)

Each state must develop a system for both secondary and post-secondary programmes, although different standards and measures may be used. The Act also provides the authority for the development of national standards for occupational competences in particular industries and trades. Further, it has established a major data-gathering operation on vocational education in the United States and its major trading partners, vested in the National Center for Educational Statistics. Thus, there has been a large, recent injection of public resources into vocational education, but of such a kind that diverse patterns will persist throughout the country.

More recently, the concerns and initiatives of the State Governors and the President have resulted in the 'America 2000' programme (Bush, 1991; National Education Goals Panel (USA), 1992). Highly controversial, and challenged by critics as a largely political exercise, America 2000 is nevertheless a recognisable extension and development of initiatives that have been gathering force for decades. It has identified six goals to be achieved by the year 2000:

1. All children in America will start school ready to learn.
2. The high school graduation rate will increase to at least 90 per cent.

3. American students will leave grades four, eight, and twelve having demonstrated competency in challenging subject matter including English, mathematics, science, history, and geography; and every school in America will ensure that all students learn to use their minds well, so they may be prepared for responsible citizenship, further learning, and productive employment in our modern economy.
4. U.S. students will be first in the world in science and mathematics achievement.
5. Every adult American will be literate and will possess the knowledge and skills necessary to compete in a global economy and exercise the rights and responsibilities of citizenship.
6. Every school in America will be free of drugs and violence and will offer a disciplined environment conducive to learning.

(Bush, 1991, p.3)

A four-part education strategy has been identified to enable communities to achieve these goals. A National Education Goals Panel will report annually on progress until the year 2000 (National Education Goals Panel (USA), 1992).

In support of goals 3 and 5 of America 2000, the Secretary of State established a Commission to identify 'changes in the world of work and the implications of those changes for learning' (SCANS, 1991, p.v). In its initial broadly based report, the Commission identified 'workplace know-how' comprising five competences and a three-part foundation of skills and personal qualities needed for a 'solid job performance' (which we have already discussed). They stress that they are not calling for a 'narrow work-focused education', but are addressing how schools prepare young people for work as one of school's several equally important concerns. An assessment system and curriculum development are flagged as items for the Commission's future effort.

All of this illustrates the general lack of support for the purely vocationalist option as a separate alternative to high school general education. The emphasis in the 'Back to Basics' movement has not been on vocationalisation, as such, but on making children work harder and more effectively, on more training and financial advantages for teachers and on standardised testing at regular intervals to assess progress and identify needs. The theme is less the vocationalising of the common school than the raising of standards of pupil performance in an academically oriented general education curriculum.

Against this backcloth of qualitative improvement of general education in the high school, however, increasing efforts are being made to maintain and strengthen a vocational strand. Thus, the role of experimentation and innovation in establishing some kind of balance between general and vocational education in the high-school years has by no means been

71

exhausted in America, and the pressure for more student involvement and response programmes continues unabated. Examples of such innovative programmes in career academies (specialist high schools combining academic and vocational learning) in one part of the USA are reviewed by de Leeuw *et al.* (1992).

In sum, the schooling model as exemplified in the USA is, despite its variability and the cross-currents of policy and practice, that of the common school with a vocational stream and a vocational overlay in general education. Only a small proportion of students are enrolled in the separate stream and vocational preparation at school is generally broad. Moves there are however, notably at the federal level, to bring a more conscious vocational orientation within general schooling and to upgrade the status of (broadly defined) vocational education with regard to academic learning.

Japan

After the Second World War, under the Allied Occupation, an Educational Reform Committee was established and a Fundamental Law of Education enacted (1947). This swept away the fifty-year-old system and ideology of the Meiji government, set forth new democratic and pacifist ideals and introduced a school system strongly influenced by American practice (Horio, 1988, Chapters 4 and 5). It was assumed by planners that the American high-school model, with its emphasis on mixing and equality of opportunity, would contribute to the dawning of a new, egalitarian, anti-imperialist Japanese culture. This is not to say that all aspects of traditional Japanese educational thought and practice were eliminated. They continued to inform the new structures, for example in the form of a highly developed work ethic, competitive exams and the respect accorded to the teacher.

The 1947 Fundamental Law of Education defines the goal of upper secondary education as 'the provision of higher-level general education and specialized education, upon the foundation of lower secondary education, and with due regard to students' psychological and physical development'. In practice, however, upper secondary education has not acted as a termination of general education so much as a bridge between compulsory schools and universities or colleges – a 'transfer' orientation. As Iwaki (1988) points out, this runs counter to jurisdictional definitions and the practical necessity of teaching those students who go directly to business. Existing general and vocational education schools were to be re-established as common schools open to children from all backgrounds and both sexes. Naturally, this imposition of a new type of school throughout the country was only possible because both the economy and the morale of the nation had been shattered. In practice, the comprehensive move proved incomplete in Japan with respect to the upper tier of schooling, with only around 30 per cent of upper secondary schools being multiple-course. Thus more than two-thirds are single-course schools, either general academic or vocational. There is a clearly recognised hierarchy among senior secondary (and indeed all) schools, with intense competition by junior secondary students for entry to the higher-ranking or more prestigious, which are the general (academic) track ones. The goal of their children reaching a 'good' university is still strong among parents. In recent years, renewed interest in comprehensive education has focused attention on some newly established comprehensive schools (HMI, 1991a).

The role models widely acceptable to Japanese children encourage them to be high achievers in school. Social forces lead Japanese parents and children to pursue the goal of 'making the grade'. Conformity to widely accepted patterns and nationally recognised norms of success in academic study are endemic. Thus we see relatively homogeneous values and goals, together with a willingness to work very hard; the children learn what they are expected to; low achievement is not blamed on the system but on the individual, who is nevertheless treated as if the ability to succeed is latent; results of an international study of mathematics achievement of 13-year-olds placed Japan ahead of all other Organisation for Economic Co-operation and Development (OECD) countries (OECD, 1992b). This so-called 'effortism' is, however, not without its critics, who range from outspoken academics like Professor Teruhisa Horia of Tokyo University to conservative members of government committees. It cannot be assumed that Japanese society will continue to treat the extreme pressures of the education system as the norm or pattern for the future. Nor should it be assumed that the much admired and highly successful Japanese industrial and commercial employment systems, to which educational values and procedures (if not content) are geared, will continue on their present course. Lifelong employment is under severe pressure and human resource management policies are criticised for their lack of direction and personal motivation (Amaya, 1990).

In 1991, some 89 per cent of 17-year-olds continued their schooling in the upper secondary cycle, with some 91 per cent completing the three-year course (OECD, 1993a). Of these, 72 per cent took general academic courses and 28 per cent of students studied special courses (mainly vocational), of which the two most popular areas were industry and business. For vocational/non-vocational specialised courses (such as agriculture, industry, business, fishery, home economics, nursing) students are grouped according to their interests, career plans, abilities, etc., from the beginning of the first grade of upper secondary education. Over 50 per cent of study in all courses, however, comprises general education.

For academic/general courses, most schools have established two or three curricular areas (such as sciences, humanities/social sciences) from the beginning of the second or third grade. These are seen as helping the schools better adapt to the diversity of the student population in an era of universalisation of the upper secondary school. Graduates of the non-academic general courses have been shown to have poorer job prospects than those of the vocational courses. Special Training Schools with a vocational orientation were established in 1976 and in 1985 these took 25 per cent of upper secondary school graduates, essentially from general courses. In that year, 31 per cent of upper secondary school graduates went to higher education, and 40 per cent took jobs.

> Most specialized education has been vocational education. Vocational programmes have had a distinctive character in that they aim to provide practical skills and knowledge in addition to general curricula. But they have been plagued with the difficulty of keeping up with rapid industrial change and inappropriately organized practical curricula. In today's information and service-oriented society, vocational education is being forced to come closer to general education.
>
> (Iwaki, 1988, p.4)

The heyday of vocational courses in the upper secondary school was the 1950s to mid-1960s, before sustained economic growth had become established. At this time the vast majority of upper secondary applicants to vocational courses were from rural areas, wishing to acquire some technical skill and knowledge in anticipation of moving to urban industrial areas. Around 1965 industry and business courses began to become less popular than academic/general courses, with vocational enrolments dropping from 41 per cent in 1960 to 37 per cent in 1975, and 28 per cent in 1985 (Iwaki, 1988, p.45).

The decline in popularity of the vocational courses apparently results from several factors, including changes in students' and parents' motivation (the generalisation of university aspiration, lowering of status of upper secondary graduates in organisations and decline in aspiration for self-employed status) and a mismatch of vocational curricula with occupational and industrial structure (their lag behind industrial change and the irrelevance of the subdivision of vocational courses). Since the mid-1960s, vocational courses have lost their most able students to the academic/general courses, and have settled into the bottom rank of the hierarchy of upper secondary schools.

Japanese employers, even more so than their American counterparts, do most of their own training, which they provide either on the job or off. Most of the large employers, accounting for some 30–40 per cent of the workforce, have taken on employees for life, and have therefore sought in new recruits motivation, a capacity for hard work, basic skills and the ability to learn and go on learning. At a more advanced level these qualities and competences are expected from higher achievers at school who enrol on the academic courses which lead on to prestigious higher education. In the same way, the content of subjects studied at university frequently has no obvious or direct bearing on the activities of the eventual employer. This is not to say that the attitudes, values, work habits and self-discipline fostered by the formal processes of education lack such direct bearing on subsequent employment. For that small proportion of students not progressing to upper secondary education (10 per cent), prefectural authorities offer one- to two-year courses in vocational training centres, according to need (Reutersward, 1992).

Two distinctive characteristics of Japanese corporations have given job preparation (for these enterprises) a somewhat different meaning from that in other OECD countries. First is the traditional internal labour market, which means that higher-level vacancies tend to be filled by promotion, and large-scale recruitment is at the level of new graduates from schools and universities – usually once a year (each April). From starting on the lowest rung, individuals are promoted on the basis of skills and knowledge acquired through on-the-job training until their retirement in the March of the year they turn 60. (Here we are talking essentially about men – women's career structure, if one can use the term, is much less clear.)

The second distinctive and very important feature of Japanese corporations is the lack of clear job demarcations.

> Workers are assigned to broad categories of jobs such as sales, clerical, manual, or technical positions, but corporations expect their employees to do any kind of task necessary for the work teams to accomplish certain prescribed goals. In addition, companies require their employees to perform a variety of jobs with differing work teams and in different places. Such job rotation helps firms maintain the practice of filling vacancies from within the organisation and may even take place beyond the broad categories of jobs. . . . New graduates are preferred because their wages are low and, more importantly, because they are presumed to have basic knowledge and flexibility, which means easy mastery of company training programmes and, consequently, reduced training costs to the employer.
>
> (Iwaki, 1988, pp.53, 55)

Despite a high value being placed on specialised school and university studies, new recruits are not regarded as 'ready for combat' workers, but as still in need of company-specific learning. The concept of readiness to learn is, in these circumstances, extremely important: the school is the agency, in association with the family and in the distinctive Japanese cultural ethos, which has this readiness as a principal outcome target.

Clearly, general ability is of major importance; the Japanese education system is, as we have seen, not highly vocationalised in terms of specific preparation for work, but is nevertheless highly functional given the nature of work organisation (Dore et al., 1989; Yoshio, 1992). Individual disciplines and the curriculum in general are not very much directed towards the world of work either in primary or in secondary school. This does not mean that the Japanese authorities have been indifferent to vocationalisation, broadly conceived, as a policy. It is a question of different means to long-term ends which, for the Japanese, certainly include a high level of success in economic and enterprise terms.

Notwithstanding its overall orientation, Japanese education does incorporate some specific elements of what in most countries would be recognisably vocational or pre-vocational. Concern with economic development meant that some pre-vocational courses were offered at lower secondary level from the period of reconstruction onwards. In the late 1950s, after Sputnik had been launched, the teaching of industrial arts (that is, machine engineering, electrical technology, woodwork) was introduced into the lower secondary curriculum (Murata *et al.*, 1985, p.531). As the number of pupils in the upper secondary school increased so also did the government develop career guidance and the quantity and variety of vocational courses and options available.

During the 'oil shock' years of the early 1970s, the authorities introduced into the basic upper secondary curriculum a new pre-vocational component, which:

> aimed to train students in problem-solving skills, to foster desirable attitudes for work and to inculcate transferable fundamental knowledge relating to specialized courses, for instance, the foundations of agriculture, the foundations of industry.
>
> (Murata *et al.*, 1985, p.533)

At the same time, work experience programmes were made available to upper secondary students, to acquaint them with the world of work and to help them acquire positive attitudes towards work. The objective of these innovations was to make young people more employable and more responsive to the needs of the then nearly flagging economy.

The advent of the new technologies is bringing profound changes to employment but, until very recently, much less so to the schools. While it is generally felt among planners that the obsession with success in academic and general education, which creates an 'examination hell', is not fruitful and that study should be directed more towards different, more co-operative and humanistic values and towards practical applications, this entails adaptation and adjustment rather than wholesale change. Likewise, emphasis on creativity, active learning through project study and the development of problem-solving aptitudes are considered to be appropriate avenues to pursue, but within the established school curriculum, not as an alternative to it. It is thought that the employers of tomorrow's labour will require job applicants to be literate in the new technologies, trained in practical pre-vocational skills and able both to work in a team and to show individual initiative. The stress on individual initiative is of interest; it seems that there is a desire to reduce the conformist pressure of educational provision, so as to promote independence of mind among young people without, of course, jeopardising their deep pride and confidence as Japanese citizens. Welcomed by some as evidence of a concern at the bad effects of formalism, conformity and excessive pressure on students, the reform initiatives in Japan are criticised by others as part of an elite-led strategy for increasing global economic dominance (Horio, 1988, Chapter 14).

The Japanese authorities are intent on revising educational practice and taking account of vocational needs, mainly through the overall curriculum. The essential point is that in the highly successful and competitive economy that is modern Japan, it is general education that is to be refocused: vocationalism is seen as but one strand within this wider reform.

> Japan puts vocational training in clear subordination to general education until the age of 15. And the standards of literacy, numeracy and oracy achieved are amongst the highest in the world – and with a smaller spread than in most countries between high and low achievers. In the vocational (technical, commercial, agricultural, etc.) high schools, continuing general education still takes up two-thirds of curriculum hours.
>
> (Dore *et al.*, 1989, pp.69–70)

How 'vocationalised', then, is the Japanese educational system or curriculum? One way of addressing this is to inquire whether graduates are equipped with immediately usable skills and knowledge. From this point of view, the Japanese education system and courses of study are not highly 'vocationalised', allowing for some exceptions. On the other hand, if one sees Japanese education as a screening system that provides students with the groundwork for subsequent employability, places them in key positions in enterprises and the public sector, and motivates them morally, it is understandable why the system as a whole has been functioning well, in terms of its goals, without an elaborate apparatus of vocation-specific preparation and training at the school level.

Sweden

In 1970, Sweden integrated into a single upper secondary school (*gymnasie-skola*) the then existing three types of parallel upper secondary education – general, technical and vocational – thereby establishing a direction for comprehensive secondary education which has attracted the interest of policy-makers and researchers in many countries. The new structure was intended to provide equal access to educational opportunities for a widely scattered population, following completion of the compulsory nine-year comprehensive school (*grundskola*) for ages 7–16 (Myrberg, 1987). In 1991, 85 per cent of 17-year-olds continued directly in the upper secondary school with 27 per cent in general and 73 per cent in vocational education (OECD, 1993a).

Most students are now in integrated schools, though some separate schools still exist, especially in urban areas. The integrated schools were established with a very wide range of 'study lines' (programmes) (over twenty-five different lines of either two or three years' duration, and more than 500 specialised courses of varying length) available within a national framework, leading ultimately to some ninety different final qualifications. This organisation led among other things to small groups of students and high costs per student (Ministry of Education and Science (Sweden) 1992).

In 1991 the Swedish Parliament passed a new School Act, which will bring significant changes to upper secondary education as it is implemented from the 1992/93 school year onwards. As with other major educational developments in Sweden, the vocational changes have followed a period of systematic experiment and research, on a trial basis, before becoming national policy (Eliasson, 1992). The changes concern two major areas: decentralisation of control for upper secondary education; and reorganisation of the course offerings within the integrated upper secondary school.

Since the 1980s, decentralisation has been a general process within Swedish society, affecting many spheres of formerly highly centralised government activity. In common with the comprehensive schools, upper secondary schools have now become the responsibility of municipal authorities. Although they must be run within the goals and guidelines established in the national School Act, schools as well as municipalities now have considerably more autonomy and freedom to vary programmes. Under the so-called 'steering by goals' model, the overall framework and direction of schooling is determined under parliamentary authority by the National Agency for Education, which in 1991 displaced the National Board of Education and the twenty-four County Education Committees. The quality of school performance is monitored and assessed against this framework, again by the National Agency for Education.

The reorganisation of courses sought to strike a balance between two requirements: to limit the number of study options; and to achieve an appropriate vocational orientation. The new structure has been simplified, and so organised as to give general eligibility for higher education to graduates of both vocational and academic courses. There are now sixteen nationally determined three-year educational programmes in upper secondary schools – two for university preparatory study (science and social science) and fourteen vocational programmes. Most programmes divide into branches in the second and third years. While a number of these branches are nationally defined, there is scope for additional locally defined branches (Ministry of Education and Cultural Affairs (Sweden), 1991a,b).

· The reforms of recent years have been driven more by industrial than by social equity (distributive) or pedagogical policies. They have led to a strengthening of vocational preparation through extending former two-year vocational courses to three years and a strengthening of general preparation for further studies by increasing the proportion of general subjects – for example, introducing English, mathematics and civics as compulsory subjects. The broad orientation is towards providing knowledge which is fundamental and generally relevant. All programmes now take the general pattern of broad introductory programmes and gradual specialisation, alongside a common core of subjects.

Vocational courses are to be built on the basis of co-operation between schools and working life. At least 15 per cent of teaching for all these courses must be located at a workplace, where specialist competence can be provided.

In addition to the sixteen national programmes, upper secondary schools must also enable students to follow individual study paths designed to satisfy their individual wishes. These individual programmes have their origins in the responsibility that municipalities have had since 1976 to provide a two-year follow-up of all students leaving compulsory schooling. In 1980, the school system became responsible for all young people to age 18, and in 1982 schools became responsible for securing youth opportunities for those who had left school, but were excluded from work. This concept of a guarantee, or net, has resulted in intensive efforts to provide appropriate, educative experiences. Up to one day per week of education and training can be part of the youth opportunities, and an experimental scheme of developing individual programmes for these young people at upper secondary schools has existed since 1986 in some municipalities. Such individual programmes – which may include modules in upper secondary school as well as work experience – are now to be a regular part of this level of schooling.

A new three-year apprenticeship programme is also to be created, comprising vocational training organised by employers with upper secondary schools providing courses in Swedish, English, civics and mathematics. In each of these ways, the integrated upper secondary school in Sweden has become the focus for both academic and vocational educational activities of a wide range for the 16–19 age range. While the Swedish policies have been increasingly industry driven, it is noteworthy that the locus of activity, for youth, is the school rather than the enterprise. Moreover, schools and municipalities have greater freedom than hitherto in educational decision-making and, presumably, a greater capacity for gearing these decisions to local needs and expectations including those of local labour markets.

France

In France, initial vocational education and training is essentially organised within the framework of a schooling system which is common to age 14, and differentiated thereafter. French public education has, since Napoleonic times, been highly centralised, but in recent years various pressures have led towards some decentralisation. Consequently, while there remains a strong national framework for structuring all aspects of education, variety is beginning to emerge in school practices in different parts of the country. In common with other industrialised countries, France has experienced increased retention rates after the end of compulsory schooling at age 16, with pressure on limited school facilities and resulting in a greater diversity in the student population. Official statistics indicate that, in 1991, 86 per cent of 17-year-olds were in full-time education, comprising 46 per cent following general education courses, and 54 per cent vocational–technical courses (OECD, 1993a). The provision of new courses to cater for this diversity and for changing employment needs has been high on the agenda. The broad directions of policy have been: to raise the overall qualification level of school-leavers (the stated goal is that by the year 2000 80 per cent of an age group should have access to a level equivalent to the *baccalauréat*); to offer more vocationally oriented education and to seek to raise its status in relation to academic and technical education; and to establish a well-articulated framework facilitating routes for individuals to continue their education and training up to and beyond commencing work.

Since 1975, after finishing primary school, French students begin a common four-year lower secondary education at *collèges*. Notwithstanding hierarchical and separatist traditions embedded in French society, which continue to have a strong impact on school structure and culture, the need for the common school with common curriculum elements for all students has been powerfully put, in terms of technological change as much as societal values (Legrand, 1983). All students study the same subjects which provide a wide base of general education, and lead to the national certificate (*brevet*). After the first two years of the *collège*, however, at age 13, a small number of students – those deemed to have a strong academic 'handicap' – are 'oriented' towards pre-apprenticeship classes, and at 14-plus a certain number are 'oriented' to a vocational lycée (*lycée professionel*). The *lycée professionel* begins to prepare these students for either a specific three-year trade qualification, the Certificat d'Aptitudes Professionelles (CAP), or a three-year general vocational qualification, the Brevet d'Etudes Professionelles (BEP) focused on vocational skills not in a specific trade, but in a single profession, industry, commercial area, administration or social sector. Some 250 different CAP qualifications are offered (mostly in the industrial sector), and some fifty different BEP qualifications.

The majority of students, however, complete the full four years of *collège* before choosing their future course. Following completion of *collège* (usually at 15 years), students may progress either to a *lycée professionel*, or to a *lycée* for general and/or technological education. At the general and/or technological *lycée*, students take a three-year course leading to one of: a general baccalaureate (*baccalauréat général* or *bac général*); the technological baccalaureate (*baccalauréat technologique* or *bac technologique* or *BTn*);

or the technical certificate (*Brevet de Technicien*, BT). A reform process begun in 1992 has streamlined the types or *séries* of *bacs* offered, with now three for the *bac général* and four for the *bac technologique*. The *bac général* and the *bac technologique* essentially lead towards higher education (that is, to university, preparatory classes for *grandes écoles*, higher technician sections, university institutes of technology, specialised schools, etc.). The BT is essentially a vocational qualification leading directly to employment. In the general *lycée*, course choices each year lead to increasing differentiation and specialisation by students.

The disproportionate status traditionally accorded the *bac général*, especially in the maths and economics *séries*, has been widely criticised for effectively narrowing study choices, given the now universal nature of upper secondary schooling. The 1992 reforms are intended to equalise the status of the different *bacs* and avoid the domination of mathematics (*une véritable 'dictature des mathématiques'*, Ministère de l'Education Nationale, 1993). How far this will be achieved remains to be seen, as reforms have been firmly resisted to date by powerful entrenched lobbies (Broadfoot, 1992). While there appears to be a parallel here with the British A levels, it should be noted that, for all its apparent imperfections, the French *bac* is indeed considerably broader than the A level system.

The *lycées professionels* receive their main intake from those who complete *collège*, and this group joins the earlier intakes to study for either the CAP or BEP, taken at age 16/17. In 1986, a new award, the vocational baccalaureate (*baccalauréat professionel* or *bac professionel* or *bac pro*) was introduced, involving two years' further study beyond the CAP and BEP. The *bac professionel* is a high-quality training for a particular profession. While it is designed to lead directly to working life, it also provides access to higher studies and stands as a major step, offering pathways for continuing study in the vocational area. Now the previously largely separate vocational, technical and academic areas each offer a *baccalauréat* qualification at 18-plus, with each *bac* intended to have equivalent standing. Like any new programme, however, the *bac professionel* has yet to establish its clientele, make its mark and overcome – if it can – the continuing status disadvantage of the vocational area (Watson, 1991). In 1992, 434,500 students gained a *baccalauréat* – for the first time more than 50 per cent of the age group. Of these, 10 per cent gained a *bac professionel*, 63 per cent a *bac général* and 27 per cent a *bac technologique*.

The *bac professionel* is offered in two modes. Mode 1 students are school-based, but have a minimum of sixteen weeks of workplace training over two years. Mode 2 students are apprentices with employment contracts, and divide their time equally between work and apprentice training centres. In 1993, thirty-two different *baccalauréats professionels* were offered with new ones being added each year.

While most of the programmes discussed have large compulsory components, differentiation into general, technological and vocational streams mean that there is no structure which aims to provide learnings which are common to all students above the age of 14. It is true, however, that in all the courses there is a substantial component of general education including – in some form – French, modern history, civics and mathematics.

Since 1969, six training levels have been recognised in France, with one-year pre-vocational courses being at level VI, CAP and BEP level V, *baccalauréat* at level IV, and levels I–III relating to different higher or further education qualifications (Ministère de l'Education Nationale (France), 1992). Noting the attachment to formal recognition through such a framework, Colardyn observes:

> In a country where the diploma is king, undertaking a course of training without gaining a diploma, a certificate or a formal qualification of some kind 'underwritten' by the state represents a radical departure and raises the question of why anyone should take a course of training without any prior guarantee that it will be taken into account.
>
> (Colardyn, 1990, p.7)

The significant strengthening of vocational education at school level in France needs to be seen as a complement to comprehensive, continuing vocational training, whereby since 1971 all French firms employing more than ten people must by law contribute to expenditures for the continuing training of their staff (Berton *et al.*, 1991).

Thus the routes to working life in France are predominantly education-led and school-based at the post-compulsory level, forming a complex structure with a considerable variety of qualifications. The move to develop the *baccalauréat professionel* provides an important linkage between the large and diverse vocational training area and higher education and training, as well as attempting to upgrade the status of vocational qualifications. It is still too early to judge the effect of a development which is state- not employer-led and adheres to traditional values of French culture: rigour, clarity, sequence and continuity of learning, whether in its literary, scientific, technological or vocational formations. The problems of status differentials and effective linkages between the vocational programmes and the labour market in an era of persistently high youth (and adult) unemployment levels, remain.

Australia and New Zealand

Arrangements for vocational education and training in *Australia* have in the late 1980s and early 1990s undergone a major reorganisation whose impact will be felt for many years. New structures are being established which are intended to develop a comprehensive national system in a federal country where responsibility for schooling and TAFE (technical and further education) have been traditionally, and are constitutionally, state matters.

Several factors during the 1980s have spurred this major overhaul. In August 1988, the Industrial Relations Commission determined that restructured industrial awards should comply with the Structural Efficiency Principle, a principle agreed by government, industry and unions aimed at improving Australian industry's ability to be competitive. A fundamental review of awards followed, including provision for skill-related career paths, multiskilling and broadbanding of occupational preparation. National consistency in training arrangements was a next step.

The national reform programme which has developed over the years following commands wide support among Commonwealth, state and territory governments, employers and unions. Extensive consultation, dialogue and partnership at each stage have been fundamental features of the consensus approach to development (Murphy, 1992).

Until the mid-1980s, apprenticeships, although in decline, formed the main avenue for industry-based youth training, with a compulsory off-the-job component at a TAFE college to achieve the requisite qualification. The plethora of other small-scale education, skills training and job creation and employer subsidy schemes were criticised in an influential report to the Commonwealth government on labour market programmes (Kirby, 1985). The Kirby Committee recommended that government programmes focus on training young people and qualifying them for skilled work or for re-entry to the education system. A subsequent reorganisation of Commonwealth programmes saw the creation of the Australian Traineeship System, combining on-the-job work experience with formal off-the-job training in areas where there were no existing traditional apprenticeships. Traineeships, open to any 16–18-year-old leaving school, have been concentrated mainly in the clerical and retail sales sectors.

Alongside these changes in the training area, Australian states made considerable efforts to improve the retention rates of students in the post-compulsory upper secondary years. In 1988, Australia had a 92 per cent enrolment at age 16 (66 per cent general education and 26 per cent vocational–technical education) (OECD, 1992b). While youth unemployment has undoubtedly played a role in making school (relatively) attractive, there have also been major changes in the upper secondary curriculum of different states, considerably broadening this beyond its traditional academic and higher education preparation focus (Australian Education Council, 1992). One common feature of this broadening has been to seek to relate schooling more closely to working life. For example, in the restructuring of curricula and examining in the upper years of secondary education which took place in the state of Victoria in the later 1980s, a general orientation to working life was placed at the centre of the newly compulsory course of Australian studies for students sitting the Year 12

Victorian Certificate of Education. In a number of states, schools provide fairly specific vocational preparation courses as options within the single state-level award offered at the end of secondary schooling (Year 12). These innovations in schooling are part of a larger reform process aimed at achieving a common national framework for the curriculum, which is discussed below.

In 1992, the Prime Minister, in his 'One Nation Statement' (DEET, 1992, pp.21–22) announced the establishment for 1993 of a new Australian National Training Authority (ANTA) to assume responsibility for all Commonwealth government involvement in TAFE. Following negotiation with the states, it was agreed that the current state-level responsibilities for TAFE colleges were to continue (that is, administration by state boards and state funding), and the Commonwealth government promised some A$700 million or more in additional funding to be administered by ANTA. As proposed, this new body was to comprise a Commonwealth–states Ministerial Council, and a Commonwealth Statutory Authority with strong industry backing. ANTA was also expected to assume responsibility for the National Training Board (NTB).

The NTB, a joint Commonwealth–states initiative established in 1990 and charged with the setting of national skills standards, moved fast to establish the Australian Standards Framework (ASF) of eight competency levels designed to provide reference points for comparing vocational training and qualifications. In expressing a 'competency standard' in 'units of competency', each of which comprises 'elements of competency' and their associated performance criteria, the NTB appears to have studied closely the approach taken by the British National Council for Vocational Qualifications (NCVQ) in establishing National Vocational Qualifications (NVQs) (outlined in some detail below in Chapter 5). Tripartite Industry Training Councils, comprising employers, unions and training authorities, are to be the means of formulating the competency standards for a particular industry sector, submitting these to the NTB, for clearance. The Carmichael Report (discussed below) initially recommended four vocational certificate levels equating with ASF levels 1–4, with the intention of moving on to a detailed study for levels 5–8.

Over this same period, another body, the Australian Education Council (AEC), comprising the state and federal ministers of education, commissioned a study into young people's participation in post-compulsory education and training. The consequent Finn Report identified six broad key areas of competence (language and communication; mathematics; scientific and technological understanding; cultural understanding; problem-solving; personal and interpersonal) which should be included in *all* post-compulsory education and training programmes for the 15–19 age cohort (Finn, 1991, p.58). The Finn Committee envisaged a commitment to at least two years of post-compulsory education and training for all young people. Thus, post-compulsory curricula and programmes must cater for ability at all levels and of all kinds, diverse interests and different initial vocational and educational destinations. Curricula must be broad and balanced, with an appropriate mix of general and vocational education and theoretical and applied studies. Both school programmes and TAFE/training programmes should be coherent and broad enough to incorporate the employment-related key competences listed above. Curriculum outcomes should be clear in terms of expected knowledge, skills and attitudes, and must be explicitly structured into standards frameworks compatible across both the school and TAFE/training sectors. Cross-crediting of learning between sectors was seen as a goal, to give young people flexibility in constructing appropriate individual learning programmes.

The Finn Committee's work laid foundations for moves to define levels of competence regarding schooling outcomes. As the Finn Committee noted, it is a considerable challenge to operationalise the key areas of competence by developing each into a usable student competency profile, and enabling each competency to be separately assessed (Finn, 1991, p.59).

Building on the Finn Report in the training area is the Carmichael Report (Employment and Skills Formation Council, 1992). This report, endorsed by the federal and all state governments, recommends a new competency-based entry-level vocational education system – the Australian Vocational Certificate Training System (AVCTS) – to be established to absorb or replace the existing apprenticeship system and traineeships, for all industry sectors.

The Carmichael Report proposed that by 1995 competency-based vocational training be established in all industry sectors and almost all enterprises. The report set as a target that by 2001 90 per cent of all young people at 19 should have completed Year 12 or an initial post-school qualification, or be participating in formally recognised education and training.

The report recommended a move by all states towards Senior Colleges for upper secondary programmes for all students, with the development of more vocational options for Years 11–12. Schools, then, would increasingly become the locus for initial vocational training for the first level of the Australian Standards Framework (ASF). TAFE colleges would move towards a predominant (but not exclusive) focus on advanced vocational education and training from ASF certificate level 2 up to diploma level.

The new training system as envisaged would focus on the generic key competences identified by Finn, seen as underpinning the acquisition of vocational and other specific competences. A flexible, well-articulated structure, enabling clear paths for progression is envisaged, to be phased in with goals set to the year 2001.

Following the Finn Report, and as already mentioned in Chapter 3, a committee was established to develop the concept of 'employment-related key competencies' (Australian Education Council and Ministers for Vocational

Education, Employment and Training, 1992). In receiving the report of the Committee, the ministers emphasised that Australia's competitiveness in international markets depended on 'developing a workforce capable of participating effectively in new forms of work and work organisation. This requires', they said, 'a renewed emphasis on the role of general education in providing the foundation of a multi-skilled, flexible and adaptable workforce and a greater emphasis on broad employment-related competences in vocational education and training' (*ibid.*, Foreword). Thus, the competences identified by the Committee were to be developed alike in school and training sectors, within a framework of common levels and consistent assessment and reporting procedures. So much for directions. The ministers, in adopting them, were implicitly accepting the need for a vast, long-term programme of development and implementation.

The scale and pace of change in vocational education signify a major reform process for Australia, with Commonwealth and state authorities in the vanguard but in partnership with employers and unions. The state education and training authorities are, however, responsible for delivery and for a considerable part of the financial commitment. The impetus for change is primarily economic, a reflection of the serious problems Australia has encountered as a primary producer and exporter of largely unprocessed minerals. The change process began in earnest in the late 1980s, but it will be many years before the substantial policy agenda has been worked through and programmes implemented on the scale envisaged. Still to be resolved is the balance between vocationally oriented education in the upper secondary school, the specific vocational preparatory role of the TAFE sector and the responsibilities of employers. However, the overall direction of policy envisages schools or colleges co-operating closely with the workplace and training agencies, as the primary sites for vocational education and training.

New Zealand, like its near neighbour Australia, is also in the process of major national changes in education and training. Fifty-nine per cent of 17 year olds studied full time in secondary education in 1991, with 93 per cent in general and 7 per cent in vocational education (OECD, 1993a).

In 1990, an Achievement Initiative for schools was announced. Following this, the Ministry of Education commissioned the development of draft statements in the 'essential areas of learning' of the new draft national curriculum, to specify clear achievement objectives for the curriculum. Eight levels of achievement are clearly identified in each area. Statements in science and mathematics were issued as draft curriculum statements to schools in 1992, for consideration and comment, with the intention that these were to be the basis for the new official curriculum from 1993 (Ministry of Education (New Zealand), 1992a, b).

A New Zealand Qualifications Authority was established in July 1990 to develop a comprehensive and coherent framework for nationally recognised qualifications within the post-compulsory education and training sectors, including, controversially, degrees and advanced degrees. Widespread consultation with the community and interested parties has been a feature of the rapid development of the new National Qualifications Framework. Eight levels have been established, with level 4 marking the end of secondary schooling or its equivalent, and level 8 advanced degrees, diplomas or higher certificates. A new common terminology will see achievement at levels 1–4 receiving the appropriate National Certificate, and levels 5–8 an appropriate National Diploma, with the new qualifications being gradually brought in from 1993. This system is designed to recognise all forms of learning, and enable them to be appropriately credited.

'Units of learning' are the basic elements of the framework, with each unit having a credit rating recognising the skills and knowledge achieved. A recognised qualification will comprise several recognised units. Unit standards indicate unit titles, level, credit rating, qualifications to which the unit relates, brief explanation of the purpose of the unit, specified outcomes in terms of skills and knowledge to be acquired, and the assessment criteria against which performance will be measured. A National Catalogue of Units will be publicly accessible. Those involved in teaching will construct, for each unit they select, a delivery statement, detailing learning and teaching approaches, content and context, resources and range and number of assessments to be used. The unit delivery statements will be part of accreditation proposals (New Zealand Qualifications Authority, 1991a, b).

Units of learning may have either a general or a vocational bias, with on-the-job training recognised and certificated. Special Maori-based qualifications within the national framework will enable appropriate crediting of learning within the indigenous Maori community.

The New Zealand reforms have, like the Australian and British, been prompted by recognition of changing economic circumstances. By the 1980s and 1990s Australia and New Zealand could no longer continue to support high standards of living on the basis of exporting unimproved primary produce – for which a minimally trained workforce had been sufficient – and means are being actively sought to upgrade both general education and skill levels in the community. The establishment of national frameworks for vocational education has been central to both their approaches.

United Kingdom: England and Wales; Northern Ireland; Scotland

In *England and Wales*, compulsory schooling finishes at age 16. About 90 per cent of students now attend comprehensive secondary schools, and 90 per cent also take the General Certificate of Secondary Education (GCSE) – the recognised 16-plus qualification through examination offered by different national examining boards. The education system is such, however, that only about one in three 16-year-olds achieves the five or more GCSEs at grades A–C which have been the standard qualification for sixth-form study. The system rewards academic ability and achievement and its history has been one in which '[v]ocational qualifications . . . are usually a route for people who have failed something' (Smithers and Robinson, 1991, p.4). Of those who achieve one to four GCSEs at grades A–C, or five or more at grades D–G, some may resit the following year, while others may take vocational qualifications. Those embarking on Youth Training and entering employment tend to be at the lower end of the scale of GCSE results. About 6 per cent have no graded results at all.

For the United Kingdom as a whole, 43 per cent of 17 year olds are in full-time secondary level education, of whom 80 per cent are in general and 20 per cent in vocational courses (OECD, 1993a). Returning to England and Wales, for those staying on, there is a variety of offerings, the General Certificate of Education (GCE) A (Advanced) level courses – mostly highly academic – being the best known and most prestigious. At all comprehensive schools, sixth-form colleges, further education (FE) colleges and tertiary colleges, students not taking the A level route have the choice of studying several rather different courses. They include occupation-specific training courses, for which a very wide range of programmes exist, offered by different examining bodies (the main three of which are Business and Technician Education Council (BTEC), City and Guilds of London Institute (CGLI) and Royal Society of Arts (RSA), which are considered in more detail in Chapters 5 and 7), and now gradually being linked into a new national framework, the National Vocational Qualifications (NVQs); and pre-vocational courses providing a broad introduction to occupational fields, offering students the recently established General National Vocational Qualifications (GNVQs). Among this collection of courses there is none leading to a broad general educational award; there are no necessarily common elements between the different programmes currently offered for students aged 16-plus within a given institution; and the multiplicity of pathways, dead ends included, has constantly baffled informed observers, let alone students faced with crucial decisions at the age of 16.

A distinctive feature of British qualifications is that they are offered by a range of examining boards – essentially non-profit companies – some specialising in offering academic, others in vocational, qualifications. While the examining boards operate in a regulated environment (the governmental body, the Schools Examination and Assessment Council (SEAC) has been responsible for overseeing them), they are still in competition with each other for examination candidates – and their fees. Educational institutions are free to choose for which qualifications from which board they will prepare students – and they often choose from more than one board at any one time. While there are some clear regional patterns of allegiance to some boards, within England and Wales, most boards examine students throughout the country.

From the 18-plus A (Advanced) level, there is a clear progression to higher educational studies. Progression within the vocational sphere has been much less obvious. A wide range of vocational qualifications has been on offer from different boards; these have been of many different standards, and the relationships between them are often unclear. This 'jungle' of post-16 awards has long been a cause of concern and attempts have been made in the past to 'map' it (Locke and Bloomfield, 1982). Failure to make real headway in defining clear pathways and a well-articulated framework prompted the Review of Vocational Qualifications, to which we return in Chapter 5. By the early 1990s, a national framework had been established for accrediting existing qualifications at recognised levels as NVQs (levels 1–4, with plans for level 5 accreditation), but this is a voluntary system, and has not changed the structure of examining bodies. Accrediting courses as GNVQs has commenced also, as we discuss further in Chapter 5.

Over recent years, an increasing number of sixth-form colleges and tertiary colleges have been established to take 16–19-year-old students. These offer a range of academic and vocational courses. Schools have for long been the responsibility of some more than 100 local education authorities, but recent government policy has been to encourage schools to 'opt out' of local control. This process is likely to keep very fluid the institutional structures of post-compulsory schooling, with – at present – no clearly discernible trends for the future.

Post-16 full-time education is also available in FE colleges, which have also been under local governance, but in 1992 were 'nationalised' and brought under national funding arrangements. Further education colleges offer the bulk of non-advanced further education (NAFE), thus overlapping with (and in this period of demographic decline, to some extent competing with) the courses offered at post-16 schools. Further education colleges also offer NAFE to adults and, as we see below, operate part-time study programmes for students aged 16-plus.

Of those students who leave school at 16, with or without formal qualifications (that is, a GCSE), many hope to enter directly into employment. It should be noted that the UK does not have a regulated youth labour market, and youth wages can be quite high. Since the 1970s, however, overall prospects for youth employment have declined, and high youth unemployment has persisted, modified to some extent by demographic change, since the late 1980s.

Faced with high numbers of unemployed youth with no formal qualifications, the government has, since the 1970s, established various youth programmes, the subject of detailed discussion in subsequent chapters. These have culminated in the Youth Training Scheme (YTS) and Youth Training (YT) ostensibly providing, at least in principle, an entitlement to training for two years for all 16-year-olds in a wide range of places of employment. Requirements for off-the-job training have often been met through FE colleges, although it is an essentially employer-led programme. Thus trainees (who receive a modest training allowance rather than a wage) gain some work experience and a variable education and training exposure during the programme. Increasingly the educational and training component of YT programmes is being so organised as to qualify trainees for NVQs through participation in recognised courses of one of the vocational examining authorities.

But participation in YT is voluntary, with no compulsion by education or training authorities to provide for all 16–18-year-olds – although the stick is to some extent wielded by the practice of denial of social security benefits to unemployed individuals under 18 who refuse a training place (Woolhouse, 1991). Apprenticeships still exist in a contracted form in the UK, and although there is no formal link between apprenticeships and YT, in practice YT is increasingly being used as the vehicle for apprenticeship training in such areas as construction and hairdressing.

Whereas the YTS started under the highly centralised Manpower Services Commission (MSC), its successor programme, YT, is now decentralised under the responsibility of some eighty-two Training and Enterprise Councils (TECs) throughout England and Wales. These are discussed in detail in Chapters 5 and 7. It is sufficient here to note that there has quickly developed between these local TECs and central government a divergence of view about the importance of YT relative to other forms of local enterprise development that many TECs have taken an interest in.

Considerable concern exists about the continuing 'jungle' at post-16, with the National Council for Vocational Qualifications (NCVQ) attempting to provide a recognised national framework for validating awards. Interest has also been expressed, as discussed in Chapter 3, in bringing academic and vocational education of the post-16 age group closer together through exploring proposals for a common core of studies. Some critics regard this as insufficient, seeing nothing short of a scrapping of the present divided system and the construction of a single 18-plus award for all students as sufficing (Finegold *et al.*, 1990). Just what the proposed new Ordinary and Advanced Diplomas will add up to, if they are indeed established, remains to be seen, as we discuss in Chapter 5. To date no action has been decided on in this area, and new proposals, like the many preceding them for the reform of the A level system, must come to terms with successive governments' perceptions of the A level as the 'gold standard' of the school system. So long as this attitude prevails, the fragmented, uneven and confused pattern of 16-plus provision and assessment will remain. Influential proposals for reform, such as those of the National Curriculum Council (NCC) and NCVQ, relate to common learnings for jobs by contrast with the Continental emphasis on a common core of general educational studies (for example, native language, foreign language, mathematics, social science) for all students, vocational included.

In *Northern Ireland*, educational provision is organised on similar lines to that in England and Wales, with some significant structural differences. Most post-primary schools are selective on the basis of academic ability, with students divided between grammar (11–18 years) and secondary (11–16 years in the main) schools. Also, there is a large voluntary school sector, with some 44 per cent of primary and secondary schools being voluntary maintained. A small number of integrated schools exist where students of both Catholic and Protestant backgrounds study together. Five education and library boards administer the education system under the aegis of the Department of Education for Northern Ireland (DENI). A reform programme broadly similar to that in England and Wales is being implemented in Northern Ireland, with the changes of the 1988 Education Act being brought into force through the Education Reform (Northern Ireland) Order 1989. The remit of the NCVQ extends to Northern Ireland, as do those of the various examining bodies operating in England and Wales.

While a number of programmes for 16–18-year-olds are offered in some secondary schools, for those students wishing to pursue studies beyond the compulsory years other than in the primarily academic grammar schools, by far the most common pattern has been to switch to FE colleges after age 16. Here a wide range of both vocational and non-vocational courses is on offer. Over the last decade, a broader range of course offerings in schools and FE has been sought, as well as closer co-operation between FE, schools and industry, and in many cases achieved (DENI, 1992a, c). By contrast with England and Wales, Northern Ireland does not have a tradition of free-standing sixth-form colleges.

With many factors bringing change to the FE environment during the 1980s, there has been a series of reports and reviews to reconsider the nature of FE provision in Northern Ireland. *Signposts for the 90s* was issued by DENI in June 1990 (DENI, 1990) as a consultative document, seeking community and professional response to the issues facing FE. Over the previous decade, there had been a significant growth in enrolments in advanced courses, together with a continuing growth in non-advanced course enrolments. Young people aged 16–18 have come to dominate as the key client group, with their participation in FE increasing. Some college courses were seen as too narrowly focused to promote flexibility and adaptability for the various client groups of FE.

In the 1990 consultative document, the development of a curriculum framework for 16–19 provision was proposed, comprising: main studies; complementary studies; educational themes (five cross-curriculum themes suggested); and core competences (six suggested). This should:

provide equivalence with 16–19 qualifications in England and Wales and ensure that our young people have the broad background necessary to compete for jobs in Great Britain and in the rest of Europe. The framework would enhance continuity and progression from the school curriculum, promote achievement on a broader front and meet some of the specific skill needs of Northern Ireland.

(DENI, 1990, p.6)

In the government's official response, *Further Education in Northern Ireland – The Road Ahead*, the theme of a curriculum framework was seen as an appropriate concern, but needing to be viewed in the broader context of schools, colleges and recognised training organisations 'to secure for all young people clear routes of progression to post-16 opportunities' (DENI, 1991, p.20).

The Curriculum for 14–19-year-olds: A Framework for Choice followed in 1992, proposing a 'curricular framework consisting of a number of components within which post-16 provision for all young people in full-time education in schools and colleges of further education might be made' (DENI, 1992b, p.12). In a brave attempt to achieve a measure of clarity and coherence in the confusing array of courses and qualifications, the Department of Education stated that 'main studies' were to be the principal subjects, units or modules taken by young people in full-time education and training post-16, and would be drawn, as appropriate, from: GCE A/AS levels; GNVQ levels 2 or 3; NVQ levels 1, 2, 3; and International Baccalaureate at Certificate and Diploma levels. 'Additional studies' would take the form of modules, units or full subjects, to complement the main studies and to broaden the educational experience of young people by giving them access to knowledge, understanding and skills in a greater range of curriculum areas than is at present available to many, and should, where possible, lead to external assessment and accreditation. Careers guidance should be provided both through the context of main and additional studies, and through counselling and information available on an individualised basis. Comparing this framework with that proposed in *Signposts* confirms an interest in seeking a common form to post-16 studies, and in fostering studies leading to qualifications, but the opportunity to identify common areas of learning for all 16–19-year-olds (with the exception of guidance and counselling), and the nature of a broad-based education have, as in England and Wales, been passed up.

To return to *Further Education in Northern Ireland – The Road Ahead*, the main thrust of the government's response was to establish aims for FE to: increase participation in vocational education (especially by adults); improve the quality of such provision; enhance standards of attainment of FE students; develop closer links with the business community and schools; and achieve cost-effective provision and equitable impact of FE pro-grammes on different parts of the community. By contrast with the position in Great Britain, it was decided that FE colleges should remain under education and library board control, but because of the large number of very small colleges in Northern Ireland, considerable restructuring and rationalisation of the sector was seen as a priority. Consequently, a Review Group on Further Education was established to advise on achieving a more co-ordinated FE system. Among other things, it proposed wideranging institutional amalgamations, but no closures of campuses (Review Group on Further Education, 1992), a direction subsequently endorsed by the relevant minister (Hanley, 1993). As in the rest of the United Kingdom, seeking increased vocational education and parity of esteem between vocational and academic studies has been a key theme.

In Northern Ireland, the Youth Training Programme (YTP) has since the early 1980s provided a two-year programme for 16-year-old school-leavers, combining training, further education and work experience in the first year and either employment with training or more specialised full-time training in the second year. The Training and Employment Agency funds a network of Recognised Training Organisations, including training centres, community workshops, FE colleges and employer-led agencies – to deliver the YTP. The first two years of apprenticeship are delivered through the YTP, with other arrangements for their completion. In 1990, major changes in the delivery and funding arrangements included greater emphasis on outcomes and recognised qualifications, increased employer involvement, and greater flexibility in programme design and financial discretion for providers (D. Gordon, personal communication). The Agency began piloting a new training programme in 1992 which within two years should replace both the Youth and the Job Training Programmes. The pilot heightens yet further the emphasis on achieving recognised vocational qualifications (Training and Employment Agency, 1992). Key issues for youth training remain: the high level of unemployment through-out Northern Ireland (on average 14.8 per cent, with a high of 33 per cent for males in one region); the large number of small firms with little expertise in, or commitment to, training and assessment in the workplace; and problems of providing suitable training programmes for trainees with special educational needs (I.H.N. Wallace, personal communication). Over and above these is the lack of a comprehensive, coherent framework for the education and training of all 16–18-year-olds, only partially compensated for by the planning approach adopted in the official documents.

School-level education in *Scotland* is under separate legislation from that holding in other parts of the UK, and is the responsibility of the Secretary of State for Scotland. The Scottish Office Education Department (SOED) (formerly Scottish Education Department, SED) is the main agency of the Secretary of State for directing, evaluating and administering education for Scotland as a whole. Considerable responsibilities have been delegated to regional and island education authorities for delivering the school curri-culum. The Scottish Vocational Education Council (SCOTVEC) works closely with the SOED and other national (Scottish) level agencies for curriculum and examinations.

A national curriculum framework, issued in 1989 in the form of guidance to headteachers (that is, not mandatory as in the rest of UK), identifies three stages (S) of secondary education: S1–S2 (ages 12–14); S3–S4 (ages 14–16); S5–S6 (ages 16–18). This framework sees, typically, S1–S2 students studying a common curriculum with a balance of subjects and activities covering eight identified modes or categories of study, as proposed by the Munn Report (Scottish Education Department, 1977): language and communication; mathematical studies and applications; scientific studies and applications; social and environmental studies; technological activities and applications; creative and aesthetic activities; physical education; religious and moral education. In S3–S4 students choose from a balanced framework of modes of study – the core comprising some 70 per cent of school time, the balance comprising options. In S5–S6 (post-compulsory) students choose a wide range of courses to suit interests and career plans. A range of key skills essential to every pupil's personal and social development have been identified as a main component of the curriculum, to be taught and reinforced by all teachers in all subjects. Communicating and learning skills involve use of language and numeracy, obtaining information and how to learn. Technology and creative skills include reasoning, problem-solving, designing and applying skills to a variety of situations. Given this continuation of Scotland's traditional commitment to broad-based education, it is interesting to note that the Technical and Vocational Education Initiative (TVEI) (see Chapters 5 and 8) was initially met with suspicion and mistrust by Scottish educators, but subsequently, and later, embraced when its breadth proved compatible with Scottish developments (Pignatelli, 1987).

The post-16 vocational curriculum has been fully revised, and schools can offer modular courses certificated by SCOTVEC (see below) in S5–S6 as well as courses certificated by the Scottish Examination Board (SEB), including the Scottish Certificate of Education at Higher Grade (age 17, following the age 16 Standard Grade) and the Certificate of Sixth Year Studies (EURYDICE and CEDEFOP, 1991).

Virtually all state secondary schools have a comprehensive intake, and some 90 per cent provide the full six years of secondary schooling (four years compulsory, two years optional). Most students continuing in full-time education at age 16 remain at school rather than transferring to colleges, which thus tend to cater more for older students. As in England and Wales, FE colleges have recently moved from the control of local education authorities to become autonomous and directly accountable to the central authority, namely SOED. From 1991 they have been supported by the Scottish Further Education Unit (SFEU).

In common with other parts of the UK, vocational education in Scotland has been strongly influenced by the direction of argument of the *New*

Training Initiative of 1981 (see further, Chapter 5 below). A major reform of certification occurred in 1984 when a single National Certificate based on modules and modular programmes replaced non-advanced FE and many non-academic courses open to 16–18-year-olds at school (Jeffrey, 1985). Comparably organised Higher National Certificates and Higher National Diplomas, corresponding to the first two years of higher education, were subsequently introduced. Both these certificates are awarded through SCOTVEC (Further Education Colleges (Scotland), 1990).

While SCOTVEC's National Certificate modules and Higher National units are units of learning and certification normally requiring forty hours of study, the award of the module is based on satisfactory performance, independent of study time – that is, a 'time-free' learning outcomes model. A unit descriptor specifies learning outcomes, performance criteria and assessment procedures, as well as advice on preferred entry level, content and context, and learning and teaching approaches. The awards are all internally assessed, and externally moderated or verified.

> Under SCOTVEC assessment arrangements it is for the lecturer to devise the assessment and to decide whether the students' performances are of the required standard for them to be credited with the achievement of each learning outcome. . . . The adoption of an internally assessed criterion-referenced approach to assessment aims to ensure that the method of assessment is appropriate to the purpose of the learning. By freeing the assessment process of the constraints of externally set and administered assessment it is possible for a much wider range of assessment instruments to be used.
>
> (Tuck, 1992, p.22)

SCOTVEC issues successful students a Record of Education and Training documenting their recognised achievements. SCOTVEC moved into modularisation/unitisation of its non-advanced and advanced FE curriculum with its 1983 Action Plan, somewhat ahead of the NCVQ, which has drawn considerably on SCOTVEC's experience.

In several other developments since the 1980s, the work of both organisations shows considerable parallels. In common with the NCVQ, SCOTVEC uses a model of occupational competence and employment-led standards of competence, emphasises assessment of competence in the workplace, recognises prior experiential learning and requires the learning of core skills (both organisations use the same list) (Tuck, 1992).

Scottish Vocational Qualifications (SVQs) have been developed based on the same standards as those used by the NVQs holding in the rest of the United Kingdom (see also Chapter 5). Both SCOTVEC and the NCVQ work with the UK-wide industry lead bodies charged with defining the relevant employment competences to which SVQs and NVQs relate (McPhail, 1992; see also Chapter 5). Equally, SVQs exist at five levels, and are occupational in focus. They have been grouped into eleven occupational areas, as have NVQs (see Chapter 5).

General SVQs (GSVQs) are being developed in parallel, and are intended to relate closely to the development of GNVQs in the rest of the UK (see also Chapter 5). These GSVQs, which relate to broad occupational areas, focusing on the skills, knowledge and understanding which underpin them, are primarily designed to provide a broad and coherent vocational education for 16–18-year-olds (although not excluding adults) in a school or college setting. Beginning with levels 2 and 3 in four areas in 1992, GSVQs are planned to become progressively available for all occupational areas and at all levels. Progression is planned from a lower to a higher level of GSVQ, and from a GSVQ to an occupational SVQ of the same level. Level 3 GSVQs will be recognised for progression to higher education.

Upper secondary education in Scotland stands to be significantly changed if proposals from the 1992 Howie Committee Report (Scottish Office Education Department, 1992) are implemented. The proposals envisage a clear identification of upper secondary education as a distinctive stage in which a much closer relationship, though nevertheless a continuing formal distinction, between academic and vocational education would develop. Two new awards would replace existing ones: a two-year, mainly vocational, Scottish Certificate based on modules, and a three-year, more academic, Scottish Baccalaureate based on subjects. A common set of characteristics would underpin both these awards. Both would:

- embrace general and vocational education;
- employ the same framework of core skills (communication, numeracy, problem-solving, personal and interpersonal skills, information technology and modern languages) [the same as advocated for England and Wales, see Chapters 3 and 5];
- prepare for entry to both employment and higher education;
- use a core plus options course structure;
- be offered in FE colleges as well as schools;
- employ criterion-referenced assessment;
- use a mix of internal and external assessment;
- allow for differentiation in student performance;
- lead to group awards;
- be jointly administered by SCOTVEC and SEB.

In this new framework, the vocational track would have a general education element built in, and the academic track a built-in vocational element. Both qualifications would be accepted for entry to higher education, an important consideration in the inevitable question about parity of esteem.

Government response to the Howie Report remains to be decided, but professional response is divided. While some see these proposals as realistically building on existing traditions of good practice, offering scope for the academic and vocational traditions to grow progressively together, others regard it as a mistake to perpetuate the academic–vocational divide in this formal fashion. For the latter group, a more radical, fully modular school curriculum offering scope for shaping to individual needs is the direction to pursue (Tuck, 1992). Whatever the outcome, there is no doubt that the direction of change will be towards seeking equal esteem for vocational as for academic learning, and a greater engagement in both these modes by individuals within a school or college setting for 16–18-year-olds.

Youth Training operates in Scotland in a broadly similar fashion to the rest of the UK, but through Local Enterprise Companies (LECs), as the Scottish equivalents to the TECs (see Chapter 7). Training credits, to operate within the Youth Training framework, are being broadened from a pilot phase as a key move in the government's continuing commitment to increase the participation of students aged 16-plus in education and training, with an emphasis on gaining qualifications (Scottish Office, 1991). Scottish Enterprise and its network of LECs, equally, believe a successful Scottish economy requires the development of world standard skills by its people. 'This will require a continual upgrading of specific skills built on a strong foundation of general education' (Scottish Enterprise, 1992, p.8).

In addition to Youth Training, many of the specific programmes through which the new vocationalism has taken shape in England and Wales, such as TVEI, compacts, education–business partnerships (discussed in subsequent chapters), have operated in Scotland. The introduction in 1989 of technology academies in Scotland has echoed other developments, in this case the City Technology Colleges.

The long tradition of respect for education in Scotland, coupled with its democratic tradition of participation and a more unified structure than exists in England, Wales and Northern Ireland, provide certain advantages in the moves to reform education along more vocational lines. Routes and directions are clearer and simpler than in the rest of the United Kingdom. It remains to be seen, however, whether Scotland can attain the levels of participation and the quality standards which are envisaged in the series of reform measures. Furthermore, it is not clear whether that intangible relationship between education, training and economic performance will prove stronger and more durable than in other parts of the UK. Certainly, the structures and processes seem clearer and more coherent than has been the case in England and Wales.

Germany

The 'dual' system of the Federal Republic of Germany (essentially the former West German system), and to a lesser extent that of Switzerland, Denmark and Austria, is the most widely discussed form of vocational education when international comparisons are made. It is frequently held up as a model for emulation, notwithstanding its very distinctive place in German life and its dependence on assumptions, values and a range of deep structures that are not normally found outside the German-speaking countries. From the time of the medieval craft guilds the dual system has evolved and changed over the centuries and has in this century become formalised in national law with reference to training apprentices for some 380 recognised occupations. This is an important point – by contrast with, for example, the USA, the UK, Australia and New Zealand. Continuing, slowly evolving and long-standing agreements among the social partners are a feature, as is the leading role of industry, in the form of the Chambers of Commerce, in determining the direction and content of vocational studies.

The Vocational Training Act of 1969, followed by the Vocational Training Promotion Act of 1981, provide the legal basis for training and define a mix of on-the-job (in-firm) and off-the-job (in *Berufschule* – part-time vocational school) training over the period of the contracted apprenticeship. A crucial point in considering the dual system is the status the ancient system of apprenticeship has retained in these countries, and the manner in which successful graduates are able – in principle at least – to move on, as it were, through the academic system. Apprenticeship is neither held in low esteem, nor is it a by-way shut off from subsequent alignment with other parts of the overall education/training system (Achtenhagen, 1992).

In 1988, some 1,658,000 apprentices were participating in the dual system. Of these 50 per cent were in industry and commerce, and 35 per cent crafts, the balance including 4 per cent public sector, 2 per cent agriculture, 8 per cent solicitors' firms, surgeries, etc. This represents some 73 per cent of the 16–18 age group (Federal Ministry of Education and Science (Germany), 1989a, p.52). In 1991, 92 per cent of 17 year olds were in full-time secondary level education (including apprenticeships), with 20 per cent following general and 80 per cent following vocational courses (OECD, 1993a).

By law, all German youth must remain in full- or part-time education up to the age of 18, although students may leave full-time schooling from the age of 15. Most students enter two- to three-year apprenticeships at age 16 directly from either the *Hauptschule* or the *Realschule* – the more practically focused German secondary schools, where students are provided with a work orientation through learning about the world of work and having work experience with local employers. At age 18, some 16 per cent of students enter apprenticeships following completion of the *Abitur*, the university entrance, awarded from the *Gymnasium*, the academically focused system of German secondary schools.

A prospective apprentice applies directly to a firm and, when accepted, signs a training contract with that firm. The firm is then responsible for ensuring that legal requirements for both on- and off-the-job training for that trainee are met; it pays the costs of tuition, plus a training allowance to the apprentice. There is no requirement that the firm employ the apprentice on completion of the course and the majority of apprentices seek work elsewhere. Nor is there compulsion for firms to take apprentices. Indeed, to do so they must become registered with the local Chamber of Industry and Commerce as an accredited training firm and have the requisite number of staff with *Meister* qualifications, enabling them to train apprentices, as well as paying all the training costs. Why, one might ask, do firms volunteer to do this?

A number of advantages for companies, although not directly financial, can be seen. Legally, only accredited training firms can take on young people in any of the 380 or so recognised occupations. Many firms train more young people than they need, enabling them to select the most able as permanent employees – a screening function. As training progresses, apprentices become increasingly productive – an economic function. In their report on the dual system, Her Majesty's Inspectorate (HMI) noted, too, a significant cultural factor: it is good for a company's image to be an accredited training firm in a society where training is highly valued (HMI, 1991b) and, it might be added, where the teacher in whatever setting still commands prestige.

In German society, the *Meister* or master craftsman/woman is a highly regarded member of the workforce and community, and this is seen as one of the reasons that dual system training is held in high regard in Germany. (If it does not quite attain parity of esteem with academic training, it is at least held in higher regard than, for example, in the UK.) Nearly one-third of apprentices proceed to *Meister* training, a qualification which enables individuals to become self-employed craftsmen/women, to practice as *Meister* for a company or employers, and to train apprentices.

This voluntary and quite rational decision by firms to train apprentices is one of the distinguishing features of the dual system and, one might argue, both an essential basis of its success and a reason for caution in expecting an easy transfer of the model to other countries. A long-standing practice, it is deeply embedded in the cultural fabric. But, alongside voluntary participation is a well-structured system which specifies the respective roles of the main players: employers, Chambers of Commerce, unions, educators and government – and, of course, the students themselves. These principles, together with the society-wide acceptance that a solid foundation of education and training for all is essential, are of greater significance for other countries wishing to learn from the dual system than the specificities of the structure; many of them are intimately connected with legal and historical features that are not readily replicable. Structural details on a comparative basis are documented in European Community publications (EURYDICE and CEDEFOP, 1991).

Apprentices spend three to four days each week with the firm and, in practice, the amount of training provided by individual firms differs substantially. Instruction here is given by a *Meister* and qualified trainers within the requirements of the Federal Training Act. Firms release apprentices for the equivalent of one to two days per week (sometimes in block) for study in the *Berufschule* – part-time vocational schools which are usually highly specialised to the requirements of a particular group of occupations. These are financed and organised by the various *Länder* (states) and are their responsibility.

Some 40 per cent of the vocational course of the *Berufschule* consists of general education, the content of which is determined by the *Land*. Commonly, this is organised into subjects such as German, politics and law and, in some *Länder*, religion. As those teaching the general education components usually also teach specific vocational skills or subjects, it has been argued that they are seen as sharing the students' 'vocational culture' and the general component appears to be well accepted and regarded in the main, especially by those without the *Abitur*. In some *Berufchulen* the general education element is increasingly integrated into the vocational specialisms. In their report, HMI observed that 'Some teachers in the FRG see the general education subjects as a common core for vocational courses which will ensure breadth across off-the-job training' (HMI, 1991b, p.28).

Since 1972 students, generally from the *Hauptschulen*, have been able at age 15 (the end of compulsory schooling) to undertake a basic vocational training year (*Berufsgrundbildungsjahr*, BGJ) which can count as a year of the dual system. Students then seek a contract with a company for the remainder of the dual system. The BGJ, generally taught full-time at *Berufsfachschulen* (full-time vocational schools), is oriented towards a career area, which comprises several recognised occupations. Students must opt for one of the thirteen currently existing career areas (which group over half the recognised occupations) (EURYDICE and CEDEFOP, 1991). Thus, at this level of training, common skill elements are taught for groupings within the dual system, but not for the cohort as a whole. The BGJ, then, delays for a year the specialist apprenticeship, but begins the specialisation process for a first broad choice of career area. We are talking, however, only about a relatively small number of 15-year-olds who enrol in the BGJ before moving into a dual system place.

While the framework for the dual system is enacted in federal law and each *Land* is responsible for providing the vocational schooling, when we turn to the assessment of student's work, and its accreditation, we find this decentralised and at the local level. The local Chambers of Industry and Commerce, which are responsible for registering the training contracts between employers and young people, are themselves responsible for assessing the performance of trainees and awarding them their certificates. Generally this is through locally set final examinations. Because training is within a national system, however, there is some equivalence in these awards and they are nationally recognised. This decentralisation and local base of assessment is also a feature of schooling, with *Abitur* assessment being essentially school-based (Sutherland, 1992).

Each *Land* is responsible for its own curriculum and assessment, and there are notable differences in both the differentiated secondary education system and in types of vocational education between *Länder*, especially where *Länder* have long-established 'progressive' or 'conservative' governments (Sutherland, 1992, p.49). The functioning of the federal system in Germany is such, however, that major qualifications obtained in different *Länder* are accepted as equivalent throughout the country. There is no system of national standards as such, although agreements of the standing conference of Ministers of Education have in many cases been implemented by legislation in the individual *Länder*. For example, common conditions have been agreed on the structure, conduct and subject composition of the *Abitur*.

The dual system of the German-speaking countries, with its specialised tracking and provision, is itself part of a well-integrated overall educational provision to age 18 based on specialised provision from the end of primary schooling with choice, for students at that stage, between three separate high-school systems. This means that pupil selection is effectively made at age 10, and although ways do exist for students to change tracks at particular points after this, in practice this is neither easy nor common, particularly in those *Länder* where the different high schools are institutionally separate. There are some comprehensive schools of different types in the *Länder* of the former West Germany, but they cater for only a very small number of students. There are, then, rigidities in the structures of schooling that many other countries have overcome.

Sutherland notes that since the 1960s, parental attitudes have been changing, and many parents are now less agreeable to their children being routed to *Hauptschulen*, on completion of which options are seen to be more limited than for *Realschulen* or *Gymnasien* graduates. *Realschulen*, which provide a general education at a higher level than *Hauptschulen*, have become increasingly popular in recent years (Sutherland, 1992).

While a conscious attempt has been made to provide an 'educational ladder' between the elements of the provision to avoid students becoming too locked into particular streams at an early stage (when interests may change and aptitudes vary and develop) it is debatable whether such a ladder is either effective or attuned to contemporary public expectations. The working life basis is very well established, reflecting a strong commitment by employers to education and training. Yet such a commitment, although strong, is not universal, is structurally easier for large enterprises and is problematic in the case of small firms. Internal critics of the system are apt to question the ability of small firms to provide the breadth of experience or access to modern equipment that the system in general treats as desiderata. It is a model that in principle will work better in conditions of social stability and consensus and in a long-term, steady economic growth cycle than when there are frequent fluctuations or long-term downturns. It also rests upon the expectation by apprentices that jobs await them on completion of their courses. By the early 1990s, after a very long period of economic growth and social equilibrium, these conditions were appearing to be rather less firm.

There has been a tendency for foreign observers to present the German dual system as a paragon of its kind, to perceive it independently of its historical and cultural roots and to avoid critical appraisal, including the growing concerns within Germany itself about the inbuilt rigidities of the system. The enormous interest other systems take in the dual system is, however, understandable. It is to be explained in part by the success of the German economy and the organic links between the industrial forces underlying German economic growth and the training regime. Also, apprenticeship is part of the historical legacy of many countries and ways of making apprenticeships more effective and more attractive will continue to enlist the interest of vocationally minded educators.

With political unification, the dual system is being extended to the *Neue Länder* – a large and costly undertaking at a time when the German economy is showing signs of strain. Important for its future functioning in these *Länder* will be the resolution of the new structure of their high schools – whether the current comprehensive structure is to be maintained or, a more likely outcome, some form of differentiated structure is established paralleling that of the *Länder* of the former West Germany.

The lesson of the dual system is not 'trans-ship and emulate'. It is too deeply embedded in German culture and institutions for that. Indeed, the lesson goes much deeper than 'follow their model'. It is the same as that drawn by the German cultural attaché and architectural writer Muthesius, who, in his celebrated early twentieth-century work *The English House*, entered a cautionary note on the question of the transferability of one national experience to another:

> the greatest merit of the English house as it stands completed before us is that it is *English*, that is, it conforms totally to English conditions, embodies totally English ways of life, is totally suited to local climatic and geographical conditions and in its artistic design it must be considered totally a product of a native artistic development. Its exemplary qualities for us are therefore limited. And as we have also to develop the German house to conform to German conditions, the prime purpose of a study like the present one must be to show how closely all the external forms of the English house meet the natural conditions obtaining in England, rather than to pick out fine examples that would be worth copying in our situation. But the great instructive value of such an investigation must lie in the discovery of

the manner in which this adaptation has taken place. To face our own conditions squarely and as honestly as the English face theirs today, to adhere to our own artistic tradition as faithfully, to embody our customs and habits in the German house as lovingly – these are the lessons we can learn from the English house.

(Muthesius, 1987 [1904], p.11)

SUMMARY: THE SEARCH FOR NEW SOLUTIONS

In moving along the continuum of 'schooling' and 'working life' models, we have touched on a wide range of topics: objectives and priorities in reform measures; changing structures; partnerships and shared responsibility; relevance; cultural relativism; motivation in curriculum and learning, whether in school or in the workplace; and the importance of countries looking into their own traditions, practices, ideals and ideas in making comparisons about relative performance and success.

What kinds of curricula, therefore, what settings for their teaching and learning, what standards of assessment are to be used, and who should exercise control? Each country gives its own answers – of a sort – yet the questions inevitably recur as systems and arrangements come under review and innovations are pioneered. They cannot be adequately answered in abstract terms, outside a socio-cultural context and except in the light of economic pressures which, while they vary, are salient in every society. The answers given or attempted are, in practice, different in different societies. But they are not unproblematic nor can we take the easy way out by saying that whatever is, must be, since the fundamental conditions of education, training, and of social and working life generally are changing.

More questions have been raised here than answers given. This reflects the questioning of policies and structures that is occurring throughout the industrialised world and beyond. The quest for context-free models is naive and dangerous; what is needed are more penetrating studies of how and why the different structures work, the problems they produce and ways in which these problems are tackled. In some countries, most notably the United States, there has been an intensive debate throughout the 1980s on the core curriculum in the high school, with a strong move, in the decade-long series of national reports and reform proposals, towards a re-affirmation of general education for all and concentration on a limited, specified set of required subjects, with a distinctively academic character, for all students. These trends are challenged but mainly from an educational standpoint – the criticisms and reform measures are still largely in the context of a redefined schooling model. Indeed, it is not only in the United States that the schooling model is treated as the norm (OECD, 1985b). In some other countries, of which the United Kingdom and France are examples, the debate has been less focused and the practice is to provide a variety of routes, separate institutions, and differentiated curricula, a variety which at times discloses marked disparities, gaps and inequalities. For adolescent students in these countries there are many initiatives for change, mainly influenced, at source, by the factors of youth unemployment, changing workplace requirements, international economic competition and the possible applications of the new technologies.

There is general acceptance among educators, and not only the critics of schooling, that the content and the organisation of the traditional secondary school curriculum and ways of teaching and learning are in need of change – perhaps quite profound change. But there the agreement stops. If a revitalised common curriculum of general education is to be sustained, it is asked, what should be its principal content and structure, how is it best organised and how is it to be related to the diverse interests of students and requirements of specialised, vocational training? To those who argue for the alternative approach, affirming the value, not to say the necessity, of differentiation and specialisation from the ages of 14 or 15 onwards, the matter can be put differently. How do we avoid the dangers of overspecialisation, including obsolescence of knowledge, how can we educate for flexibility and transferability of skills, and how can we ensure that the democratic ideal of a common, shared culture is not lost to sight? Here the value of comparative analysis takes on a different hue: how well does each country formulate its aims and goals in its attempts to strengthen the links between education and working life, what are the benefits that can be identified and what losses must also be taken into account? Since 'no nation is an island' and links of all kinds are becoming closer, such questions lie at the heart of the growing internationalisation of education and training. This is a process whereby countries and systems – researchers, practical educators, policy-makers and the social partners – share information and ideas but map out solutions and future plans according to their specific needs and responsibilities, not some all-embracing, supra-national master plan.

Among these common issues in countries considered in this chapter are:

- the balance between general, foundation studies and specific forms of work preparation including increasing consolidation of the latter into broad bands or fields;
- the quest for well-defined, interrelated vocational pathways with linkages and crossovers among them and with the general education system;
- close attention to the nature, content and control of the processes of assessment and certification;
- the continuing problem of a social–educational 'underclass' of unqualified or underqualified school-leavers and drop-outs;
- the overall status of vocational education and training;

- the development of partnerships whereby the employment sector maintains or strengthens its role in guiding and providing vocational education and training.

In all systems, whatever their location on the schooling–working life spectrum, there is, at least at the policy level, an acceptance of the need for improved quality and relevance of programmes that aim to embrace all youth up to and beyond the age of 18.

5

NATIONAL MOVES TOWARDS A NEW VOCATIONALISM IN ENGLAND AND WALES

> The resilience in Britain of youth jobs, full time further education, non-employer based training, casual part-time jobs and unemployment, has proved remarkably strong.
>
> (Brynner, 1992)

INTRODUCTION

The strength and resilience alluded to in the above quotation are indeed part of the problem since they constitute barriers to needed change. Overcoming such barriers is an important part of the search for new directions and structures in education which has marked British policy since the mid-1970s. Internal review, critical appraisal, construction and reconstruction and, increasingly, assessment of the potential relevance for national policy of international experience have been particularly acute in the sphere of vocational education. Despite these endeavours and the enormous investment of resources, there is still a lack of clear and broadly agreed purpose in the new vocationalism, especially the unresolved policy issues of obligatory education and training post-16 and the relationship between the numerous strands and pathways in provision and their attendant qualifications (or absence thereof). Uncertainties remain about both the appropriate structures and the contents of and procedures for delivering vocationally oriented programmes, although much hope is held out for the emerging structure of National and General National Vocational Qualifications (NVQs and GNVQs).

In this chapter we move from the broad, international patterns of vocationalism and core curriculum thinking, to developments during two decades in the specific setting of England and Wales, the focus of some of the most far-reaching programmes and innovations over this period.

NEW INITIATIVES OF THE 1980s

As we saw in Chapter 1, a series of initiatives in the field of education, training and preparation for work, can for various purposes be lumped together under the heading the *new vocationalism*. Those words require clarification; the policy innovations amount to much more than can be summarised by a convenient term. There has been an ample supply of official documents and policy statements whose frequency of production and assorted collection of comments and proposals testify equally to unresolved issues in practice and a high degree of fluidity not to say ambivalence of thought.

Following the rapid growth of proposals and action programmes in the 1970s, designed to raise the profile of vocational education and training and overcome long-standing weaknesses, in the 1980s a new policy framework was erected. A series of government White Papers – *A New Training Initiative: A Programme for Action* (DoE/DES, 1981); *Training for Jobs* (DoE/DES, 1984); *Education and Training for Young People* (DES, 1985b); *Better Schools* (DES, 1985a); and *Working Together: Education and Training* (DoE/DES, 1986) – together have constituted major new policy directions. The 1988 White Papers, *Employment for the 1990s* (DoE, 1988a) and *Training for Employment* (DoE, 1988b), together with *Education and Training for the Twenty-first Century* (DES/DoE/Welsh Office, 1991) carried this process further while substantially modifying certain of the then recently established programmes and structures. Most striking has been the shifting balance of centralisation and decentralisation of control and operation of aspects of the new vocationalism as different policies and interests prevail.

Support for the new vocationalism has been strong among employer groups, the trade union movement and the Labour Party. The influential 1989 report *Towards a Skills Revolution*, of the Confederation of British Industry's Vocational Education and Training Task Force, as we have already noted, criticised the skills level of the British workforce and argued that 'individuals are now the only source of sustainable competitive advantage' which Britain has in seeking to improve its economic position. In a wide-ranging review of 'world class targets' for action, including a blunt call to all employers to become investors in training for these, a key recommendation was 'offering more relevant transferable skills and broad based qualifications to British youth' (Confederation of British Industry, 1989, p.9). Accordingly, the CBI called for greater emphasis on core skills in both the national curriculum and specific training programmes, including its own list of 'core elements'. These comprise a heterogeneous set characterised as 'measurable outcomes': values and integrity; effective communication; applications of numeracy; applications of technology; understanding of work and the world; personal and interpersonal skills; problem-solving; positive attitudes to change. In 1993, the CBI followed with its

Routes for Success. Careership: A strategy for all 16–19-year-old-learning (Confederation of British Industry, 1993). Here, the CBI laid strong emphasis on foundation, employment-related skills for *all* young people: core transferable skills within a single framework for all 16–19 qualifications; a 'careership' profile following on the 1991 National Record of Achievement; career education and guidance for all; and a financial incentive (cash credits) to increase participation in structured learning.

The Trades Union Congress too, responding to changes in work, the workforce and the global economy, affirmed the need to draw on the full potential of the workforce: 'By the year 2000, we will be either a superskills economy, or a low-skill, low-pay society' (Trades Union Congress, 1989, p.2). The TUC views on the matter were outlined in Chapter 3.

Among many other statements, mention may be made of the Royal Society of Arts report *Learning Pays* which, like the CBI reports, aims to set a clear standard for action and explains the implications of acceptance of 'a national expectation that everyone should continue learning (full-time or part-time) at least until the age of 18, and that all should aim to reach NVQ level 3 (the equivalent of BTEC National Diploma, or GCE 'A'-level) during the course of their lives' (Ball, 1991, p.29). The Labour Party, in its 1992 policy statement on the subject, drew attention not only to a low average standard of educational/training attainment but also to its policy objectives of a system which established a coherent set of pathways for all students, 16–19, through the proposal of a new Advanced Certificate of Education and Training (Straw, 1992).

New educational and training arrangements of great range and diversity and covering both secondary schooling and post-school training have been proposed and many of them introduced from the early 1980s. They include the Youth Training Scheme (YTS); the Certificate for Pre-vocational Education (CPVE), the Technical and Vocational Education Initiative (TVEI), the Review of Vocational Qualifications (RVQ) and the consequent National Council for Vocational Qualifications (NCVQ), the replacement of GCE Ordinary level by the General Certificate of Secondary Education (GCSE), City Technology Colleges (CTCs), the national curriculum enshrined in the 1988 Education Act, the emerging structure of National Vocational Qualifications (NVQs), the introduction of General NVQs (GNVQs) into schools and colleges, and the attempts to establish parity relationships between GCSE, A level and NVQ qualifications.

This kaleidoscope of schemes and proposals, sometimes only distantly related to one another, and the divided responsibility of different and frequently competing agencies, bear witness to an unparalleled scale and intensity of activity, amounting to a substantial if still confused overhaul of the framework for and much of the practice in national education and training. Why has there been this policy upheaval and what have its different schemes been designed to achieve? The first part of the question has already been addressed in a general way in the preceding chapters; to understand what the different schemes aim to and might achieve we need to consider them in turn.

The Youth Training Scheme (YTS), taking its first entrants in April 1983 and incorporating elements of previous programmes, was introduced as a one-year (extended to two in 1985) *work-based* scheme of broad vocational preparation for 16-year-olds. Open to all young people aged 16 and 17 who had left full-time education, and to 18-year-olds with special needs, it in practice attracted mainly those who, lacking nationally recognised qualifications or underachieving at school, saw it as a route to obtaining a job. Realisation of the job expectation was militated against from the start by changing labour market conditions together with the inherent weakness of what some of its critics have complained was an essentially remedial job-substituting school–work transition programme (Finn, 1987; Ainley, 1988; Lee *et al.*, 1990). In 1990 the YTS was succeeded by what was presented as the more flexible Youth Training (YT), a scheme whose fortunes, like that of its predecessor, have continued to fluctuate.

The Certificate for Pre-vocational Education (CPVE), introduced by means of pilot courses in 1984/85, aimed to provide a national, *school/college-based* pre-vocational qualification for an approved one-year full-time programme after compulsory schooling, consisting of core and vocational studies. It was targeted at those who needed a post-16 course which was neither GCE nor preparation for specific occupations. In practice the popularity of GCE courses and retakes, after 16 (and more recently the restructured GCSE), on the one hand, and the relative attraction of the YTS for those who wanted to secure a job as soon as possible on the other, threatened from the outset to leave the CPVE without a distinct catchment. In turn, the CPVE is now being replaced with a new Diploma of Vocational Education (see Chapter 8).

The Technical and Vocational Education Initiative (TVEI), announced in 1982, financed the introduction of technical and vocational education into *schools* with the objective of greater employment relevance in the curriculum of pupils of 14 years and upwards. The first pupils entered pilot courses in 100 schools in fourteen local education authorities (LEAs) in September 1983; starting in 1986 this was extended on a progressive basis to other LEAs, aiming at national coverage. Available to pupils of both sexes and all abilities and incorporating a number of innovatory practices such as profiles of pupil achievement, these courses were intended as a four-year programme, though in practice many pupils have tended to split off either into academic or YTS/YT courses at 16. The TVEI has proved popular; it offered many benefits, not least additional finance, to schools. But it, too, attracted critics, one of their arguments being that the broad aims of schooling were in danger of co-option by a narrow set of job-related, short-term ends (Holt, 1987).

The rapid introduction of these three vocational or pre-vocational programmes highlighted existing problems of articulation of separate structures and progression of students. In 1985, in recognition of this and of the importance of developing standards of competence, the government set up a Review of Vocational Qualifications (RVQ) under the chairmanship of the then Manpower Services Commission (MSC). Its major recommendations, published in May 1986, were accepted by the government who announced the establishment of a National Council for Vocational Qualifications (NCVQ), an independent body, charged with securing standards of occupational competence, and the design and implementation of a new national framework for vocational qualifications. In the name of coherence – ostensibly of levels and standards of attainment ('outcomes'), but also of the supply of programmes and qualifications – the NCVQ has moved beyond the task of rationalising the tangle of post-16 awards to that of drastically reforming those awards, requiring significant changes in courses and methods of assessment, essentially through the devices of NVQs for vocational qualifications and, more recently, GNVQs for school-level qualifications, as we see in more detail later (Jessup, 1991).

All these initiatives put emphasis on facilitating access to vocationally related programmes and the acquisition of competence and marketable qualifications by pupils of all levels. Another sought-for addition to the new vocationalist programme is at the level of wholly new institutions. This is the provision for the establishment, through what the government hoped would be private sponsors, of independent City Technology Colleges (CTCs). These are intended to provide, for 11–18-year-olds, a broad-based education with a strong technical and practical element, ostensibly for pupils over the full ability range. A stated objective is 'to secure the highest possible standards of achievement, both academically and in other ways' (DES, 1986b, p.4), and considerable attention has been given to the integration of CTCs into the existing education and qualification system. There is more than an echo in the idea of CTCs of the old technical education stream deriving from the 1944 Education Act, hence an indication of less than enthusiastic support by central government for a fully comprehensive system. Another illustration of this is government encouragement of secondary schools which specialise, for example, in science and technology and the arts. Such specialisation, not necessarily vocationalist, nevertheless has the potential to strengthen links between schools and particular occupational fields.

The innovatory programmes and policies are a mixture of direct inputs into the education and training system and models or proposals for its reform, the most radical in that respect being the NCVQ with its constant theme of 'outcomes' and a unitary national framework of domains (knowledge, skills, etc.) and levels (of student performance). In the same period there have been major curriculum development proposals for schools, in addition to the TVEI, which appear to be infused with similar values and objectives – for example, the emphasis on higher and measurable standards of achievement in schools; the call by the then Education Secretary Sir Keith Joseph at the North of England conference in 1984 for a broad, balanced, relevant and differentiated curriculum; the increased emphasis on problem-solving in the criterion-referenced new GCSE; the announcement of a national curriculum and procedures for its assessment comprising distinct subject areas (domains) according to a model of levels, at ages 7, 11, 14 and 16, in the 1988 Education Act.

Efforts have been made to overcome the difficulties arising from status differences and the weak national co-ordination of the numerous and varied elements of national education and training. The issue of 'parity of esteem' between vocational and academic qualifications among schoolleavers, is addressed if not resolved in the 1992 White Paper (DfE, 1992). Papers from both the National Curriculum Council (NCC) and the NCVQ, as we saw in Chapter 3, have addressed the issue of a common core of skills among all school-leavers, whether studying for A levels or BTEC or similar courses. While it is well beyond the limits of this book, or any other single volume, to analyse in any detail the vast array of qualifications and the myriad courses leading to them, in examining the new vocationalism, attention must be paid to signs of a similar philosophy at work in those parts of the system and those policies that are not directly vocational.

A style of thinking has permeated large parts of the education and training systems even though the new policies of the period under scrutiny have been assembled piecemeal by a variety of agencies through a number of often uncomfortably overlapping and competing initiatives. At the expense of close attention to the structured, balanced and sequenced content of teaching and effective ways of learning, innumerable schemes relating to structure, organisation and qualifications have flourished. At least until the late 1980s, the greatest single weakness has been the dearth of systematic curriculum-mapping exercises by contrast with the proliferation of policy proposals and organisational schemes and awards. Despite all the effort, by contrast with the A level route into higher education, taken by only a minority, for the majority there was no *mainstream* post-16 education; an 'absence of coordinated technical and vocational tracks from school into employment and higher education' (Smithers and Robinson, 1991, p.45).

The confusing nature of what emerges should not, however, be allowed to obscure either the extent and scale of the change or an evolving direction of policy. The full extent of these changes has still to be realised. While it is not yet possible to assess the innovations thoroughly, we can use statements of objectives on the one hand and early developments and tendencies, reports and reactions on the other, to analyse and appraise these innovations; and, where relevant, a historical slant or a comparison with European or other practice to elucidate the nature of the events.

FOUNDATIONS: THE NEW TRAINING INITIATIVE

The innovations and policy initiatives of the new vocationalism have emerged from many minds and several agencies, yet there is one seminal document, namely the *New Training Initiative* (*NTI*) generated by the MSC and published by the Departments of Employment and Education (DoE/DES, 1981). The *NTI* demanded a coherent approach to training for the 1980s. During the late 1970s it had become apparent that the existing courses for 16-plus students not taking A levels, then beginning to stay on at school in appreciable numbers, were either inappropriate (O levels) or presented in the form of a very confusing array for potential students to access. It was urgent to rethink provision (Dean and Steeds, 1981). One influential example of this rethinking was the Further Education Unit's (FEU) document *A Basis for Choice* (FEU, 1979, see Chapter 8). The authors of the *NTI*, while paying tribute to *A Basis for Choice*, sought, from the perspective of the employment sector, to offer their own 'new look' in education and training policy.

The contemporary debate on the purposes of schooling and its relationship with training and the world of work goes back even further, to at least the then Prime Minister James Callaghan's Ruskin College speech of October 1976. Callaghan, in this, voiced an already widely held view that the comprehensive schools were somehow reluctant to prepare children specifically for their place in an industrial society.

> The goals of our education, from nursery school through to adult education, are clear enough. They are to equip children to the best of their ability for a lively, constructive place in society and also to fit them to do a job of work. Not one or the other; but both. . . . There is no virtue in producing socially well-adjusted members of society who are unemployed because they do not have the skills. Nor at the other extreme must they be technically efficient robots.
>
> (Callaghan, 1976, p.333)

Indeed, earlier that year the government had published a statement, *Unified Vocational Preparation: A Pilot Approach*, committing it to expand learning opportunities for 16–18-year-olds through a number of experimental vocational preparation schemes (Wray *et al.*, 1980). Earlier still, in 1974 the Labour Government had established the MSC. The sentiment of Callaghan's remarks finds echoes, too, in a long historical line of government inquiries and reports, which we discuss in Chapter 6.

In openly restating utilitarian aspects of education, and declaring a causal link between skill level and unemployment, Callaghan's speech helped to prepare the ground for the *NTI*, although it and subsequent policy developments give the utilitarian orientation not equal validity so much as favoured treatment. The basis for this favoured treatment was then, and remains, problematic: 'to fit them to do a job of work' is a phrase that resonates practicality, usefulness and common sense yet it raises questions that, after nearly twenty years of sustained effort and massive expenditure, are still unanswered in youth and education policy.

The *New Training Initiative*, the 1981 consultative document of the MSC, addressed all those interested in training, with the familiar proposition that, historically and culturally, training for working life has not been given sufficient priority in the UK. It sought to obtain agreement from those interested, in particular, government, employers, trade unions and the education service, about priorities and objectives for the future, and to launch major new initiatives to transform the situation. The problem was stated primarily in terms of competitive economic performance:

> For prosperity and growth we need to invent, to innovate, to invest in and to exploit new technologies. We must have products and services people want at prices they will pay. We must exploit new and growing markets to replace those that are declining. All that we do must be at least as well done as it is by our competitors and there are more and stronger competitors now than there used to be. There are and will be great opportunities in the 1980s for both industry and commerce. To take advantage of them we need to adopt the new technologies. . . . Our standards of production and services must be every bit as competent, efficient and reliable as those of our competitors.
>
> (MSC, 1981a, p.2)

It is interesting to observe the similarity in sentiment and style to the American report of the same period *A Nation At Risk* (National Commission on Excellence in Education (USA), 1983) which, as we have seen, stands for its country as a seminal document in the realignment of much national educational debate during the 1980s. The touchstone in both documents was economic efficiency to meet the new requirements of international competition. Jobs requiring employees with very limited skills were disappearing rapidly in the late 1970s and early 1980s. New markets and technologies would require a more highly skilled, better educated and more mobile workforce in which professional and technical staff would have to be supported by workers trained to perform a range of tasks which involved processes rather than repetitive assembly. Even at a time of high unemployment, skill shortages existed and firms wishing to exploit new economic opportunities had (or preferred) to change or upgrade the skills of their existing workforce. As we have seen, this was precisely the kind of analysis being made in a number of the OECD countries as well.

The difficulty in Britain has been one of encouraging long-term perspectives among both employers and employees, a planning and co-ordinating mentality, a readiness to forgo the satisfaction of some present wants in the interests of investing in the future and an awareness of a common national interest. Employers, whether in good times or in difficult economic circumstances, have usually chosen a short-term solution and saved on training costs, hoping to buy in skills when needed. Unions have, until recently, seldom taken industry-wide training seriously. Young people, not always adequately prepared for working life by their schools, had in the past found that their training opportunities, where any were sought at all, mainly consisted of apprenticeships. These had become outdated and time-serving, limited to a few occupations, and had not been developed in the newer, rapidly growing sectors of the economy. Often even good apprenticeships were not popular.

In the analysis made in the *NTI*, it was pointed out that while further education (FE) colleges offered a range of post-school education and courses of training leading to national examining or validating body qualifications (see Locke and Bloomfield, 1982), the overall provision of this non-advanced vocational education was limited to about 30 per cent of the workforce. Courses were generally associated with craft/technician levels of training (usually via apprenticeship) for young people, mainly male, of average or above average academic ability. The curricula were generally determined by the major examining boards and syllabuses largely concerned with technical knowledge and skills. Learning might be classroom-based, laboratory-based and/or workshop-based. Not all the content was necessarily immediately relevant to the trainee's job, but it reflected the job culture and certification was a significant factor in career progression. The *NTI* inferred that new policies and programmes were needed for the large unskilled sector of the traditional workforce; and that improved economic performance demanded a workforce with identifiable, measurable, transferable skills. The problem was both quantitative and qualitative.

The *NTI* constituted a challenge whose profundity was at times masked by glib phraseology and its detachment from the underlying realities, dynamic and static, of British society. But there were and are few who would disagree wholly with the *NTI* analysis; it hit upon many of the underlying weaknesses of the British approach to training. Like *A Nation At Risk*, it offered a serious challenge that could not be ignored. Nonetheless, it was after the publication of the *NTI* and in the drafting of the objectives and contents of the national YTS which came out of it, that the beginnings can be observed of a process of oversimplification and reductionism which characterises a number of the new vocationalism initiatives.

The first confusion arises in failure to reconcile economic, industrial/commercial, social and educational policy objectives. Too little time and effort then went into and since has gone towards this very demanding analytical activity. A heavy price has been paid for the often superficial and always over-hasty decisions that were substituted for the hard, time-consuming analysis that was needed at the beginning of the 1980s. Hence policy has too often seemed to be partial, shallow and poorly integrated.

There has been a marked tendency to latch on to factors which, while they are closely associated, may not be causally related and in any case have only very limited explanatory value. Inadequate training and motivation of the unskilled young people themselves is regarded by some policy-makers as the cause of the problem, and economic recovery seen to depend on improved motivation at that level and the skills necessary for working life. Education and training must make young people respond to this and enable them to be drawn into the enterprise culture. Education from 14 to 18 must be active, practical, relevant and vocational. The key to better economic performance is the better preparation of a large slice of human capital. In this sense the new vocationalism is a highly focused aspect of economic policy, which, while highly relevant, distracts attention away from factors such as the more selective and prestigious parts of the education system, social structure, industrial investment, job restructuring, and other dimensions of structural adjustment, world trade patterns, cultural mores and other interpretations of Britain's economic ills. The focus of the new vocationalism has too often been the unskilled worker; as Smith (1984) and others pointed out, the economic problems facing Britain require strategies which pervade the whole society and require a new quality of management, administration and leadership.

The focusing of attention on one, but by no means the only, cause of youth unemployment and poor economic performance has critical implications for the education system, notably for central government strategies for reform. Again these are highly controversial bases for policy making – the schools, it is alleged, have failed, are not providing value for money, are offering irrelevant curricula. The *NTI*, very much a creature of its time, was part of a process of transformation whereby, in education generally and in vocational education and training, national ministries and agencies have taken the initiative throughout the 1980s, combining an adherence to the theories of neo-liberalism, the market and individual choice with highly centralised, government-led, system-wide change strategies.

The training initiatives need to be set against this wider background, since, taken by themselves, they are too limited and sectional to achieve the wider economic and social ends to which they are ostensibly addressed. It is hardly controversial to claim that adequate education and training of the workforce is a precondition of improved economic performance, and that one of the major objectives of education policy, the preparation of pupils for the world of work and adult life, is important for the individual. However, it *is* highly controversial to expect substantially improved economic performance to result from better training of the less educated part of the workforce. Notwithstanding some two decades of policy planning, innovation and targeted programme funding, insufficient evidence exists to conclude that increased vocational education in either quantity or quality, or any particular form of vocational education, will guarantee improved economic performance. It is, however, reasonable to suggest that attention to overall policies for and provision of education and training, combined with comparable efforts in all other dimensions and with a concerted attack on such other factors as overall economic management, improved conditions for investment especially in research and development and infrastructure generally, would produce results.

The *NTI* consultative document rightly drew attention to comparative figures of activities of young people after compulsory schooling in Britain, France and West Germany which showed Britain's relative numerical weakness at the beginning of the 1980s in all forms of training. While numbers in full-time general education were not markedly different for the years 1977–80 (27 per cent France, 25 per cent West Germany, 32 per cent Great Britain), the picture was remarkably different for full-time vocational education (40 per cent France, 18 per cent West Germany, 10 per cent Great Britain), apprenticeship (14 per cent France, 50 per cent West Germany, 14 per cent Great Britain) and young people in work or unemployment (19 per cent France, 7 per cent West Germany, 44 per cent Great Britain). A decade later, Britain still suffered from such comparisons (Smithers and Robinson, 1991).

Evidence of possible links between satisfactory economic performance and high levels of higher education has been largely ignored by exponents of the new vocationalism. Judged by the first major innovation of the new vocationalism, the YTS, proponents placed disproportionate faith and resources in practical, skill-based vocational preparation for the less academic. In this as in other respects, a broader policy framework and wider perspectives will ultimately be required if the basic objectives – economic, social and cultural – are to be achieved.

CONSOLIDATION AND CONCENTRATION OF POWER: THE MANPOWER SERVICES COMMISSION AND ITS SUCCESSORS

The new emphasis on vocational education and training, although evident in most developed countries, has in its UK form been associated with the ability and willingness of central government to devise, and pay considerable sums for, large-scale initiatives such as the introduction of the YTS. The directive role of central government has proved characteristic and its full dimensions have only slowly emerged. This has been demonstrated particularly in the pioneering activities of the (now defunct) MSC, which set up and was responsible for the financing and management of the YTS, took over the financing of much non-advanced further education in the process, introduced itself into schools by direct financing and the laying down of criteria and arrangements for the TVEI and its extended programmes, undertook a major review of vocational qualifications – and

116

absorbed large tranches of public funds during years when the education system generally suffered progressive budget cuts.

Even supposing the MSC's activities in the training field and their replacement of certain areas of local authority provision by direct financing were to be regarded as in principle catalytic rather than permanent, the intervention itself was revolutionary. Through the distribution of relatively large sums of money in an era of government financial stringency, the MSC influenced not just the organisation of education and training but what pupils learned. The purchase by cash of areas of the curriculum has been, so far, a feature of the new vocationalism.

The MSC, established in January 1974 under the Employment and Training Act 1973 to run public employment and training services, was funded by, and accountable to, the Secretary of State for Employment, after what one commentator at the time characterised as a struggle for control within the government in which Margaret Thatcher, then Secretary of State for Education and Science, was the loser (Low, 1988). It was created to address Britain's lack of skilled workers, poor economic performance and anticipated rising unemployment levels. Its chief executive functions were defined then: 'to help people train for jobs and to obtain jobs which satisfy their aspirations and abilities; and to help employers find suitable workers' (MSC, 1977, inside cover). The main aims for its first five-year plan (that is, until 1982–83) were:

a. to contribute to efforts to raise employment and reduce unemployment;
b. to assist manpower resources to be developed and contribute fully to economic well-being;
c. to help to secure for each worker the opportunities and services he or she needs in order to lead a satisfying, working life;
d. to improve the quality of decisions affecting manpower; and
e. to improve the effectiveness and efficiency of the commission.

(MSC, 1977, p.23)

Since none of these objectives, as stated, meet the criterion of well-specified performance outcomes, debate about whether or not they have been 'reached', or 'adequately reached' will be inconclusive. They do, at any rate, point in directions which were followed in many different ways throughout the 1980s. Although only obliquely touched upon in the initial aims statement, youth training became a very large and significant part of the MSC endeavours, an indication of the growing recognition that the education factor is crucial in human resource and economic development.

The MSC initially appeared to interpret its role as tinkering with the system, making small adjustments and financial contributions, as, for example, in its programmes of training in special skills (Unified Vocational Programme, UVP) and of increasing school-leavers' chances of getting jobs

(Youth Opportunities Programme, YOP). At this stage there was nothing to suggest that the MSC would come to play such a substantial role in the nation's education and training system as it was to assume during the 1980s. In its early years it was at pains not to stress its financial involvement. Its role in public training was 'to intervene in, or to provide, training only where that is necessary to support or supplement employers' efforts' (ibid., p.25). Employers should not 'come to rely on training at public expense instead of doing their own proper share' (ibid., p.25) – a piece of unintended irony in view of the widespread failure of employers throughout the 1980s to contribute their full share to training. The MSC would complement the efforts of the Industrial Training Boards in sectors not covered by them (MSC, 1977). In practice, the 'partners' did not accept the depth of the challenge; there was a widespread assumption that training is a public responsibility, and the MSC's role expanded from gap filling to much more positive intervention (and funding).

In its rapid rise to power in the early 1980s and its impact upon national education policy and practice the MSC, naturally, attracted a great deal of criticism (Low, 1988), perhaps too much for the comfort of government. The MSC was always in a state of flux. The speed of its initial growth was matched by its rate of decline in the late 1980s. In 1987 the MSC lost responsibility for employment services, becoming purely a national training agency. At this time its name changed to the Training Commission. The Training Commission in turn was abolished, its functions (including YTS responsibility) absorbed in 1988 into the Training Agency within the Department of Employment. By 1990, even the smile of the Cheshire Cat could scarcely be discerned, as the Training Agency, succumbing to yet another reorganisation, became translated into the Training, Enterprise and Education Directorate (TEED) of the Department of Employment. Administration of most of the former Agency's programmes was taken over by the locally based Training and Enterprise Councils (TECs) and quality and control of vocational education and training transferred to the NCVQ. This final dissolution was but the last of a bewildering succession of structural changes which marked the MSC from the beginning to the end of its meteoric career.

Reverting to the programmatic developments as distinct from the structural metamorphoses of the MSC, we notice that in the post-*NTI* era the first set of MSC objectives was refined and developed, and the restrictions abandoned in a veritable cornucopia of government funding. Again the *NTI* marks this change. After identifying and analysing Britain's economic problems, the MSC set out a series of most ambitious targets which it would take the responsibility for achieving:

1. we must develop skill training including apprenticeship in such a way as to enable young people entering at different ages and with different educational attainments to acquire agreed standards of

skill appropriate to the jobs available and to provide them with a basis for progression through further learning;

2. we must move towards a position where all young people under the age of 18 have the opportunity either of continuing in full-time education or of entering training or a period of planned work experience combining work-related training and education;

3. we must open up widespread opportunities for adults, whether employed, unemployed or returning to work, to acquire, increase or update their skills and knowledge during the course of their working lives.

(MSC, 1981a, p.4)

Of these three it is the second that provides a platform from which, with sufficient willpower and application, it would be possible to achieve the much needed integration of education–training–work. Throughout the 1980s efforts were made to achieve this but there were powerful barriers to contend with. Some, like traditional A levels, were fought for with the zeal of revolutionaries at the barricades even though their retention as the so-called 'gold standard' signified a fundamental conservatism and resistance to reform when the need for reform was so evident and, in broad terms, widely agreed.

The *NTI* analysis had implied that the schools had somehow failed their pupils, and a clear element of punishing the schools, and the LEAs responsible for managing them, can be detected in the activities of the MSC. In subsequent years financial provision was diverted from local authorities, or bargained for in return for MSC intervention in the school curriculum, as in the TVEI. The MSC took responsibility for a large slice of non-advanced further education in 1985; the new City Technology Colleges, however, were intended to be financed and managed by local industrial sponsors.

EDUCATIONAL IMPLICATIONS OF THE NEW VOCATIONALISM

No explanation of the actions of the MSC and the general character of the new vocationalism can overlook their origins, which were not the fruits of a carefully thought out and judiciously developed collaborative educational policy, but strands in a partial economic and political strategy – with constant undertones of ministerial and bureaucratic rivalries. This is the strategy which approaches the curriculum and organisation of education with the objective of improving British economic performance through improvement of skill levels in certain parts of the (prospective) workforce. The strategy considers the overall needs of the pupils only as hastily contrived afterthoughts responding to or anticipating criticism, or assumptions that pupils' requirements are limited to their immediate need for jobs, rather than the development of their long-term potential, even though in policy documents acknowledgement was made of the need for continued learning into adulthood. Educators, including those of only a generation before, have generally taken a much broader view. One of them, Ben Morris, opens his 1955 essay on 'The Personal Foundations of Education' with these words:

> Let us start from the perspective that education is an enterprise concerned with the development of persons – with persons growing up. This implies that it is concerned with the care and nourishment in young persons of their distinctively human powers. Inevitably then, considerations of personal maturity, of well-being, of mental health, must enter into discussions of both ends and means in education.
>
> (Morris, 1972, p.103)

Right as he was in sentiment, however, Morris was wrong in his sense of the inevitable. Young people were not seen as persons so much as figures in a grand if fragmentary design for national recovery. Insofar as the strategy has been centralist, directive, cash driven and one-sided in its instrumentalism, it has shown a dangerous – and ultimately self-destructive – tendency to bypass the very structures, processes and personnel that, properly enlisted, might have ensured the long-term gains so badly needed. Progressively, however, perspectives have broadened; it is acknowledged, for example, that education is not reducible to pre-specified learning outcomes (Jessup, 1991, pp.128–131) and broader strategies involving wider partnerships have more recently emerged. But the process has not as yet led to conviction that policies and programmes are adequately comprehensive and coherent either in structural or in content terms (Raffe, 1992).

While many parents and pupils would doubtless support the assumptions of the new vocationalism in preference to traditional objectives, it is again necessary to be aware of the implications. Contained within it are the seeds of that nineteenth-century principle (as we see in Chapter 6) that the acquisition of a job, and the skills necessary to perform it well, judged by standards of competence laid down by the employer, is an appropriate and sufficient objective for certain sectors of the population. A democratic philosophy which incorporates the personal goals and aspirations of pupils, a vision of the good life and society is by no means inconsistent with the goals of economic revival and redirection. However, lacking in the new vocationalism is any serious attempt to interpret these values and approaches. Consequently, the seeds of social and economic segregation have been sown in the new vocationalism philosophy, compounding the structural problems.

DIVISIVE TENDENCIES?

The new vocationalism has been accused on several counts of being divisive. The very number of major initiatives in recent years, conveniently grouped under that heading, suggest that something is being provided for every level of pupils – perhaps YT for the least academic, A level for the most academic, and other courses for those in between or who have not quite decided what they want. The possibility that linkages might be developed between programmes, courses and the students and young workers involved, to produce an educational/training ladder has not been ruled out, but nor has it been, until very recently, brought into the centre of policy-making. The NCVQ saw this, quite rightly, as a highly significant priority for a national education and training system and, from its inception, has worked to develop means to achieve it. This task must continue to be addressed and barriers removed through collaboration between the numerous parties and interests involved.

Close analysis of the objectives of the early vocational initiatives (see Chapters 7 and 8) suggests that the potential was there from the beginning for a comprehensive and unified system of education and training for all. For example, while the TVEI has been deliberately tightly controlled financially, schemes are potentially flexible in form and content. That flexibility has already promoted creativity in the curriculum and access to all abilities in the TVEI in some schools. The clarification and simplification of vocational qualifications achieved by the RVQ and subsequently NCVQ may be viewed as stratifying, but in theory it equally encourages progression and the changing of career tracks and therefore implicitly the level of target qualification. The appraisal in the following chapters attempts to judge whether the process of acquiring skills, competences and vocational qualifications given prominence in the courses tends to free or rather to restrict and divide/segregate.

NEW VOCATIONALISM CONTENT

In examining the focus of the new vocationalism of Britain in the 1980s, it is worth recalling how widely the traditional definition of vocational education can be drawn if the will is there. Any learning can and perhaps should be vocational in part, emphasising, as would be the case for example in Italy, learning at home and in the family and not only that in the school or workplace (Barnabo, 1985). A definition tied to immediate job preparation is quite inadequate, for reasons we discussed in Chapter 3. Depending on how it is treated and related to the wider environment, any content has vocational potential; the wider the definition of competences required for workers who are to be 'flexible', 'enterprising', 'self-reliant', 'adaptive', 'co-operative', 'responsible', 'task-oriented' and so on, the broader is the range of curricula and learning experiences that can be shown to be relevant. The new vocationalism in its general policy statements and goals follows this path; but in its treatment of educational content, it frequently goes in the opposite direction, adopting on the whole rather narrow objectives, and confidently basing some directive and specific policies on tenuous assumptions. The national YTS, rapidly introduced in response to the *NTI*, marked also the beginning of an emphasis on certain aspects of course content, for example: specific attitudes and motivation; work-based learning; the acquisition of measurable skills and standards; increasing opportunities to obtain nationally recognised qualifications. Successive initiatives have also contained some or all of these items. There are many unexamined assumptions about the relevance and applicability of learning in such initiatives. The problem of content cannot be resolved while effort is devoted to specifying for measurement purposes a separate, job-specific domain of vocational knowledge. The resolution will lie in systematic work to map the vocational dimensions and potential of a wider strategy of education and training and their complex relationships – as learning/ teaching tasks – to a small number of principal domains or fields of working life. These are strategic tasks which should be undertaken by national and regional research and development agencies working closely together and not by examining and accrediting bodies alone. In practice, course content and methods are too often a function of the highly specific requirements of these bodies. Large numbers of modularised, examinable courses provide a stock for various groupings and combinations, at the institutional level. In the process, as an HMI report observed,

> Too often the broad aims of a course are lost, teachers abandon lesson plans and schemes of work and teach only to specified objectives. The result is that a teaching style predominates which has as its main objective the transmission of information.
>
> (HMI, 1984, p.33)

By contrast, a later HMI review of *work*-based learning as distinct from *classroom*-based learning within the college itself conveyed a highly favourable impression:

> The students derive considerable satisfaction and motivation from their work-based learning in colleges and it provides them with a valuable foundation for their subsequent careers.
>
> (HMI, 1990b, p.3)

As far as it goes, this latter point is satisfactory but it still does not meet the need for a coherent, vocationally relevant curriculum for all youth.

WORK-BASED LEARNING

Advocates of the new vocationalism argue that the needs of the employers and the economy have never been given sufficient priority in the UK. The stated objectives of the YTS, CPVE, TVEI and particularly of the CTCs (see Chapters 7 and 8) all emphasise familiarity with the world of work and positive attitudes to it. Motivation, according to some forms of the new vocationalism philosophy, will be improved by learning through work, in the workplace, with trainers and workers in industry rather than with teachers of what are sometimes viewed as irrelevant subjects in a school setting. The work-related (as distinct from work-based) curriculum for schools made considerable progress during the 1980s to the point where its value was affirmed in the preamble of the 1988 Education Act and in the guidance given for the cross-curriculum theme of economic and industrial understanding. Many local authority Curriculum Statements acknowledge the value of linking the school curriculum with working life. If tokenism or the downgrading of the work dimension in mainstream secondary education are to be avoided, however, a detailed curriculum design grounded in the principles of 'entitlement' and 'universalisation' is needed (Saunders, 1992). The national curriculum for schools does not succeed in this respect, due to its traditionalist approach to subject disciplines and the weakness in practice of the curriculum themes.

The new vocationalism is firmly associated with a new emphasis on work-based learning conceived as structuring learning in the workplace and providing appropriate on-the-job training/learning opportunities. To these, Levy in her seminal work for MSC on core skills added 'identifying and providing relevant off-job learning opportunities' (Levy, 1986, p.1).

The case for work-based learning rests on the expectation of increased motivation of pupils, who, it is claimed, are more inspired by concrete than theoretical activity; and on the likely benefits of association with people doing a job. These are not new arguments but have been advanced and demonstrated in practice by such notable pedagogical pioneers as Victor Della Vos, director of the Moscow Imperial Technical School in the 1860s and 1870s, who influenced President John Runkle of the Massachusetts Institute of Technology in the 1870s and Calvin Woodward, who in the 1870s became a leading critic of the genteel culture of the American public schools and founder of a university-based manual training school (Cremin, 1961, Chapter 2). Later, in Germany, Georg Kerschensteiner used the Munich continuation schools for which he was responsible as a vehicle for a new kind of civic education based on trade training (Connell, 1980, pp.139–143). It is ironic that at the beginning of the present century, British official reports were extolling the high degree of organisation of the Munich system (Simons, 1966, Chapter 9).

Work-based learning has long been known to have intrinsic advantages which can confer a sense of partnership. Trainees are motivated by the real nature of the activity and learn from its direct consequences. Performance in the workplace is felt to have relevance. Trainees can learn to act systematically and efficiently, to fit naturally into the team in which they find themselves; and it may be better for them to train for working life by means of work-based learning because they believe in it. On the other hand there can be and often are disadvantages. The work can be repetitive and limit the learning process; the supervisor can exercise a negative function. In Germany, where work-based learning is most developed, considerable weight is also given to the complementarity of off-the-job vocational education. In the UK, the YTS, in associating itself clearly with work-based learning, has demonstrated more about its possible uses in creating job chances than its wider educational value. Certainly the spotlight put on work-based learning in individual schemes will increase understanding of its potential and practice. What is sorely missing, however, in the programmes that followed the *NTI*, is that wider sense of social, civic and educational purpose, that understanding of the relationships that must be developed between knowledge, values and practical accomplishment, so evident in the thought and practice of the early advocates of work-based learning.

COMPETENCY-BASED NATIONAL QUALIFICATIONS: THE NATIONAL COUNCIL FOR VOCATIONAL QUALIFICATIONS

'One thing is certain, labelling by qualifications is becoming more common and more necessary.' Thus did George Tolley, one of the architects of the NVQ system, state his thesis, adding that qualifications were too often in practice a barrier rather than a help to learning (Tolley, 1986, p.709). The new vocationalism gives priority, not to a broad-based development process for either individuals or society, but to the acquisition of measurable skills and levels of competence and the construction of frameworks for their validation. It is a major aspect of the policy that more young people should be qualified, in their own interests, it is said, but particularly for the sake of the economy. In its initial statement of purposes and aims, the NCVQ drew attention to the fact that only 40 per cent of the UK workforce held relevant qualifications, a considerably lower proportion than in other major industrial countries with which the UK was competing (NCVQ, 1987). From these concerns have followed two major developments: emphasis on accessibility of appropriate nationally recognised vocational qualifications; and a partial link-up with the school system.

It is not of course necessary to defend prior and existing arrangements for the education and training of the 16–19 age group in assessing the contributions of the MSC and its successors. There is much evidence to support the MSC belief that the pattern of vocational qualifications needed reform and rationalisation, for example *Mapping and Reviewing the Pattern of 16–19 Education* (Locke and Bloomfield, 1982), which recommended clarification and review of the courses and provision for the age group. In describing the existing set-up as a jungle, the authors commented:

> The number of qualifications offered is huge. They can be pursued through differently conceived courses in differently organised institutions. They serve overlapping purposes and often reflect different schools of educational thinking. The different systems of qualifications offered by the dozens of certificating bodies do not readily reveal compatibility in sequence, standards or structure. There is no unifying principle, no underlying structure to be uncovered by the inquirer. The provision looks complex at first encounter, and remains complex on close investigation.
>
> (Locke and Bloomfield, 1982, p.9)

This confusion produced obstacles for students in making well-informed choices, in progressing from one course to a more advanced one, and in transferring from one 'track' of qualifications to another when deciding to change career. It denoted a fundamental confusion or, rather, lack of national policy and a failure to come to grips with the necessity for large-scale reconstruction – not destroying but producing clear patterns of relationship, articulation and an overall intellectual coherence in provision for and requirements of students.

In the interests of a better qualified and more mobile workforce, it was natural that the new vocationalism should set about tackling these obstacles. The introduction of a YTS, which stressed the acquisition of vocational qualifications, gave added momentum. The RVQ, which took less than a year to complete, was instructed:

> To recommend a structure of vocational qualifications in England and Wales which:
> - is relevant to the needs of people with a wide range of abilities
> - is comprehensible to users
> - is easy of access
> - recognises competence and capability in the application of knowledge and skill
> - provides opportunities for progression, including progression to higher education and professional qualifications
> - allows for the certification of education, training and work experience within an integrated programme.
>
> (MSC/DES, 1986, p.i)

This highly influential review group proposed a unified national framework for vocational qualifications classified according to levels of student attainment or competence, and the accreditation of existing awards by a new National Council for Vocational Qualifications.

The simplification and articulation of vocational qualifications and the facilitation of progression from one course to another were long overdue. The centralistic and energetic, not to say directive and one-sided, way in which the problem of formal qualifications has been tackled has nevertheless provoked antagonism. Whether this could have been avoided, given the deeply entrenched interests at stake, is a moot point. Power-coercive strategies have become widespread in British education at the national level. Governments no longer believe in the necessity of carrying the research, scholarly and teaching communities with them in large-scale change programmes for which, they rather tenuously argue, they have the mandate and the at least tacit support of the wider community. The risks of failure in such an approach are high and, the need for reforms notwithstanding, their design and implementation require a more consensual approach if they are to take root.

Characteristically, the NCVQ, established in October 1986 following the RVQ's report, acted swiftly in staking out territory and establishing a strategic role for itself – partly, one suspects, as a means of survival. It lacked legal powers and, at this stage, was dependent on support and co-operation from the award agencies, industry, the professions and the educational and training establishments. That dependence necessitated an emphasis on developing a framework (competence types and levels) to which other bodies, retaining a high degree of independence, could nevertheless relate.

By the early 1990s, the NCVQ had established a comprehensive framework for validating – or giving its imprimatur to – those vocational qualifications offered by other agencies which met its criteria for National Vocational Qualification (NVQ) status. The NVQs are related to both a *level* and an *area of competence.* Five levels of NVQ have been defined within an overall framework and their parity of learning, from GCSE to higher degree level, also established. Areas of competence have been defined in broad terms across a wide spectrum of fields of employment.

An NVQ is defined as:

a statement of competence clearly relevant to work and intended to facilitate entry into, or progression in, employment and further learning, issued to an individual by a recognised awarding body.

The statement of competence should incorporate specified standards in:
- the ability to perform in a range of work related activities and
- the underpinning skills, knowledge and understanding required for performance in employment.

(From *NVQ Criteria and Procedures*, quoted in Jessup, 1991, p.15)

An NVQ statement of competence is thus a kind of performance profile which specifies *units* of competence and, within each unit, usually between two and four *elements* of competence. Performance criteria have been established as the standard for each element of competence, and each is individually assessed. Units of competence are independently recognised and certificated, and unit credits are accumulated towards achieving a statement of competence, or NVQ, at a particular level. During the late 1980s students could purchase from the NCVQ a National Record of Vocational Achievement (NRoVA) which included details of their existing qualifications, unit credits and current programmes of study. In 1991, this was replaced by a National Record of Achievement (NRA) issued by NCVQ, which is a summary record in common format for both school- and non-school-based education and training achievement (NCVQ, 1992b). The NRA, now widely issued to Year 11 school students as well as trainees, builds on the experience of both the NRoVA and of the education-based movement of the 1980s which saw Records of Achievement issued locally by many schools.

In common with Scottish Vocational Qualifications (SVQs), NVQs have been grouped into eleven occupational areas: tending animals, plants and land; extracting and providing natural resources; constructing; engineering; manufacturing; transporting; providing goods and services; providing health, social care and protective services; providing business services; communicating and entertaining; developing knowledge and skill.

The competence standards for different NVQs – as for SVQs – have been derived from analysis of employment functions, by the NCVQ – and SCOTVEC – working with the some 130 national industry led bodies established by the then Training Agency; that is, they rest on the intersubjective judgements of the principal 'consumers'. According to Jessup (the figure behind many of the moves during the 1980s to create a performance/outputs template for use across the wide range of programmes and agencies) there have been some difficulties in achieving what the NCVQ, many educators, the CBI and various other groups regard as sufficient breadth in some of the standards. For some industries, statements of competence have been criticised for reflecting 'the current, often narrow jobs which people perform', and 'considerable effort' is now being exerted to broaden this concept of competence (Jessup, 1991, p.25). However, such effort will need to be Herculean since 'the underpinning skills, knowledge and understanding' defined as a necessary component of NVQs are not at all obvious, nor do they exist in some ready-made form. They should be defined through the kind of curriculum-mapping we discussed in Chapter 3, which, while it would include, would certainly go beyond, the interests of institutionalised bodies of 'consumers'.

The competency-based NVQ framework shows a much greater concern for outputs and outcomes than, to use its own system assumptions, inputs and processes. While it is largely unconcerned with how students reach certain specified levels of competence, the nature of competences specified is biased towards those which are achieved in work-based rather than school-based situations. This tendency is probably encouraged by the fact that industry rather than education representatives have the main role in drawing up competences.

Some years of development, implementation, systematic research and evaluation will be required before firm judgements can be made about the overall value and impact of the NVQ framework in establishing nationally recognised standards for existing vocational qualifications, providing clearer pathways for individual progression between qualifications and meeting good standards of curriculum development and assessment. In their 1988–1990 report on national vocational qualifications in further education, HMI were suitably cautious, preferring description to appraisal in dealing with the NCVQ (HMI, 1991d). The NCVQ, at least, is determined that the framework will indeed become well established in British vocational education.

In this effort it is well supported by the national education and training targets of 1992. This presents yet another formulation of goals, such as higher basic attainment, more high-level skills (for example, 'by 2000 51 per cent of young people to reach NVQ3 (or equivalent)') and lifetime learning (for example, 'by 2000, 50 per cent of the work-force to be qualified to at least NVQ3 (or equivalent)'). The targets give considerable prominence to NVQs (National Training Task Force, 1992). They have been adopted by central government, major education and training interests and widely endorsed by business interests. According to Sir Brian Wolfson, Chair of the National Training Task Force, the targets are intended to

> focus our full attention on the need to raise standards of achievement in education and training in Britain so that we can secure the competitiveness of the British economy and a higher standard of living for Britain's people. The Targets are necessary, urgent and ambitious. If they are to be achieved, everyone in business, education and training must be involved.
>
> (ibid., introductory letter)

Thus would the NVQ framework come to play a major role in defining the nature of new vocational awards and revisions to existing vocational awards. Such a prospect calls into question some of the basic presuppositions of the framework. Can or should curriculum planning, teaching and learning be determined by 'outcomes' which of necessity are abstractions from their social contexts of use and application? Is it sufficient to define as an 'outcome' a skill or capability free of its human, mental context of will, disposition, preference, choice, value? Are there robust and widely agreed routes or sequences whereby outcomes can be linked or related into learning and teaching pathways? Is 'level' an artifact of the norm established by performance tests on large groups, a pragmatic device agreed by committees or a derivative of some cognitive theory? What is the nature of the process whereby courses are 'mapped' on to or through 'levels' and is 'course' equated with syllabus or the experience of learning? Should educational designs be the result of the 'pull' of assessment and certification, or should not assessment follow from comprehensive designs for and development work on goals and purposes, curriculum and teaching-learning processes? The greater the visibility and impact of the NCVQ framework, the more urgent will it become to address these and similar questions in the public marketplace of well-informed educational discussion and debate, even at the risk of denting somewhat the image of collective enthusiasm and the rather excitable promotional apparatus that have been built up in the effort to gain 'endorsement' for the outcomes approach.

The NCVQ has been active in developing a programme of General NVQs (GNVQs) aimed at the 16–19 age group in schools and colleges. These have been piloted during the 1992/3 school year, initially in five broad occupational areas with others to follow later. Their aim is, by combining three core skills (communication, application of number and information) and a particular vocational area, to provide a broad-based vocational education as a foundation from which students can progress either to further and higher education or into employment and further training. With the level 3 GNVQ designed to be of comparable standard to A levels, GNVQs are intended to provide 'a genuine alternative to A level qualifications' for the increasing number of 16-year-olds remaining in full-time education (NCVQ, 1992a, p.1). Indeed in 1993, Education Secretary John Patten set as an objective 'having a full half [sic] of our 16- and 17-year-olds studying for General National Vocational Qualifications . . .' with one in four 16-year-olds taking GNVQs by 1996 (DfE, 1993, p.1).

Like NVQs, the GNVQs are related to levels and areas of competence, specified in the form of outcomes to be achieved, and modular in nature, with credits accumulating individually towards the final award. The GNVQs are set out in a 'statement of achievement', rather than a 'statement of competence' such as provided by the NVQs. The new avenues opened up by GNVQs were soon seized upon by the course-providing and examining bodies. Thus, in a full-page advertisement in national newspapers, BTEC urged readers to take up the opportunity presented by 'the first vocational qualifications recognised throughout the country that carry the same respect as GCSEs and A levels' (*The Times*, 7 December 1992, p.8). Many questions remain not only about the comparability of level 3 GNVQs to A levels but also about the linkages with NVQs and other parts of the youth and adult training world and their acceptability in practice in schools (Walker, 1993).

It is instructive to compare the emerging structure of vocational assessment and accreditation with the moves during the same period to establish the national curriculum in the state schools of England and Wales following the 1988 Education Act. The outcomes-based structure of the national curriculum has ten foundation subjects, of which three are 'core'. English, mathematics and science are core subjects, and the other foundation subjects are technology (including design), history, geography, music, art, physical education, and for pupils in key stages 3 and 4 (that is, 11–16 years old) a modern foreign language. The much disputed assessment design for the national curriculum envisages that each subject area is broken up into a number of attainment targets, for each of which up to ten levels of attainment may be specified, in the form of statements of attainment (remniscent of the elements of competence of the NVQ framework). National curriculum assessment, as intended in the initial design, occurs in relation to each statement of attainment, paralleling the NVQ assessment of each element of competence. Four national curriculum key stages are defined between ages 5 and 16 (5–7; 7–11; 11–14; 14–16), and students are assessed at the end of each stage on a criterion-referenced basis (DES, 1989). In face of strenuous criticism, the government in 1993 established a committee chaired by Sir Ron Dearing which has recommended considerable simplification, but not an abandonment, of the basic framework for school curriculum and assessment (Dearing, 1993). Both in terms of the fundamental assumptions and the procedures adopted to outline national frameworks for local action (whether in school or enterprise) there is, at least in principle, a growing convergence between the school and training institution, between models of general education and models of specific vocational preparation.

This convergence was taken further by the 1991 proposal by the Secretaries of State for Education and Science, for Employment and for Wales, to integrate academic and vocational qualifications into a new system of Ordinary and Advanced Diplomas. An Ordinary Diploma might represent an achievement of four to five GCSEs at national curriculum levels 7–10, or equivalent vocational qualifications, or a mixture. An Advanced Diploma might represent two A levels at grade C or above, an equivalent combination of A or AS levels, or equivalent vocational qualifications, or a mixture of all three (DES/DoE/Welsh Office, 1991, para 4.4). The Secretaries of State indicated they would consult widely on the proposal, and at the time of writing, the Diplomas remain under consideration.

The growing convergence of general and vocational education as such is to be welcomed, but it does bring into question the nature of the common ground thereby created. Does it constitute an educationally sound and defensible response, or is it a retreat into an ultimately self-defeating redoubt where critical thinking, creativity, knowledge and understanding are constantly cramped by hypothesised job needs? There is, moreover, a depressing familiarity in the introduction of yet another battery of qualifications. What needs are served? Will the public, the students, the employers, further and higher education institutions understand and take to the new layer and how will the new credentials relate in practice to what already exists? Such questions will resurface many times as we examine one of the principal emblems of the new order, namely 'core skills'.

CORE SKILLS

The character and objectives of the YTS, the first major initiative in the new vocationalism, deserve detailed study because its development most clearly reveals the single-mindedness of interpretation and the now familiar philosophical oversimplification which tends to follow. Later developments fit increasingly easily into it. The multiplicity of objectives and, most clearly, the switches of emphasis of the YTS reveal the evolution of what can now be quite distinctly seen as a major platform in the new vocationalism; and nowhere more clearly than in one of its four objectives – the acquisition of competence in a range of transferable core skills.

As we saw in Chapter 3, 'core skills' is a term that was widely used by the MSC in the YTS. The notion of a definable set of core skills to underpin all learning also attracted the attention of the DES, but it has in practice played a larger role in the training debates initiated by the MSC than in the national curriculum work of the DES. Interest in core skills emerged from earlier studies of the idea of skill acquisition, but the idea of a determinate, clearly definable set of core skills that could provide a common base for and thread in the structuring of separate vocational courses had not reached the stage of development necessary to satisfy the functions attributed to it by the MSC in the YTS, let alone to make progress towards an interpretation of core learnings which is relevant to both education and training.

The long-established training term *basic skills* had by the time the YTS was launched broadened into *generic skills*, mainly under the influence of work abroad, particularly in North America. The MSC drew on this and experience from their special programmes, for example Unified Vocational Preparation (UVP), which appeared to demonstrate that individuals performed better and were more able to adapt to change if they had developed competence and practical experience in a range of related jobs and skills rather than in one context only. Studies on grouping work skills, intended to develop checklists to make the most of training opportunities for preparing young people for working life, were being undertaken in a variety of contexts, some financed by the MSC. A number of different ideas were being investigated and functions for core skills identified, for example:

- as a frame of reference for supervisors/teachers;
- as an instrument confirming acquisition of a range of skills;
- to identify ways of extending learning opportunities of trainees;

- to supplement induction and guidance;
- to produce a matrix of skills applying to different training activities;
- through this to highlight commonality of basic skills between jobs and hence transfer;
- to help in monitoring and recording individual progress;
- by providing information on accomplishment, to be useful as a trainee credential;
- as a tool for self-assessment.

This array of functions was appearing in pilot work contracted by the MSC. The *Basic Skills Analysis* of Freshwater (1982, p.3) was intended as a 'simple and quick analytical tool with which to examine any job or training activity'. However, it seems unlikely that this objective could be achieved considering the number and variety of situations in which such activities occur. Too many variables were being concurrently addressed and the framework for analysis was at one and the same time too complex and lacking in rigour.

Thus the word 'skills' came, in an abstracted way, to incorporate areas of social and life skills, process skills and even learning skills. There were skills as descriptors (checklist of core skills); there was the idea of generic skills or skills to take into working life, and there were process and learning skills (learning how to learn – and personal effectiveness); there were 'transferable' skills and 'transferring' or meta-cognitive skills. The term was broadened to an alarming extent, and in danger of losing any clear reference. It was as if a whole educational/training philosophy and set of programmes was to be encompassed by the single term 'skill'. What is important to hold on to in the terminological – and often conceptual – confusion is the idea that knowledge can and should be applied, that there are practical tasks to perform and that knowledge, education and training can be so managed as to facilitate application and use.

In supporting or undertaking analytical and development work relating to skills, the MSC was not alone. Similar developments were evident in various sectors of the education and training world. An example is the City and Guilds of London Institute (CGLI) Vocational Preparation General 365 examination introduced in 1981/82, which contained a basic core of skill clusters including: communication skills and numeracy; economic, social and environmental studies; vocationally oriented studies; extension studies (individual interests); guidance; process skills and non-compulsory work experience. Assessment of this course was partly by tests, partly by ratings recorded on a profile. The concern of the Institute with industry-based definitions of competence, which attempt to identify the transferable aspects, was reflected in this course. Such definitions identified occupations in industry and duties in occupations which need competences. Each required a combination of skills, knowledge, attitudes and experience. 'Skill' has been used here, as elsewhere, in a wide and often confusing sense.

Concern with 'core skills' was emerging simultaneously in the education world. In the design of the CPVE the single most important ingredient is the core of ten 'competences' designed to yield essential capabilities for successful adult life including employment and further vocational or academic study. These 'competences' are: personal and career development; industrial, social and environmental studies; communication; social skills; numeracy; science and technology; information technology; creative development; practical skills; and problem-solving. They were to function as a checklist for achievement, a stock of course objectives and to integrate with vocational studies. Yet again, 'skills' were loosely defined and used ambiguously. Considerable work had also been done by Her Majesty's Inspectorate in their studies of 'core entitlement'. In this, work skills are treated as elements within – and given meaning and value by – areas of experience, for example, scientific, technological, spiritual (DES, 1979).

The idea of 'core skills' or 'generic competences' has also been drawn into the NVQ framework – if still in a somewhat awkward fashion. Seen as a way of helping establish and maintain breadth in the statements of competence of different areas of learning, core skills are incorporated into the NVQ system in the same format as modularised units of competence, thus attracting unit credits within the national system of credit accumulation and transfer. The core skills of problem-solving, communication and personal skills, would be, as a matter of course, developed as an integral part of occupational competence leading to an NVQ (Jessup, 1991).

Core skill units in communication, application of number and information technology are incorporated into all GNVQs and are separately assessed from the vocational units at both levels currently offered (GNVQ 2 and 3).

As already noted in Chapter 3, the then National Curriculum Council in March 1990, following a ministerial request, identified six core skills (problem-solving, communication, personal skills, numeracy, information technology, modern language competence) which it argued should be promoted in post-16 curricula. It could not, however, at the time see how they could become an integral part of all A/AS levels. Once more, the term 'skill' is used extremely loosely and in a manner that fails to distinguish either non-skill elements in 'competences' or the different nuances of 'skill' in different contexts (interpersonal relations as against numerical analyses or written communication).

TRANSFERABILITY

The *NTI* interpretation of the requirements of economic recovery always recognised the need for a trained workforce able to move from one job to another, and perhaps from one sector of industry to another as technological change and other factors kept the labour market in a state of constant change. Having identified a need, it is characteristic of the new vocationalism to come forward rapidly with a solution – of sorts. The opportunity to obtain measurable skills built into the YTS would in itself facilitate worker mobility, it was believed, because they would have general currency, but in order to make an exact fit of the objectives of the YTS and perceived economic need, the core skills had to be defined as 'transferable core skills'. Stating the objective of the YTS in these terms passed the problem – possibly the key training problem – on to those responsible for defining transferable core skills in individual training schemes, and the trainers who provided the opportunity for learning them. This was to locate a quite fundamental intellectual and developmental problem in a part of the training system which was not equipped to handle it. Thus the idea of *transferable* core skills implied an almost magical ingredient in what otherwise might be routine measurable competences. Not surprisingly, in practice, the YTS had difficulty achieving this, as we see later.

The suggested way forward was to identify the skills regarded as *common* to a number of jobs, and place significance on their acquisition in a strategic way – that is, as meta-cognitive instruments or tools of learning and not only as specific accomplishments for given situations (and this is what the YTS originally intended in core skills). This is consistent with the body of research on transferability that we referred to in Chapter 3, but is still at a level of generality that trainers in particular occupational settings found difficulty in interpreting. Consciousness of the trainee's mastery of the skills, both by trainee and trainer, so the argument ran, should lead to recognition by each that the trainee *can* (but not necessarily *will*) do other things than those he has performed. The relationship between situations of application and use, consciousness, the reflective use of skills and the specific mental or mechanical accomplishments denoted by individual skills is, however, far from clear. Research on how skills are *understood* as well as *used* in the workplace and of the meta-cognitive structures and processes involved is essential to the success of teaching transferability. Attention would need to be directed at the conditions for learning and application in the new environment and this raises the question of a continuing training function related to job mobility.

True transferability is based on functions and processes that operate at a deeper level than observed performance in test conditions. As we saw in Chapter 3, transfer is possible, at the surface level of performance, because cognitive and other mental structures are developed to the point where larger amounts of quite varied information can be processed, or experience reflected upon and analysed. Many factors affect the operations of these structures, both personal to the individuals pursuing them, and environmental or interpersonal. Awareness of the possession of a skill and the possibilities for its transferred use must also be present. Research on meta-cognition suggests that 'people can become self-aware if they are placed in a situation where they have the opportunity to be, are motivated to be, and are suitably trained' (Biggs, 1985, p.321). It follows from this argument that transfer of skills can be taught as a tactic or as a strategy, not independently of subject content and practical application but in such a way as to render such content meaningful and useful for the learner (Bridges, 1993).

> What is common to all situations is the individual who enters them. In order to maximise transfer, then, it would follow that one should maximise the strategic capability of the individual doing the transferring, that is that individual's ability to metacognize.
>
> (Biggs, 1985, p.322)

That ability to metacognize may be developed more easily through concrete examples, and so training has to be conducted 'in a manner such that the individual trainee is encouraged to be self-aware, to plan, to monitor, to match strategy with task demands' (ibid., p.323). What we might emphasise in this approach is the use of core skills as themselves a meta-cognitive strategy. Transfer, then, is sought through the development of the individual's cognitive awareness of tasks and their interrelationships. The YTS, as originally defined, might have facilitated transferability, but in its later form, as described in Chapter 6, seems to offer less potential. Greater attention to the forms and processes of meta-cognition, to the complex tasks that students must undertake and research on the structuring, processing and application of work-related knowledge are needed if more powerful frameworks for mapping and assessing competences are to be erected. Such research and analytical work should be at least as high a priority for the national agencies, especially the NCVQ, as the development efforts going into schemes for classifying competences and tying assessment procedures and qualifications to them.

Jessup discusses the issue of how to assess students' ability to transfer learnings from one context to another within the range required by elements of competence within the NVQ framework. He notes that:

> Coping with variation, as opposed to performing routine and proceduralized functions, provides a primary distinction between low level and high level occupations in the NVQ framework. In particular, coping with variation which cannot be anticipated is a characteristic of the most demanding jobs, at the forefront of development and innovation in a profession.
>
> (Jessup, 1991, pp.122–3)

He argues that in practical terms:

> for most assessment decisions, particularly those at higher and professional levels, the sum of the performance evidence is unlikely to be sufficient to ensure that the candidate could cope with future varia-

tions which might occur. This is where demonstrations of performance need to be supplemented by assessments of knowledge.

(ibid., p.123)

Such knowledge should concentrate on:

(a) the knowledge of the variation in circumstances that might be expected and how practices and procedures should be modified to meet different circumstances, over the range which is expected;
(b) an understanding of the principles or theory which explain the nature of the function or activity to be assessed.

(ibid., p.123)

Reference to knowledge and theory, although not entirely absent, were sparse in the early days of the YTS; the acknowledgement of the part they play in skill formation thus represents an important step beyond the dominant elements in the skills debate of the 1980s. Links are being adumbrated, if yet to be fully worked out, between: the research on transfer; theories of meta-cognition; competence in the NVQ sense; and knowledge frameworks. This is a potentially fruitful line of inquiry, analysis and development work. Still to be developed are powerful curriculum frameworks that, for the major occupational fields, bring together knowledge content, student competence and student–teacher learning strategies, all in a well-marked landscape of the changing world of work.

SUMMARY

Trials and experiments have been taking place to determine appropriate forms and content of education and training at the centre of a rapidly evolving government policy for youth. Scarcely have needs been defined and agreed upon, and experimental projects launched, than structures for managing and organising new strategies and programmes have been erected and others dismantled. The introduction of the TVEI, YTS, CPVE, GCSE and curriculum reforms in schools hasten the collapse or contraction of one kind of education and training and access to working life, and foreshadow a new pattern likely to take effect nationally in the years ahead. Such far-reaching and rapid changes on the scale envisaged are unusual in any national system and always difficult to accomplish. Some changes are taking place in other countries too, but the rate and extent of developments in the UK throughout the 1980s is very largely explained, if not necessarily justified, by the crisis in youth unemployment of the early 1980s and, at a deeper level, long-term structural weaknesses in the economy and dissatisfaction with the education and training systems.

The new vocationalism is, not least, a political phenomenon. Britain has been bracing itself and changing direction. Thatcherite Conservatism was a

136

driving force in the 1980s, but it was not the whole story. There has been for some time a sizeable body of public opinion in the UK, not only on the political right, which supports the charges that schools have been failing to prepare pupils for economic reality; that standards of achievement, discipline and motivation have been allowed to fall; that, judging by results, public expenditure on education is not efficient. The case for reform of training and the structure of vocational qualifications was strong; existing apprenticeships were increasingly out of date, too few young people had formal training, a sense of lack of purpose was common among the non-academic. What were introduced for the 1980s and beyond were centrally devised schemes for training young people – pre-work, in the workplace and throughout the years at work. What must be evaluated is what they are intended to do (their hidden as well as their published objectives), and the nature of the relationship between these vocational initiatives and 'education', and, to use the favoured term, the outcomes of the reforms as distinct from their stated objectives.

The various initiatives undertaken mainly at the behest of central government and its agencies in Britain have been considered. Together, they constitute what has become familiarly known as the new vocationalism. Appraisal of these initiatives must acknowledge the inadequacies of many traditional practices and the incoherence of the structures that had been added to, piecemeal, over the decades prior to the establishment of the MSC. These inadequacies have not been fully addressed, however, and the rapid succession of half-formed programmes and incomplete changes has created many difficulties for students, employers and employees. At the same time, the intensive drive towards vocational relevance has resulted in a decontextualising of skills and an undue narrowing of goals and values. The issues arising can be more fully analysed if we see them against the historical background: the contemporary problematique of the education–training nexus has roots deep in the national culture. Its resolution will not be independent of the continuing impact of that culture.

6

HISTORICAL ROOTS
Origins of vocationalism in England and Wales

In 1570 Sir Humphrey Gilbert, Sir Walter Raleigh's step-brother proposed to the queen a curriculum for the education of Statesmen which included mathematics, geography, physics, surgery, moral philosophy, Greek, Latin, Hebrew, logic and rhetoric, as well as Spanish, Italian, French and High Dutch. 'By erecting this Achadamie' (he argued) 'there shal be hereafter, in effecte, no gentleman within this Realme but good for some what, Whereas now the most parte of them are good for nothing'.
(Early English Text Society, Extra Series VIII (1869), 1–17, quoted in Armytage, 1955, p.78)

INTRODUCTION

The difficulties England has encountered in recent decades in finding new directions for education and in establishing a system in which preparation for working life has a full and honourable part in the scheme of things cannot be understood if attention is confined to the present. The educational tradition has been inhospitable to a broad and comprehensive vocational philosophy just as it has resisted the educational implications of liberal democratic theory. The paradox, yet to be explained, is that Britain has been home to practical and liberal values and to parliamentary democracy.

The English, as we saw in previous chapters, have never before established a national system of vocational education, the mosaic of provision and practice notwithstanding, but are now doing so. While schools have had overt and hidden purposes and objectives beyond the general liberal one of developing the mind and potential of the child (maintaining the status quo, social engineering, etc.), not until the 1980s has the preparation of children for the world of work in order to improve British economic performance been a major declared objective upon which government has vigorously acted. Among the industrialised nations, England was also late in establishing a fully-fledged national, publicly maintained school system, relying for most of the nineteenth century on voluntary effort chiefly by religious bodies and for a good part of the twentieth century on a system which produced elites but left the masses under-educated and inadequately, if at all, trained. Only gradually was the move made from gap filling and subsidy to the establishment of full public education and the beginnings of a well-articulated national system of training.

Regarded by many as evidence of a deplorable myopia or failure by the state to make the necessary connections between economic well-being, the conditions required for personal fulfilment and the erection of a national education and training system, others relate the British attitude to education and training to enduring and more positive cultural values. Longden, for example, argues that 'the political philosophy of *laissez-faire* inherent in British life since the Reformation . . . dictated that education was essentially voluntary and the responsibility of the individual' (Longden, 1987, p.42).

A random look at examples of vocational schools or training programmes for children of school and immediate post-school age in the past indicates that they were intended for highly specific purposes and flourished for limited periods of time. What is clear is that they grew up outside the emerging 'normal' system, such as it was, even as responses to omissions in it. They had much to contend with, including a firmly entrenched belief behind the provision of education in England that an academic – until recently classical – education made the pupils who managed to complete a secondary education, whether to age 14, 16 or 17/18, good for everything they might do. The discipline and learning of an academic education produced, or so it was supposed, 'transferability'. In that academic education, Latin traditionally performed the function of a general training or furnishing of the mind.

At the other extreme, and as a separate, parallel system until well into the twentieth century, elementary education in the rudiments of knowledge was believed to suffice for the masses. This bifurcation of the 'genteel' and the 'popular', like the *laissez-faire* mentality, was deeply rooted. It is reflected, for example in pedagogical writings in the eighteenth and nineteenth centuries, in views about the 'mentalities' of the higher orders and lower ranks. Shapin and Barnes draw out this distinction with reference to three sets of dichotomies which have long persisted in educational assumptions: 'the *sensual* and *concrete* character of the thought of the lower orders against the *intellectual, verbal* and *abstract* qualities of the thinking of those above them'; 'the *simplicity* of the thought of the lower orders and the *complexity* of that of their betters'; 'the *active use* of knowledge and experience by the higher orders, contrasted with the *passive* and *automatic* way in which the lower ranks were assumed to react to experience' (Shapin and Barnes, 1976). A Victorian proverb which G.M. Young used as the text for his *Victorian England: Portrait of an Age*, puts the matter in a nutshell: 'Servants talk about People: Gentlefolk discuss Things' (Young, 1953).

Despite the most devastating criticisms of the consequences of these assumptions about the natural order and of the cramping mean-spiritedness that coloured the elementary school system, including those of a notable Chief Inspector, Edmond Holmes (Holmes, 1911), remnants of the elementary tradition persisted up to and indeed beyond the 1944 Education Act. This Act, for all its value in laying foundations of a post-war system of secondary education, maintained, under a quasi-psychological guise, traditional distinctions between mental, manual and technical work, enshrining these in what proved to be an unstable and cramping tripartite system of secondary schools. The legacy of a stratified and status-ridden national system of education has remained and is still a serious impediment to achieving a unified approach in which there will be a place for work-related education and other common learning experiences for all students regardless of ultimate destination.

As we have seen, the range of recent changes in education, particularly in the vocational field, together amount to a sweeping reform of national education in Britain. During the last 150 years there have been several periods of major discussion and reform – but, significantly, none has previously confronted the issue of national education in its role of preparing pupils for the world of work. Even when, between 1860 and 1900, major commissions were alerted to the requirement, the practical results were usually insignificant and a short-sighted conservatism prevailed. Vocational preparation did exist, beyond the school years, in technical colleges and institutions of continuing and higher education. Important as this provision has been and is, however, it has never been articulated and integrated with the mainstream. Provision at this level is not the main concern of this chapter or book, where the focus is on the middle and later years of secondary education and on the transition years of 15–18. It is precisely this period of adolescent development which has been inadequately provided for and which is the focus of the major national and international initiatives outlined in the previous chapters.

LACK OF A SUCCESSFUL VOCATIONAL EDUCATIONAL TRADITION

Historians have painted a picture of generally modest efforts and lack of attention to education as a significant national force or asset. Nevertheless, from its medieval and Renaissance origins, education did perform a variety of broadly defined vocational functions which must be borne in mind in considering the historical background of the new vocationalism. The European universities were, from their inception, centres for screening and preparing for the liberal professions; their teaching was based on systematic knowledge, and grounded in the classical tradition. They prepared for the vocations of law, theology, medicine, administration and higher education. England, however, had only two universities, Oxford and Cambridge, until the early nineteenth-century establishment of University and Kings Colleges in London, and the University of Durham, and for long periods the ancient establishments were far from dynamic centres of learning. While charity schools at the elementary level and grammar schools prepared students for vocations ranging from domestic service to clerical duties, the provision was patchy and access to them limited.

Education and teaching overall in Britain, the evidence suggests, changed slowly from the sixteenth to the eighteenth century. There were, however, some significant developments. They included university endowments for the teaching of mathematics and the activities of notable schoolmasters, such as Richard Mulcaster at Merchant Taylors' and St Paul's, to establish this subject; the Elizabethan Statute of Artificers (1563) which imposed a seven-year apprenticeship on some thirty crafts; and the Elizabethan Poor Law (1601) which empowered churchwardens and overseers of the Act to apprentice pauper children (Armytage, 1970). Educational reformers were not lacking and there is a rich thread of analytical and hortatory literature running from such notable Renaissance and post-Renaissance figures as Thomas Elyot, Roger Ascham, Richard Mulcaster, William Petty and John Milton to John Locke, precursor of the American and French revolutions and founder of British empiricism (Quick, 1895). Their impact on educational practice, insofar as it can be ascertained, was uneven, falling well short of the reformist ideals they espoused.

Notable innovations in curriculum and pedagogy occurred through the establishment of the dissenting academies, themselves the outcome of powerful intellectual, social and religious movements. The academies, established in the second half of the seventeenth century to train dissenting clergy, were soon broadening their curricula to include science and the vernacular language. It was one of the leaders of the movement, the notable chemist Joseph Priestley, who stressed the need for an education which is a preparation for 'the business of manhood', for 'active life' (Simon, 1960, p.38). They were, naturally, opposed by the established church and the historian W.H.G. Armytage has characterised the period of their hey-day (1660–1732) as 'the national religion versus national needs' (Armytage, 1970, p.27). Notwithstanding the development of different kinds of schools to meet the need for more practical subjects (such as surveying, navigation, chemistry and physics, and schools of industry – joinery, knitting, spinning, shoemaking, etc.), and the freely voiced criticisms of the predominance of the liberal arts, the classical grammar schools dominated.

The entry requirements laid down by the ancient universities of Oxford and Cambridge set targets for the grammar schools. The preparation for the professions happened to coincide with the view that a general classical education was a proper training for the ablest minds and for the young men of upper-class background (women were excluded), because that was what the universities required and because the grammar schools, being endowed, were relatively free from public pressure.

In seventeenth-century continental Europe the demand for a vocational education for the needs of a governing class who wanted training for posts at court, in diplomacy and higher appointments in the army did not result simply in more classical education, as in England, but in the establishment of courtly academies where horsemanship, the use of arms, modern languages, geography and the application of mathematics to civil and military engineering were studied. Nothing of this kind developed in England in spite of evidence of a demand for it, although, given the penchant of the English for exploration, colonisation and warfare, there was clearly a large element of on-the-job training and, of course, the English played a major role in the scientific revolution of the seventeenth century, notwithstanding the generally poor provision for science education.

Towards the end of the eighteenth century, however, to meet the needs of manufacturers and merchants, Non-conformists established a large number of new private schools, including the dissenting academies, especially in London and industrial towns. They represented a renewal of interest in applied, practical knowledge – what Brian Simon terms 'the revival of an educational outlook which had been obscured for over a century; one originally associated with the name of Francis Bacon and widely propagated during the revolutionary era 1640–1660' (Simon, 1960, p.26). It was another revolutionary era, that of the late eighteenth century in America and France, which provided the stimulus on both sides of the Atlantic for a more secular, practical and socially oriented approach to education. Despite frequent setbacks, science and other modern studies, such as history, geography and economics, as a result began to gain a foothold. Of more fundamental importance, the Enlightenment confidence in the capacity of any form of social action, a national system of education included, to effect improvement of the human lot depended upon the repudiation of deeply rooted Christian doctrine concerning God's grace and the individual free will (Passmore, 1970, Chapter 8). This was not so much abandoned by the populace but only very gradually vitiated, before the onslaught in the late nineteenth century of post-Darwinian scepticism.

The radical strands of Non-conformist religion in eighteenth-century England fed the demand for self-education, especially literacy skills, and contributed to the popularisation of science and other forms of useful knowledge. The identification of Non-conformity with natural science and political radicalism, however, proved disastrous and the onset of the French revolution provided an opportunity for a conservative resurgence, including attacks on and closures of some of the most notable of the dissenting academies (Armytage, 1970). The attack on dissent continued well into the nineteenth century. In a letter in 1833, the Duke of Wellington, with characteristic forthrightness, put the matter starkly in terms of class war:

The revolution is made, that is to say, that power is transferred from one class of society, the gentlemen of England, professing the faith of the Church of England, to another class of society, the shopkeepers, being dissenters from the Church, many of them Socinians, others atheists.

(Aitken, 1946, p.144)

With the rise of the full-blown industrial society from the late eighteenth century onwards, new challenges arose: work requirements were changing as were the social system and its demands for new kinds of citizen roles. The challenges were responded to haltingly and incompletely. It was the industrial revolution that made possible and pointed to the necessity for a popular education which connected the idea of the school with that of working life (Jarman, 1963, Chapter XIII). As we have seen, more practical subjects fought for a place in the sun from the Elizabethan period, in response to changes in Britain's role as an industrialising, trading, seafaring and colonising nation and to the development of modern, that is, seventeenth century onwards, science. The narrow range of studies both provided by the endowed schools, and insisted upon as entrance requirements by Oxford and Cambridge, was increasingly criticised from the beginning of the nineteenth century. Although not insulated from new trends, especially in scientific thought and experimentation, they, and the grammar schools, fought for the traditional values of the classical heritage and the liberal professions. The increasing dissatisfaction of the middle classes with the curriculum stimulated the development by subscription of cheaper day proprietary schools such as University College School (London) and similar institutions in major industrial centres which, unrestricted by old-fashioned statutes of founders and not normally endowed, were obliged by public pressure to respond to what were seen as the needs of the time. These schools tended to combine a liberal education with vocational aims often expressed in specific terms.

Efforts, at first unsuccessful, were made to redefine the concept of 'liberal education' to incorporate within it modern studies in science, mathematics, geography, history and English. There were other developments which were to contribute to a steadily growing but still small stream of technical education. These we will return to after considering the role of major governmental inquiries. The spontaneous development of a more useful curriculum in the proprietary day schools coincided with the establishment of the two major commissions which examined schools in the 1860s – the Clarendon Commission on the principal public (that is, private) schools (1861–64) (Clarendon Commission, 1864) and the Schools Inquiry (Taunton) Commission into the other endowed schools (1864–67). The Taunton Commission, in addition to its twenty-one-volume report in 1868 (Schools Inquiry (Taunton) Commission, 1868), issued a one-volume *Report Relative to Technical Education* in 1867 (Schools Inquiry (Taunton) Commission, 1867).

The Clarendon Commission on the public schools, set up in the teeth of opposition from the major independent (public) schools, drew attention to gaps and weaknesses in the curriculum, in particular the absence of natural science teaching, 'a plain defect and a great practical evil' (Clarendon Commission, 1864, Vol. 1, p.32), and recommended that in addition to the fundamentals of classics and religious teaching, the curriculum should include arithmetic, mathematics, at least one modern language, at least one branch of natural science, either drawing or music, a general knowledge of geography, English history, modern history and pure, grammatical English. This represented both a broadening of the curriculum and attention to modern subjects.

G.M. Young, in his *Victorian England: Portrait of an Age*, neatly draws more than one set of mid-nineteenth-century tensions:

> when Lord Clarendon summed up all the charges against the public schools in a question to the Headmaster of Eton, 'We find modern languages, geography, chronology, history and everything else which a well-educated Englishman ought to know, given up in order that the whole time should be devoted to the classics, and at the same time we are told that the boys go up to Oxford not only not proficient, but in a lamentable deficiency in respect of the classics', the Headmaster could only answer, 'I am sorry for it'. But public opinion did not want knowledge. It wanted the sort of man of whom Wellington had said that he could go straight from school with two N.C.Os. and fifteen privates and get a shipload of convicts to Australia without trouble.
>
> (Young, 1953, p.98)

Notwithstanding its criticism, the Clarendon Commission was far from proposing to dislodge classics from its position as a principal branch of study: 'we should certainly hesitate to advise the dethronement of it, even if we were prepared to recommend a successor' (Clarendon Commission, 1864, Vol. 1, p.28). And the successor, or rather the idea of a successor, was the problem. What the Clarendon Commission sought was a strengthening of education for the upper and middle classes, through a broader – but not a science-based – curriculum and through a reform – not a replacement – of the teaching of classics. It is interesting to note the attack launched by one of Britain's greatest practical scientists, Michael Faraday, who was among the many notable scientific witnesses:

> Who are the men whose powers are really developed? Who are they who have made the electric telegraph, the steam engine, and the railroad? Are they the men who have been taught Latin and Greek? Were the Stephensons such? These men had that knowledge which habitually has been neglected and pushed down below.
>
> (Clarendon Commission, 1864, Vol. IV, p.377)

In the same year that the Clarendon Commission reported, the Schools Inquiry Commission, chaired by Henry Labouchere, 1st Baron Taunton, was established to examine the other endowed schools. This Commission enjoyed a unique opportunity to consider the desirable content of secondary education nationally. Whereas the Clarendon Commission addressed the problem of the public schools, the target for the Taunton Commission was the bulk of the old endowed grammar schools.

After carrying out the most far-reaching of all educational inquiries, the members of the Taunton Commission, describing the work of the endowed schools as highly unsatisfactory, concluded unanimously in favour of general education versus preparation for special employment, which was thought to break up teaching and confer only temporary benefit on the pupils, arguments that still carry weight. However, still cleaving to the deeply stratified nature of British society and education, and with more than a touch of the Platonic division of men of gold, silver and iron, they accepted the principle of a differentiated education in envisaging three grades of school above the primary level, seeing this sociologically rather than psychologically, in terms of the social position of parents and likely career destination rather than individual ability or aptitude. Schools of the first grade were for the upper middle and professional classes. Their target was university entrance. Schools of the second grade were for the mercantile and trading classes, preparing pupils to age 16 for the army, the medical and legal professions, the Civil Service, civil engineering, business and commercial life. Third-class schools were for the children of smaller tenant farmers, small tradesmen, and superior artisans, who would complete their education at age 14. Vocational education of different types had some sort of place within this framework, not only for third-grade schools, which would have a special function of training boys and girls for higher handicrafts or the commercial activities of the shop and town. For them a general education would enlarge on their elementary education, and at the same time provide instruction for the hand and eye of the craftsman and define and illustrate the principles thus learnt. For the Taunton Commissioners, education was to be sustained in its roles of social stratification and screening, but it was, nevertheless to have a distinct vocational bearing for all three grades and classes.

What is disappointing, although not at all surprising, about the major reviews of the 1860s is that they uncovered the problem without being bold enough to tackle questions of curriculum in a genuinely open manner free of already outmoded social attitudes and the incubus of a class system which was taken to be, if not the natural, then certainly the proper, order of things. The need for more teaching of the natural sciences, for technical education, for vocational preparation, for provision of practical subjects, were known but were in practice lumped together with a sort of fastidious distaste as suitable for certain classes and abilities. Yet these were 'the boys who were to be the executive of the late Victorian industries and professions, and could be fairly described as the worst educated middle class in Europe' (Young, 1953, p.89). A heavy price has been paid for all this in the century and more that followed.

The very success of the industrial revolution seems, paradoxically, to have stood in the way of the development of a system of vocational and technical education, and the provision of links between a general education and training for work in industry, particularly manufacturing, in which Britain's international competitiveness was already in decline in the latter years of the nineteenth century while it still dominated the world economy (Landes, 1978; Smith, 1984, Chapter 3). The critical response to the worst features of nineteenth-century industrialism, by Dickens and William Morris, by Carlyle, Ruskin, Matthew Arnold and Patrick Geddes among others, could have fostered another kind of humane, practical education that drew together the elements of modern life in a new kind of cultural and social unity. In spite of much good analysis in the 1860s' reports and many individual writings then and subsequently, nothing like this happened. The classical influence of the public schools was seen as elite rather than outdated; the teaching of applied science and practical or vocational skills as more suited to the lower and poorer classes. The middle classes could manfully carry their philistine and imperial burden with a modicum of classical and modern learning. The analysis contained in the technical education volume of the Taunton Commissioners did not lead to a prestigious form of national provision for an industrial and commercial future. These educational values and attitudes perhaps reflected the continuing power and influence of a landed and monied aristocracy, whose power and wealth were never really supplanted by the new money of industrialism. Contrary to popular impressions, wealth and power did not reflect the industrial transformation. A new industrial culture did not take hold (Rubinstein, 1977; Wiener, 1981).

INDUSTRIAL NEEDS AND GOVERNMENT RESPONSES

It is therefore not so difficult to explain the lack of government action to confront the educational implications and consequences of the industrial revolution and of Britain's changing economic role, already weakening well before the end of the nineteenth century.

The Taunton Report explains:

Our attention has been incidentally called to the evidence considered to be afforded by the International Exhibition at Paris, of the inferior rate of progress recently made in manufacturing and mechanical industry in England compared with that made in other European countries. It has been stated to us that this alleged inferiority is due in

146

a great measure to the want of technical education, and we have therefore thought it desirable to ascertain from many eminent English Jurors in this department [that is, judges of manufactured goods at the Paris exhibition] whether they agree with this opinion.
(Schools Inquiry (Taunton) Commission, 1867, p.3)

We see also this concern more than a century later, coming from concrete evidence of poor performance in competition with other countries, but without, in the latter case, resort to jurors, the evidence being too painfully obvious.

Dr Lyon Playfair's submission to the Taunton Commissioners stated that 'the one cause upon which there was most unanimity of conviction is that France, Prussia, Austria, Belgium, and Switzerland possess good systems of industrial education for the masters and managers of factories and workshops, and that England possesses none' (Schools Inquiry (Taunton) Commission, 1867, p.6).

William Dampier, the historian of science, has said that the nineteenth century 'was the beginning of the scientific age', by which he meant that whereas in previous eras inventions and other improvements had largely proceeded independently of science, or set the pace for science to follow, now science led the way and practice followed, as with Faraday's electromagnetism and the dynamo (Dampier, 1946, Chapter VII). Several of the Taunton Commission jurors mentioned that the Continentals had taken over British inventions and improved and outstripped British performance. Dr David S. Price blamed the lack of 'a higher scientific culture . . . so that when discoveries are made they may fructify and not stagnate and decay, as has too often been the case, for want of intelligence on the part of those who command capital and works to perceive their merits' (Schools Inquiry (Taunton) Commission, 1867, p.22). This has been a recurring theme ever since in appraisals of scientific discoveries and their applications, almost a comforting reassurance that things remain much as they have always been.

Despite the constraining social assumptions under which it operated, the Taunton Commission was clear about what was needed: proper elementary education on a national scale; technical education for skilled workers; a prestigious scientific and technological education for the future managers of industry which would be shared and appreciated by those who would become financial backers of industry, public service and legislators; provision for high-level science and technology at universities. The question to ponder is why sufficient action was not taken to put the situation right, why Britain accepted the slow and inadequate development of compulsory elementary education, and the energetic, continued monopoly of classical education in the prestigious public and endowed schools which acted as a model for the later growth of new, state grammar schools.

Although there was legislation in 1869 covering some aspects of the Taunton Report (the Endowed Schools Act), the erection of a structure for national secondary education did not proceed until after the Royal Commission on Secondary Education in 1894 (Bryce Commission), with administrative legislation in the Board of Education Act 1899, Education Act 1902 and Regulations for Secondary Schools 1904–5. By comparison with France and Germany, government response in Britain was piecemeal and late.

Developments there were, to be sure, notably in science and technology: the establishment of the great provincial universities, many of whose applied science departments had close links with industry (Armytage, 1955). Voices there were that supported the changes needed in second-level education. The Bryce Commission was one such, arguing for a strong central authority and for a wide view of secondary education to include commercial and technical education. Some took action, such as Sidney Webb in his role as Chairman of the London Technical Education Board and as indefatigable campaigner, writer and 'permeator' of the political power bases (Webb, 1903). These and other more positive achievements were indeed of considerable importance but were nevertheless minority movements. We refer to them later in the chapter, after sketching in the normative framework for and government attitudes towards the overall development of the educational system.

The endeavours of the activists notwithstanding, no national educational system was established until the turn of the century; and secondary schooling was not compulsory before the Second World War. An almost complete lack of government involvement in technical education for workers was coupled with a slow growth of high-level scientific and technological education. Furthermore, in spite of occasional brief outbursts of enthusiasm for technical education, and science and technology – usually in response to dramatic evidence of successful international competition – provision came from outside central government, from Mechanics Institutes, for example, to help fill a vacuum. In spite of regular reports drawing attention to the ill effects of neglect – for example, Matthew Arnold's devastating criticism of the inadequacies of secondary education – in later years government typically lacked the impetus to tackle the problem. When, in 1904, Regulations for Secondary Schools were issued by the recently established Board of Education (the central authority following the Bryce recommendations) it was to the traditional academic secondary school that the Board turned for its model. Technical or vocational education, and the practical scientific and non-linguistic education recently evolved in higher elementary schools, were firmly discouraged. 'English secondary education became grammar school education' (Connell, 1980, p.41). Subsequently, four-year central schools for pupils from 11 to 15 years were established in London and Manchester, and these were given a commercial or industrial bias. Despite their success, they were still exceptional and of a lower standing than the academic grammar schools.

Through a slow, evolutionary process, in the first half of the twentieth century, the foundation of what is, as the century comes to a close, close to a universal system of further, continuing education and training, were laid. The Fisher Act of 1918 firmly established state schools and a universal minimum leaving age. Following the Spens Report (1938), which considered the provision of universal secondary education from 11 to 16, the Education Act of 1944 enshrined the right of all to free education regardless of social class, parental background and job destination. Given the late appearance of state-sponsored secondary education, relative to France, Germany and the USA, and the fact that by the time it developed it was wholly under the shadow of the traditional public, grammar and endowed schools whose ideals dominated it, we may have some understanding of the absence of a natural and deeply embedded strain of technical and vocational education.

TECHNICAL EDUCATION: A SERIOUS, IF MINORITY, CONCERN

Thus far, we have drawn attention to a powerful, if often implicit, cultural tradition which gave to the emerging educational system a character that was generally demeaning to practical forms of vocational education. But a tradition of technical education related to both old and new crafts did exist and, as we have seen, at periodic intervals the need for reform and development was highlighted, if not acted upon. Endeavours, particularly from the mid nineteenth century onwards, to build on and strengthen this tradition were inadequate and often faltering but they provide the foundations for many of the new vocational initiatives of the late twentieth century.

Such technical education as existed before the industrial revolution was work-based and took place through craft apprenticeships. Then master craftsmen often became capitalist employers without the time, experience, skill or inclination to undertake what amounted to training. The industrial revolution was led by practical and commercially minded men – ironmasters, craftsmen, etc. – who achieved much by individual effort and without the advantage of theoretical or academically formalised knowledge. The workers, mainly peasants forced into overcrowded and insanitary towns, were, with some notable exceptions, ignorant and unambitious. From the first they were exploited and did not see themselves as contributors. Offered neither reasonable conditions nor education, their approach to their work was often negative and their eventual aim, comprehensible though ultimately unsatisfactory, was to protect themselves, for example, through their unions against further exploitation. There was, nevertheless, a nucleus of formal technical instruction, assessment-led. 'In the 19th century, technical and scientific instruction was largely moulded by the examinations of the Science and Art Department and the City and

Guilds of London Institute' (Curtis, 1967, p.501), an interesting pre-figuring of the role the National Council of Vocational Qualifications sees for itself. At the beginning of the twentieth century, the tradition was firmly established that the school should concentrate on theory and the workshop on practice. The Technical Instruction Act of 1899 specifically stated that technical instruction should *not* include the practise of any trade or industry. Technical education, although not lacking practical correlates, was conceived as a variant of academic instruction.

During the second half of the nineteenth century the fate of technical education was tied up both with that of a fragmented and restricted national secondary education generally, and with the inability of policy-makers to devise a mainstream tradition of secondary education incorporating technical and practical work-related learning. While the succession of commissions we have discussed above continued to believe that the best preparation for technical activity was a good general education, no reconstructed concept of general education addressing the foundations and significance of technical learning or the great forces transforming late nineteenth- and early twentieth-century society, was forthcoming. The general education that was advanced, as we have seen, was still cast into the mould of the established culture.

The need for modernisation and modification of apprenticeship was ignored because of the apparent but ultimately misleading evidence of industrial success and, especially, of the secure markets and supply sources of Empire. From the 1820s the provision of technical and technological education was mainly in the hands of independent bodies such as the Mechanics Institutes; and individual contributions such as Whitworth Scholarships (established 1868).

The emergence of the two university-level science and technology institutions in London (Imperial College and University College) and the major civic universities promoted at last a high-level education in science and technology but, characteristically, they were funded largely through private endowments and not supported by the state till 1889, and then only sparingly (Armytage, 1955).

Notwithstanding the limited and fragmentary nature of the developments referred to above, significant initiatives, led by relatively small groups of innovators, did take place. In 1836 a Select Committee of the House of Commons recommended the establishment of a Normal School of Design and voted £1,500 for this purpose. Starting in 1841, annual grants were made for promoting provincial schools of design of which, by 1852, there were seventeen in operation. The Normal School of Design eventually became the Science and Art Department of the Board of Trade which did much through grants and examinations to promote the teaching of science and art – a system which, one historian has argued, eventually degenerated into examination cramming and credentialism (Curtis, 1967).

During the nineteenth century, the creation of public, non-government examination bodies was an important stimulus to technical education. For example, the Society of Arts (founded in London in 1754 and receiving royal patronage in 1908) introduced its system of examinations, including chemistry, mathematics and mechanics, in 1854. This examination system was extended to technical subjects in 1872 and at a still later stage the concentration was towards commercial subjects.

Other initiatives to provide and regulate examinations were the Union of Lancashire and Cheshire Institutes (1829) and the London City Livery Companies, which appointed a committee to draw up a national scheme of technical instruction, the result of which was the City and Guilds Institute founded in 1880. The 'City and Guilds' has for more than a century played a major role in encouraging the teaching of sciences and technical subjects in schools and further education institutions. The emergence of the polytechnics is another example of significant innovation. Under the influence of Quintin Hogg, founder of the Regent Street Polytechnic in 1880, polytechnic institutions were established in different parts of the country, teaching technical and practical subjects in day and evening classes.

In response to alarm over industrial progress in the German empire and competition from the United States, finally a Royal Commission on Technical Instruction was established in 1881 (Samuelson Commission, 1884). This Commission went through the familiar process of discovering that provision was inadequate, recommending more and better secondary education and technical instruction, while concluding that the best preparation for technical study was a good modern secondary education (thereby supporting the provision of the third-class Taunton schools). It recommended the provision by Charity Commissioners of schools and departments of schools in suitable localities where the study of natural science, drawing, mathematics and modern languages should take the place of Latin and Greek; and that local authorities, if they thought fit, should contribute to the establishment and maintenance of such schools and colleges. Following the Commission's report, the Technical Instruction Act was passed in 1889. The Act empowered local authorities to levy a rate in support of technical instruction, but the relationship of technical to other secondary education was still not tackled. The idea of teaching the practice of any trade, or of preparing pupils for industry or employment, was not acceptable as part of the curriculum.

The Royal Commission on Secondary Education (1895) (Bryce Report) addressed the task of considering 'what are the best methods of establishing a well-organised system of Secondary Education in England' (Royal Commission on Secondary Education, Vol. 1, 1895, pp.iii–iv). This Commission unanimously rejected any early specialisation, regarding instruction in special subjects as inadequate in itself, and as inducing too utilitarian a spirit. Special preparation for employment was provided by the appearance of new subjects in the curriculum which acted as pre-apprenticeship education. The difference between technical and other secondary education after much soul-searching was deemed to be not one of kind but of emphasis.

The Bryce Commission did recognise that technical education had a right to exist because of 'its practical utility in days when industrial and commercial competition grows constantly more severe', but then almost contradicted itself: 'Technical instruction must be considered not as the rival of a liberal education but as a specialization of it . . . and will be most successfully used by those whose intellectual capacity has been already disciplined by the best methods of literary or scientific training' (Royal Commission on Secondary Education, Vol. 1, Part IV, 1895, pp.284–285). Had liberal or general education itself been redefined in a quite fundamental way, rather than treated as an established doctrine which could be refurbished by reference to 'modern studies', England might have found the middle way that some of its thinkers were seeking, between a broad general education and specialised, applicable knowledge and skills for everyone.

The 1902 Education Act, although a milestone in the establishment of a system of secondary education in Britain, still left many problems unresolved and could not be regarded as the legislative foundation of an integrated and comprehensive system of education for all. Such a structure was not in fact put in place until the 1944 Act and even then many weaknesses in national provision remained, some of them still being addressed today. After 1902 Britain still retained parallel systems of elementary and secondary education. There was a gap between the age at which students completed elementary education (13–14 years) and that at which they could commence apprenticeships (16 years of age). In recognition of this the Board of Education authorised grants to day technical classes. These new junior technical schools fell into one of two groups: (1) those which prepared pupils for particular trades and occupations (trade schools); and (2) those preparing pupils wishing to enter a specific trade but not a specific occupation (pre-apprenticeship schools). Both types were to provide for a continuance of the general moral, intellectual and physical education given in elementary schools – but were not recognised as secondary schools until 1938.

Developments such as these represented a serious intent on the part of certain sections of the community to address profound needs and break the grip of what had become an effete educational tradition. They were, however, minority movements, illustrating the fragmentary and inadequately articulated approach to the provision of educational and training opportunities for young people. In both structural and curriculum terms discontinuities and imbalances have characterised the evolution of public provision. The middle way was not found then, and still has not been found. As a consequence the growth of specialist and technical studies continued to inspire the concern that such education might be too narrow and specialised and that schools should not send out pupils with un-balanced or neglected development of faculties. The Regulations for Secondary Schools 1904–5 recommended in favour of a four-year course which provided a complete general education.

It was generally felt that wider development of experiments in vocational learning and practical activities belonging to the small sector of technical schooling, rapidly growing but outside the mainstream of secondary educa-tion, should be limited to the independent technical schools. But in recog-nition of their rapid growth and importance, the Board of Education recognised the independent full-time junior technical schools which had developed in certain areas to prepare young people for certain trades and occupations, under special regulations in 1913. Offering vocational train-ing, they prepared young people to go into unskilled industrial or domestic occupations, by means of practical work in appropriate subjects. Trade schools offered the equivalent of apprenticeship for specific skilled occu-pations – such as printing, silversmithing, etc. – with one to three years specialised vocational education after completion of elementary schools.

Although pupil numbers in junior technical schools doubled between 1925 and 1937, the total reached only 30,000 at most. Time and attention were devoted to general subjects and physical and social welfare, and their capacity to adapt their curriculum to local needs was their strength. The standardisation of external examinations in 1917, and the high prestige acquired by the First School Examination in the eyes of employers, had the general effect of stereotyping and narrowing the school curriculum, and putting the technical schools outside the mainstream of national schooling provision. They never recovered and when, in the 1960s, the compre-hensive school movement took off, the vestiges of the technical schools were too insignificant and piecemeal to provide the basis of a new technical culture within the mainstream, comprehensive movement. The contem-porary concept of City Technology Colleges (CTCs), has echoes of the technical education strand of the 1944 Education Act.

The Spens Report, the *Report of the Consultative Committee on Secondary Education with Special Reference to Grammar Schools and Technical High Schools* (Spens, 1938), noted with approval that the curriculum in junior technical schools in engineering was based on learning broad scientific principles while English subjects were offered on a basis comparable to grammar schools; it concluded that the response of some children to a vocational and practical approach was proof of its educational effectiveness. But the technical schools took children at 13 when the most gifted academically were already in grammar schools:

The natural ambition of the clever child has been turned towards the Grammar School and the professional occupations rather than towards Technical High Schools and industry. This tends inevitably to create a disproportion in the distribution of brain power as between what may be broadly termed the professional and industrial worlds. Furthermore, there is a regrettable and undesirable difference in social esteem.

(Spens, 1938, p.274)

In recommending a five-year course for technical high schools and a selection procedure involving tests, parental choice and headmaster's report, the committee no doubt hoped to change this. But the truth is that the desire to incorporate technical education into the system of universal free secondary education established in 1944 came too late and was insufficiently vital. The impact of the schools was diluted by the fact that they did not exist in all areas of the country, and by their having to compete as newcomers with the traditional grammar school. They were part of an artificially differentiated system which claimed there were three types of children – those suited to learning for its own sake; those preparing to take up applied sciences or applied arts; and those interested in concrete matters rather than ideas. Though achieving an advance on a philosophy of the classics or of self-help, Britain failed, as Naylor (1985) argued, to solve the problem of cultivating intelligence without demeaning manual and practical skills and activities. The technical schools had considerable academic success – small schools with committed staffs and motivated pupils – but found themselves competing for the same outcomes as grammar schools. They lost the status battle and their influence never penetrated to the inner recesses of government or the Civil Service. Few of the most academic children entered them, and in spite of excellent results they did not enjoy equal esteem even among educators.

The technical schools developed independently and were incorporated into state secondary provision in the 1944 Education Act. Had they been established earlier within a national system they might have formed the grounding for the development of successful industrialists and a preparation for prestigious university-level education in science and technology. Appearing belatedly on the scene they were not able to compete in terms of recognition with prestigious grammar schools and so failed to attract the all-ability intake essential to win for technical education an equal status. Whether or not their absorption within comprehensive schools in the secondary reorganisation introduced in 1965 theoretically gave technical subjects an increased chance to capture recruits of all ability and social levels, in practice curricula in comprehensive schools generally perpetuated an unstreamed version of the general liberal grammar school tradition. Just as in the late 1860s the inability of policy-makers to deal with questions of differentiation was obscured by providing a new or modern curriculum, the 1960s made much of adjusting the general liberal

154

curriculum in favour of 'integrated' studies, social sciences and 'relevant' subject matter, while conspicuously failing to reappraise the curriculum in the light of the aptitudes, needs and destinations of different children and the great social, economic and cultural changes of the post-war era.

As we have seen, independent bodies such as the Royal Society of Arts (RSA) made provision outside the national system for examinations in technical subjects in the last quarter of the nineteenth century. So too in recent years have the RSA, City and Guilds of London Institute (CGLI) and the Business and Technician Education Council (BTEC) offered technical and vocational courses and qualifications in further education colleges and in schools to those not motivated by, or suited to, GCE and academic courses. In response to the Newsom Report, *Half Our Future* (Central Advisory Council for Education (England), 1963), and with encouragement from the then influential and prestigious Schools Council for Curriculum and Examinations, schools themselves increasingly responded to the needs of the less academic pupils. But until the upheaval caused by the innovations of the 1980s, the fact that technical and vocational courses appeared to increase the motivation of the less academic has served to confirm the impression that they were suitable for such pupils – and to reinforce their status as still basically inferior to academic subjects. As Benson and Silver aptly remark:

> The vocationalism of further education was identified with the lower status of the institutions, courses and qualifications, the most commonly male focus of its orientation, the part-time nature of much of its work, and its 'training' role. Its qualifications, derived from bodies like the Royal Society of Arts and the City and Guilds of London Institute, were seen from the vantage point of elite sectors of education and from some policy directions as low-level hangovers from nineteenth-century industrial training needs.
>
> (Benson and Silver, 1991, p.4)

Here too the significant interest and value of the new vocationalism of the 1980s is the sustained bid to break the sorry pattern of past negligence and the attitudes that it resulted from. Technical and vocational education in these initiatives have been placed firmly within the mainstream of national provision, available for pupils of all ability and shown – already in the Technical and Vocational Education Initiative (TVEI) and perhaps also to be in the CTCs – as potentially prestigious areas of the curriculum. The central innovation is that, for the first time on any scale in English educational history, they have been given not only substantial central government backing but positive discrimination in financial and prestige terms. It is not clear that the 1988 Education Act will in practice sustain and strengthen this momentum. With the absorption of the Training Commission and then the Training Agency (short-lived successors to the

Manpower Services Commission (MSC)) into the Whitehall bureaucracy, there is, once more, a need to question the adequacy of the national policy structures and institutions in the face of the historical trends and forces we have outlined. Indeed, it is questionable whether structural adjustment, even when supported by large injections of funds, gets to the heart of the matter at all. Deep-seated attitudes, a particular cast of values and the sub-stratum of British culture have all to be changed if the transformation of education and training that is sought is to be achieved. In these circumstances, and notwithstanding the critique we and others have made of the Youth Training Scheme (YTS), the innovations of the 1980s represent a bold and badly needed departure from a depressing historic norm.

TRAINING/APPRENTICESHIP

One more strand needs to be touched upon in this overview of the historical antecedents of the reforms of recent decades. Apprenticeship in Britain dates from the Statute of Apprentices of 1563 and remained in being, albeit in more recent years in steady decline, until the Industrial Training Act of 1963 – a period of 400 years. In the intervening period it was weakened by the industrial revolution but then revived, perhaps artificially. In Elizabethan days it was geared to small-scale domestic production and involved concrete tests of competence on completion. Inadequate in that form after the industrial revolution because of new conditions and new areas of activity for which it did not exist, it failed to take root in the new factories, a significant contrast with the German-speaking countries of Continental Europe.

By the 1870s, there was a serious problem of standard of workmanship demonstrated in shoddy products and successful foreign competition. There were no regulations and no centrally devised system of education and training although the trade unions (then as now) were pressing for both. In 1878 certain City livery companies invited six men, including the notable Darwinist and science educator Professor Thomas Henry Huxley, to recommend how they should most profitably spend their money on the 'extension and improvement of technical education'. It was Huxley, incidentally, who, in a public lecture in 1854, caustically remarked on 'the utter ignorance as to the simplest laws of their own animal life, which prevails among even the most highly educated persons in this country' (Huxley, 1906, p.279). The conclusions of the consultants to the City livery companies revived the old apprenticeship system and in one sense confirmed the separation of theory and practice – of the responsibility of industry for practical training, and colleges and institutes for formal academic learning. Notwithstanding Huxley's own belief in the intimate relations between theory and practice, Wellens (1963) notes that this unduly circumscribed idea entered the country's nascent education system and stayed there harmfully, to be reaffirmed in 1958 by the Carr Committee in their report *Training for Skill* (Ministry of Labour and National Service, 1958). Trade unions reimposed controls over age of entry, duration of apprenticeship and the proportion of apprentices to skilled men. Perhaps even more harmfully in the long run, the new complex processes in manufacturing meant that few workmen saw a process through to its conclusion, and the original idea of a 'masterpiece' and with it the test of competence was lost.

Whether a well-grounded, structured and comprehensive system of apprenticeship could or even should have been established is perhaps an idle question, except that the fading of the 400-year-old tradition was a function, yet again, of the lack of a sense of national purpose and direction for education and training. Be that as it may, apprenticeship was no longer a major option in the decades following the Second World War.

Training for Skill in 1958 addressed the challenge of the baby boom years. At least in quantitative terms, it was obvious that apprenticeship was inadequate for training young people. It did not apply to more than half of the 15–17 age group who entered semi-skilled occupations; it omitted girls and commercial workers altogether. The Carr Committee had to choose between the modernisation of apprenticeship with the addition of a recognised test of competence, or fundamental reform. The Committee judged – or, more accurately, misjudged – that the birth of apprenticeship in new occupational areas demonstrated its vitality, although action had to be taken to improve quantity and quality.

Surveying recent good practice in a number of foreign countries, which could usefully be disseminated in British industries, the Committee concluded with more than a touch of complacency, that

> we should build upon foundations that have already been laid rather than attempt to construct *something entirely new*. We consider that, as a general principle for the future, the existing division of responsibility between Government and Industry for the education and training of apprentices should be maintained.
>
> (Ministry of Labour and National Service, 1958, p.6)

The efforts of the government, it said, should be directed to the expansion and improvement of facilities for technical education, while the responsibility for the industrial training of apprentices should rest firmly with industry. All the nineteenth-century qualities – *laissez-faire*, diffidence, fear of state interference and the profound desire to keep the culture of industry separate and apart from what is truly treasured – were manifest once more. Not surprisingly, apprenticeship as a principal mode of industrial training did not enjoy a renaissance.

CULTURAL VALUES AND PREPARATION FOR WORK

> They [the great majority of professional men and poor gentry] would, no doubt, in most instances be glad to secure something more than classics and mathematics. But they value these highly for their own sake, and perhaps even more for the value at present assigned to them in English society. They have nothing to look to but education to keep their sons on a high social level. And they would not wish to have what might be more readily converted into money, if in any degree it tended to let their children sink in the social scale.
>
> (Schools Inquiry (Taunton) Commission, Vol. 1, 1868, pp.17–18)

Education in Britain has been influenced more by traditional, class-related cultural and social pressures than by national economic ones, or by a concern for the personal growth and development of *all* children as individuals and future citizens. The tireless endeavours of reformers as diverse as Matthew Arnold, Sidney Webb and a range of industrialists and scientists have been insufficient fully to overcome these deeper forces in the nation. In a characteristically pointed sally, as late as 1907, George Bernard Shaw remarked: 'Nobody can say a word against Greek: it stamps a man at once as an educated gentleman' (Shaw, 1907, Preface).

In spite of the industrial revolution, historically the majority of the best academic students have been directed away from business by the education system, and the old universities have in general presented the route out of, not into, industry and business. The industrial ethos was briefly admired in the mid nineteenth century, but the values of an industrial society never succeeded in ousting those of the old aristocracy. So runs the persuasive argument of Martin J. Wiener in *English Culture and the Decline of the Industrial Spirit 1850–1980* (Wiener, 1981). The strength of the English public school and the culture from which it derived diluted the values of the industrialist and brought into question the virtue of productive work in manufacturing or even commerce as a way of life for intelligent, educated people. Because there was no prestigious form of scientific and technical education in existence at the time, industrialists used their money to send their sons to schools which were prestigious in social terms. The successful industrialist was persuaded that the best way to use his money was to buy land, which was acquired not to be developed but to be enjoyed; to become accepted as a member of the 'gentry' and to absorb his son into the public school system. The values that brought the fathers material success – zeal for work, inventiveness, material productivity and interest in money-making – gave way in a couple of generations to 'the more aristocratic interests of cultivated style, the pursuits of leisure, and political service' (Wiener, 1981, p.13).

Characteristically the new generation moved out of the modern industrial town to the old, preferably historic, home. Wealth was extracted from industrial progress, rather than ploughed back in. Thus the industrial revolution led, in a bizarre manner, not to the rise of a modern industrial education and ethos but to the rise of the modern professions – the proliferation of institutes and associations for lawyers, accountants, doctors, public officials, journalists, professors and men of letters. These of course were a necessary part of the urbanising society. However, as Bill Rubinstein, the authority on wealth accumulation in the nineteenth century, says, 'The process of incorporation, acquisition of an expensive and palatial headquarters in central London, establishment of an apprenticeship system, limitations on entries and scheduling of fees, are all manifestly designed to "gentrify" the profession and make it acceptable to society' (Rubinstein, 1977, p.122). The arcadian ideal, 'the myth of the happier past', deeply embedded in the culture, and forcibly contrasted with the evils of those quintessential products of industrialism, London and the provincial cities, lost none of its persuasiveness in the nineteenth century (Williams, 1975).

But, as we have seen, there was a deep ambivalence in nineteenth-century British society. It was not only a pre-industrial past that presented ideal landscapes. Comparisons of a more contemporary kind were drawn with other industrialised countries. Neither vocational and technical, nor modern forms of secondary education were believed to be accorded the importance attached to them at the same period in France, Prussia, Austria, Switzerland and the USA among others (Samuelson Commission, 1884; Sadler, 1902). But it must be remembered that from the mid nineteenth century onwards, many countries engaged in comparisons with others and often found themselves wanting. In the British case, both technical and vocational education, in a classical Greek view of the matter, tended to be associated with an undesirable and lower-class way of life. This in spite of commission reports identifying the pernicious consequences of such attitudes and the evidence linking them with poor economic performance.

By the time of the 1944 Act, although the ideas of a liberal education had long since been extended to include modern languages, science, modern history and geography, the idea of vocational education had, if anything, been further diminished. It had become identified with preparation for various practical occupations, such as typing and shorthand, book-keeping, tool-making, auto mechanics and so on. 'Liberal' and 'vocational' were, however, linked – as the upper and lower levels of a hierarchy of jobs, rewards and social status. Institutional dichotomies corresponded with these levels and were further compounded by the 1944 Act. This negative association of ideas has persisted up to the present day. The education and training initiatives of the 1980s, and the influence of the MSC on the provision of both training and education, whatever their limitations, represent a genuine assault on this culture, its doctrines and institutional correlates. Their ultimate success is therefore of great importance. Even more important is the establishment of a unified system of education, with education for productive work and the values of work impregnating the whole system and no longer confined to the lesser margins.

SUMMARY

In the light of a brief review of selected educational and curriculum developments, and of features of vocational and technical education, and training for work, over the last century and a half, certain remarks can be made about the context of the 1980s' innovations, the new vocationalism. In focusing on an interpretation of Britain's poor economic performance which blames the education system, the new vocationalism echoes the findings of the Technical Inquiry attached to the Taunton Commission and others since. But it breaks with tradition in acting energetically upon its conclusions. The difference between the major review and upheaval of secondary education in the 1980s and those others since the 1860s (the Clarendon and Taunton Commissions, the Spens Report, the 1944 Butler Education Act, comprehensive reorganisation) is that vocational and technical education have been officially welcomed and given priority rather than neglected. Vigorous attempts have been made to bring them into the educational mainstream. Prominent figures in political and public life, in the enterprise sector, in higher education and the professions have established common ground in affirming and supporting these changes. Yet it is still too soon to be at all confident that the historical situation has been transformed. Continuing efforts over many years will be required, and these cannot be confined to the education and training systems but must address a wider array of factors in British society and its cultural underpinnings.

During the nineteenth century the influence of the classical tradition and of the public and endowed schools, compounded by anti-democratic sentiments and arcadian ideals, was dominant and, whether as cause or effect, policy-makers were reluctant to construct a national education system to educate the nation's workforce beyond elementary level. Furthermore, they showed a distaste for a genuine evolution of the curriculum to meet new needs and in particular to include practical, technical or vocational learning except at a low status. The comprehensive school reform of the 1950s and 1960s onwards, while addressing many of the defects of secondary education, did not include a fundamental transformation of the curriculum or the incorporation of an industrial culture. Pressure for that has come, as we have seen, from the economic, employment and industry sectors of government and from industry itself.

Britain still has a bifurcated education system, whose separate parts are not integrated through national policy or through a common understanding in the community about the nature and purposes of education. Vestiges of the old stratifications and status differences remain. There is still a lack of consistency and coherence in the goals and procedures of reform. Historically informed reflection and analysis are all too rare among policy-makers and system developers.

Today's changes have, however, been firmly backed by an interventionist style of government which regards vocational and technical education as suitable and necessary across the ability range, and which has been determined to increase their status. If negative cultural attitudes, or a certain conservatism among policy-makers, played a crucial part in keeping a spontaneous strain of 'useful' learning out of the mainstream of secondary education in the last century, and consequently relegating technical and vocational education to an inferior status, then the very different thrusts of the 1980s' innovations should be noted. The old grammar school type of curriculum, which, persisting into comprehensive schools, met with a significant lack of motivation and underachievement by pupils, and lack of confidence by parents, has now been replaced by a national curriculum with a significant corpus of common learnings for all students. Perhaps the most important aspect of the new vocationalism is the impetus for the first fundamental curriculum reform, free of the influence of the nineteenth-century tradition. And this is perhaps partly explained by the new type of policy-makers who themselves stand outside a persistent classical tradition.

The innovations of the 1970s and 1980s mark the beginnings of a profound break with a firmly entrenched historical tradition. While this has its risks, for a number of reasons the priority given to technical and vocational education may be more in accord with public attitudes than ever before. This priority also accords with another strand in the historical tradition whereby practical, useful knowledge and a high standard of universal education have been affirmed by intelligent and far-sighted, if often disregarded, figures in public life. One question from history, upon which there must be real doubt, is whether the new vocationalism of the 1980s is an educational strain which can produce its own momentum, its own natural growth. Will the new vocationalism influence the independent schools, will it meet with understanding and support from higher education, where will it stand as the national curriculum of the 1988 Education Act takes shape in school practice? Most important, will the potential segregationist tendencies themselves prove stronger than the measures taken to give technical and vocational education an improved status?

This brief overview of the historical context underlines the significance and drama of the upheaval that has occurred during the past decade or so. The combination of good intentions, narrow vision, torpor, complacency and class-based resistance to change that blunted and defeated reform initiatives is an enduring cultural phenomenon whose impact must continue to be addressed. Many of the fundamental features in the structure of British society that compounded the 'do nothing, or as little as possible, in case loss is incurred' mentality of governments have disappeared or changed: the economics of post-imperialism, the collapse of a significant global role, the decline of industrial power, the transformation of aristocratic governance into bourgeois democracy have forced a radical reappraisal. But nostalgic traces remain and too little has been done during the past decade to weld a national coalition for reform out of the still divided education and training interest groups. If any one lesson emerges it is the need for energetic, sustained, comprehensive and unified strategies, with government providing intelligent, well-informed leadership, shared through active partnerships with those who have major stakes and must be involved in implementing their strategies.

7

NEW SCHEMES FOR TRAINING BRITISH YOUTH

Afterward, other tigers will appear.

(Borges, 1979, p.137)

INTRODUCTION

After the prolonged period of neglect or limited activity as outlined in the previous chapters, and a series of initiatives mainly through the certification bodies such as the City and Guilds of London Institute (CGLI) and the Royal Society of Arts (RSA), in the 1960s the national government in Britain began to take steps which were to result in sweeping changes in educational and training policies.

Following the criticisms aired in the Carr Report of 1958, the government in a White Paper in 1962 announced proposals for industrial training (Department of Labour, 1962). Legislation in 1964 (Industrial Training Act) resulted in the establishment of twenty-three Industrial Training Boards for the major industries, with responsibility both to prescribe and to improve training schemes (Cantor, 1989, p.117). A Central Training Council was also set up to co-ordinate activities of the boards. The boards had some success in structural matters, the enhanced professionalism of training and pioneering new approaches to assessment (Ward, 1987), but the board framework did not prove to be the means needed for developing new ideas, or responding to emerging technologies and innovative work practices. Its administrative burdens were resisted by employers and so it was substantially dismantled. The Industrial Training Board structure was the immediate forerunner of and was displaced by the Manpower Services Commission (MSC), a central government agency.

In Chapter 5 we briefly outlined the steps whereby the MSC emerged from its uncertain fledgling status to become a powerful national force with immense resources at its disposal and the capacity to mount and sustain major national initiatives in youth and adult training. It is one scheme – a

163

flagship of the many MSC initiatives – that is our concern in this chapter. The Youth Training Scheme (YTS), in its ambitions, proposed scale of operation, key concepts and strategies for training, expresses most fully and comprehensively the central ideas of the new vocationalism in Britain, its strengths and its weaknesses.

The YTS during the 1980s was on a scale which few other schemes anywhere match and was pursued with great vigour and determination at the highest political level. We have already indicated (see Chapter 5) that the YTS went through a rapid series of changes as policy-makers and developers sought adjustments to the changing work scene and struggled to produce a scheme which adequately met a multiplicity of demands, both economic and political. Whatever its limitations – and critics have not been slow to identify them – the YTS warrants careful consideration both as a dramatic demonstration of government determination to restructure the training environment in a period of continuing high youth unemployment and because it has been the main test bed of ideas for the National Council for Vocational Qualifications (NCVQ) and its framework of National Vocational Qualifications (NVQs) (outlined in Chapter 5).

With its replacement by Youth Training (YT) in 1990, the highly visible profile of youth training under YTS has diminished somewhat, as youth unemployment, while remaining disturbingly high, has moved downward in the national policy agenda. Because of its intimate links with the field of employment and its social, cultural, financial and political implications, it should come as no surprise that there has been continuing criticism and even a cynical reaction to the fluctuating fortunes of the scheme and the priority – and finance – accorded to it. The YTS, after all, was promoted and funded, not as a relatively short-term adjustment measure but as a profound shift in policy, provision and resource utilisation – and as a permanent feature of British life. Its permanence is now very much in question although its impact will long be felt.

In this chapter we briefly review the origins of the YTS, then look at the evolving design of the scheme in its early stages up to the establishment of its two-year programme. We consider three trends evident during the evolving design process, before reviewing in turn each of the four outcomes defined for YTS. Finally, we locate the YTS in a wider setting, drawing some conclusions about its significance and legacy.

FROM THE YOUTH TRAINING SCHEME TO YOUTH TRAINING

The YTS occupied a central position for nearly a decade in the government-sponsored philosophy of the new vocationalism in England and Wales. Driven from a single site in central government, and with substantial funds to dispose of, it is, together with the Technical and Vocational Education

Initiative (TVEI), the clearest demonstration in modern educational training policies in Britain of a strategic determination to overcome the historical gap between 'schooling' and 'working life'.

The YTS, as we have seen in Chapter 5, did not spring fully formed on to centre-stage. National schemes to cater for the needs of the young unemployed have existed since the Work Experience Programme was established in 1976 to provide a six-month-long programme of work experience for young unemployed school-leavers. This was replaced in 1978 by the Youth Opportunities Programme (YOP) which provided young people with a mixture of on- and off-the-job training, provided not just by employers on their premises (as had been the case with the Work Experience Programme), but also in schemes established by public authorities, voluntary and community organisations, and youth agencies. Thus a broader range of training contexts began to be provided, with training workshops, community service agencies, environmental improvement projects and information technology centres providing training as well as employers (Ball, 1988).

In its turn, the YOP was replaced by the YTS, the product of the *New Training Initiative* (*NTI*) analysis in its clearest and purest form. The introduction of the YTS was the first major government response to the second training policy target of the *NTI* (see Chapter 5), that of enabling all young people under the age of 18 to continue in full-time education, or enter training or a period of planned work experience combining work-related training and education. The YTS was designed to offer opportunities to young people to acquire the skills they lacked and industry needed; and the motivation and positive attitudes to the world of work which the schools had contrarily somehow failed to develop. Thus the YTS had a great deal to deliver.

The YTS guaranteed an early offer of training to school-leavers who were unemployed. Taking its first trainees in April 1983, the scheme was intended to provide what the *NTI* called 'a period of planned work experience combined with work-related training and education' (MSC, 1981b, p.4) to all young people aged 16 and 17 who had left full-time education, and to 18-year-olds with special needs. A minimum of thirteen weeks off-the-job training was to be provided during the one year of the scheme – in its initial form. Crucial to an understanding of the YTS is the dominance of a philosophy of technical rationalism whereby education and training were conceived as instruments in a wider programme of economic and industrial reform. Hence its political significance, its rapid expansion, nationwide, and the scale of funding it was able to attract from government to support its growth.

The YTS was thus as much a socio-economic policy as an education or training one, emerging from an interpretation of Britain's poor economic performance that highlighted the lack of skills of young people entering employment, with only some 40 per cent having recognisable qualifications. It had, therefore, from the beginning two entirely different and, at times contradictory, responsibilities – to the economy and to the young potentially unemployed. In both respects it ranked high on the political agenda throughout most of the 1980s. A full understanding of the nature and content of the scheme requires that it be seen in this wider context.

It is not only the actual introduction of a national youth training scheme offering a broad-based vocational training to 16-year-old school-leavers, but also the role and the operations of the MSC (cutting across many existing authorities and funding arrangements) that has been characteristic of the new vocationalism. We have noted in Chapter 5 the speed with which the MSC launched its national youth training scheme in 1983 and the scale, backed by considerable sums of scarce government resources, requiring massive co-operation – or compliance – from employers and other local sponsors. Whatever the quality of the early activities within the YTS, this was a remarkable achievement fuelled by the rapid deterioration in youth employment levels. It marked the transformation of MSC from catalyst and backer of small-scale manpower and training programmes to a strategic management role of training on a very large scale. The sheer level of MSC activity associated with the start of the YTS – the finding of sponsors to manage schemes, of work placements for trainees, the establishment of teams of inspectors, advisers and quality assessors and of research and development activities, the financing, the publication of quantities of advisory material – emphasised the break with the education and training tradition whereby there was a lack of or only limited direct intervention by central government. In this sense the use of money as a policy tool, the direct central government intervention, the sheer energy and singlemindedness of the new vocationalism demand attention. Whatever else has been achieved, the government has been fortified in the exercise of its own powers and emboldened to extend them, as in the 1988 Education Act and the subsequent surge of interventionism from successive Ministers of Education.

In March 1985, less than two years after its introduction and before there had been an opportunity for serious evaluation of initial performance, the YTS was extended from a one-year to a two-year programme (for those beginning at age 16), effective from 1986. Insofar as it was possible at so early a stage in its development, the YTS or some variant of it was also officially confirmed as a semi-permanent feature of vocational preparation in the UK in the context of the government target of offering opportunities for obtaining qualifications relevant to employment, whether general or work-related, for *all* young people (DES, 1985b). The government committed itself to making available some £125 million in additional resources in 1986–87 and £300 million in 1987–88. Thus the total exchequer contribution to the YTS already envisaged at that stage was £925 million in 1986–87 and £1,000 million in 1987–88 (DES, 1985b). These very considerable sums, provided against a background of reduced government spending in many areas, indicate the significance attached to the policy of providing training for young people – and the riskiness of a venture that proceeded nationwide on such a rapid timescale. Sceptics might remark that expenditure of this order was bound to have an impact; there have been no studies on the global, comparative cost effectiveness of the YTS as a national strategy and it seems unlikely that there will be.

Already by January 1984 nearly 25 per cent of the 16-year-old age group was on the YTS books (DES/DoE/MSC, 1985), as well as some 25,000 17-year-olds, and some older trainees with special needs. By the end of March 1986, 265,000 young people were on the YTS; and in March 1987 318,000, including 52,400 on continuation places under the two-year version of the scheme. By 1988/9, some 407,500 were participating in the YTS. By the end of the decade in which it was launched, some 2,400,000 trainees had been recorded as taking part in the scheme (DoE, 1990b). With what effects or outcomes, either for the participants individually or the economy, it is impossible to say.

The YTS continued as a major national programme, although its responsible authority underwent several metamorphoses from the MSC to Training Commission 1988 and to the Training Agency later that year. In 1990 the YTS was superseded by Youth Training (YT), with its management becoming decentralised into the Training and Enterprise Councils (TECs), of which eighty-two were established in England and Wales (and twenty-two Local Enterprise Companies in Scotland) by the end of 1990 (DoE, 1990b).

TECs are employer-led, locally based private companies which – through a contract with the Department of Employment – are responsible for the detailed management and provision of training in their area, including YT and compacts (see also Chapter 8). Based on the Private Industry Councils in the USA established in the early 1980s to run federally funded training programmes, the TECs have a chief executive, and larger ones employ up to sixty staff. Membership of the TECs comprises two-thirds employers at top management level drawn from the private sector, and one-third senior figures from local education, training and economic development activities, voluntary bodies and trade unions (DoE, 1988a). They are legally independent but work in association with local education authorities, further education colleges, enterprise activities, business organisations, Chambers of Commerce and the Confederation of British Industry (CBI). It is noteworthy that, almost as soon as the TECs took over responsibility, the interest of many of them began to move from the primary purpose for which they were established, namely the development and management of youth training, to local economic development with or without a training focus.

Central responsibility for YT lies with the Training, Enterprise and Education Directorate (TEED) of the Department of Employment, which replaced the Training Agency in 1990. There are echoes, here, of some features of the Training Boards of the 1960s and of the structures of local education authorities whose powers central government has substantially reduced.

How substantially – and in what form – YT will continue into the 1990s is unclear, but some recent developments (see further below) suggest its less

167

prescriptive nature than the YTS has yielded more diversified and regionalised programmes, in style, duration and management. The 'Youth Guarantee', by which the government guaranteed to provide two years of training for all 16–18-year-olds through the then YTS, is seen by some, however, to be undermined by the freedom that has been given to – and taken by – TECs to vary and reduce the time requirements for YT.

THE EVOLVING DESIGN OF THE YOUTH TRAINING SCHEME

The YTS from its inception included the main curriculum objectives associated with the new, employment-led interpretation of the training needs of the country: work-based learning; increased motivation and positive attitudes to work; emphasis on acquiring definable, measurable skills and nationally recognised qualifications; an attempt to make these skills broad-based and transferable. Apart from some dubious assumptions about 'skill' and the ability to analyse skill independently of broader contexts (subject matter; field of application; personality; social context of values), the main curriculum objectives of the YTS have related well and contributed to the new directions being taken by the country's educational and training systems.

The content of the YTS was the responsibility of the MSC, with room for local diversity of implementation. Individual schemes have been a matter for individual managing agents – originally local employers and local authorities in about equal numbers – within guidelines laid down by the MSC and influenced by local MSC advisers and quality controllers. The extension of the YTS to a second year, and the momentum of the scheme, engendered change, principally increasing standardisation and regulation. The MSC was in a hurry and the YTS developed as it went along without the benefit of trialling or systematic evaluation, and always driven by political responses to the currently perceived state of the labour market and to the economy more generally.

The aims of the YTS were formulated not as straightforward training objectives, or as a curriculum or syllabus as commonly understood in education and training circles. The contents were initially expressed in the accountability movement's instrumentalist language of *inputs and outcomes*, an approach retained, although subsequently refined. A confusing aspect of the early YTS was its lack of clear language and therefore of intention, probably explained by its possibly conflicting responsibilities. A major problem, as in all schemes based on the oversimplification of 'input–outcome' analysis, is to relate these to a diverse *context*, to the interests and needs of various *actors* and to an uncertain *impact*, to name but three of the dimensions of change which educators need to examine in planning and assessing reform movements.

Its design passed through several distinct stages in the early years: the first YTS scheme design and content (YTS, 1984b); the revised design framework

(YTS, 1984a); and the proposals for the two-year YTS (MSC, 1985c). These represent a progressive refinement of the design, as well as crystallisation of the characteristics of new vocationalist policies. An initial uncertainty about what was intended in curriculum terms – which bewildered, or was ignored by, those providing the training – nevertheless served to foster a creative potential, a distinct feature of the original design. Subsequent designs have

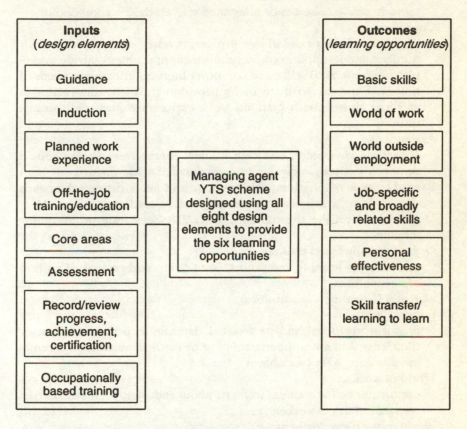

Figure 7.1 The first YTS design and content
Source: YTS (1984b, p.5)

been progressively clearer, more vigorous and more familiar to employers. The elements of the design framework for the initial YTS, as shown in Figure 7.1, were elaborated as follows:

Inputs (design elements)
Guidance
    every trainee must have a named person responsible for reviewing
    progress

Induction
> planned induction to meet needs of trainees on entry to scheme, and at each new stage

Planned work experience
> planned work experience, major locus of learning, will enable the trainee to learn by doing in a work context

Off-the-job training/education
> requiring close liaison to be integrated with on-the-job components

Core areas
> five areas of skills needed to a greater or lesser extent in all jobs: number and its application; communication; problem-solving and planning; practical skills; and computer literacy/information technology. Exposure to them to be provided through work-related activities during both planned work experience and off-the-job training

Assessment
> systematic assessment, involving trainees themselves – initial, continuous to gauge progress, and summative of achievements

Record/review of progress, achievement and certification schemes
> should have a systematic reviewing and recording process. All trainees to receive the standard MSC YTS Certificate on leaving scheme

Occupationally based training
> introductory training and skills related to a broad group or family of occupations

Outcomes (learning opportunities)

Basic skills
> practical, technical and personal skills basic to progression and transfer within employment, training or further education. These include core skills (see above)

World of work
> opportunities for trainees to learn about industry, their role and responsibilities as workers, etc.

World outside employment
> contribution of individuals and companies to the community, development of trainees' own interests and abilities outside work, understanding of community as a whole

Job-specific and broadly related skills
> opportunity to acquire a broad range of skills related to a family of occupations

Personal effectiveness
> opportunity to develop as workers and adults in key areas such as problem-solving and planning, interpersonal skills, responsibility for own lives, etc.

170

Skill transfer/learning to learn
> opportunity for trainees to identify and learn skills built on and used in new tasks, jobs or occupations, and develop own learning skills
>> (Source: YTS, 1984b, pp.3–6)

Notice that the outputs were characterised as learning opportunities, not learning *per se*. This feature, together with the generality of the analysis and the initial lack of detailed guidance, provided ample scope for trainers to develop their own schemes. During its first period, the main YTS effort was in launching the scheme nationwide – a considerable achievement in itself. Once the YTS was safely in operation, the MSC gave priority to a greater specificity of both 'inputs' and 'outputs', improving quality and tackling the increasingly pressing questions of assessment, recording and certification.

The notion of 'core areas' featured from the beginning, in the expectation that a common foundation of competence could be defined for all jobs regardless of their specific content requirements. However, the core concept as introduced through the YTS into the vocational tradition of job-specific skills perplexed trainers from the start, and the Core Skills Project, which ran from July 1982 to December 1985 within the MSC, was set up to develop the concept and show its applications in training practice. Partly financed by a grant from the European Social Fund (ESF), it was itself to experience difficulties in the first of its objectives – namely, to provide a list of transferable core skills that might underlie all of the particular schemes whatever their substantive content. As we have seen in Chapters 3 and 5, great importance was attached by both the MSC and the NCVQ to the role of generic or basic skill acquisition in providing a broad-based training with genuinely transferable qualities. But the fact that these skills were not, indeed could not be in the time available, clearly defined from the outset weakened their potential influence on the content of the YTS and left something of a vacuum, or at least some ambiguous ideas, at its centre. We return to these issues arising from the Core Skills Project below.

REVISED DESIGN FRAMEWORK

Figure 7.2 shows how the YTS design framework (YTS, 1984a) was revised after the first year of operation.
An ostensibly simpler, clearer and more coherent framework for delivering the outcomes was planned, reducing them to four:

- competence in a job and/or a range of occupational skills;
- competence in a range of transferable core skills;
- ability to transfer skills and knowledge to new situations;
- personal effectiveness.

171

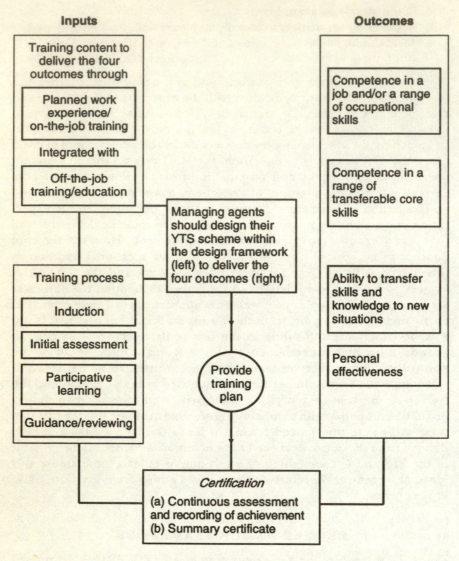

Figure 7.2 The revised YTS design framework

Source: YTS (1984a)

There were no longer 'opportunities' but expected learnings. Even if the average manager responsible for training was bewildered by some of the wording, the familiar areas were easier to pick out: the acquisition of occupational skills and job competence through planned work experience; and reaching agreed standards of performance in a range of tasks. What was less easy to grasp was the nature of the experiential process which, in the varied and numerous field settings (to say nothing of individual differences among trainees), would constitute the vital bonds between 'inputs' and 'outcomes'.

A consequence of the sharper focus and greater concentration achieved through the revised design framework is that the aforementioned dimensions of 'context' and 'impact' were driven even further towards the periphery of the design frame. On the other hand the YTS managers were conscious of the need to give greater attention to process. A renewed focus was also evident on assessment, recording and certification procedures, intended to clarify standards. Certification was to be related directly to the four outcomes and recorded in a new instrument – the Record of Achievement – which gave guidance on the different kinds of standards which could be applied to performance in each outcome. Inputs were also clarified and more tightly structured. There was a distinguishable tilt in design and content towards developing occupational skills and job competence as vehicles for the other three outcomes. This consequent unbalancing of the originally equal line-up of objectives was emphasised by reducing the role of off-the-job training and education in schemes run by companies. Though an integral part of YTS philosophy from the beginning, participatory learning was identified separately for the first time as:

• experiential learning, learning through doing, emphasis on skills and tasks rather than abstracted knowledge or theory;
• involving the trainee in solving problems, reviewing progress, negotiating activities, etc.

CORE SKILLS MANUAL

In September of the same year, the manual *Core Skills in YTS* (MSC, 1984a) was published, but not generally available to managers and trainers until December 1984 or January 1985. This lists 103 skills (organised into fourteen skill groups – see Table 7.1) as common to a range of tasks and necessary to the satisfactory completion of them. Despite the increased refinement of the design, as evidenced in the recognition of such concepts as activity and experiential learning, molar learning processes (for example, problem-solving and negotiated inquiry) and more responsive procedures for assessment (for example, the Record of Achievement), the list of skills and the enthusiasm for a set of national norms whereby they might be referenced underlined a continuing faith in an extreme form of rationalistic planning. The message was: specify the skills, define the norms, design the tests. On the one hand, the list of skills was too lengthy and detailed; on the other, the actual problems of curriculum design and implementation are a deal more complex than this oversimplified, instrumentalist approach implies and guidance on them was lacking, in the early days at least.

173

Table 7.1 Core skill groups proposed by the MSC Core Skills Project

Number

1 Operating with numbers
2 Interpreting numerical and related information
3 Estimating
4 Measuring and marking out
5 Recognising cost and value

Communication

6 Finding out information and interpreting instructions
7 Providing information
8 Working with people

Problem-solving

9 Planning: determining and revising courses of action
10 Decision-making: choosing between alternatives
11 Monitoring: keeping track of progress and checking

Practical

12 Preparing for a practical activity
13 Carrying out a practical activity
14 Finishing off a practical activity

Source: MSC (1984a)

The four major core skill areas adopted in the 1984 revision were: number, communication, problem-solving and practical skills, with the fifth – computing and information technology – set on one side because the skills required were considered to be of a different order. (Details on this area were subsequently published separately: see MSC, 1985a.) In order to enhance the objective of transferability of the skill between one job and another, each individual core skill had an active verb built into it (estimate, interpret, handle, etc.) and was located in one of the fourteen skill groups (such as 'Interpreting numerical and related information'). The list derived from an empirical investigation of skills said to be needed in a variety of jobs and occupations. It bore little resemblance to other contemporary approaches to the term 'core', such as core learnings or a core curriculum, which, as we have seen in Chapter 3, focus on learning which is formative and developmental in a broadly defined educational sense. Furthermore, despite aspirations, there was no systematic effort to look ahead and to project the kinds of 'skills' that might be of most value in the society of the future. Admittedly a formidable task, it is a logical consequence of the underlying strategy: train now for an effect on employment over the next decade or so. In two senses, therefore, core skills proponents were venturing into uncharted seas: seeking on the one hand a 'Northwest passage' from the known territory of vocation-specific competences to content-free, generic skills, and, on the other hand, aiming to anticipate future skills needs of industry.

Core skills were not optional, but were from the start a part of the minimum criteria for training schemes. Initially formulated as both inputs and outcomes, they were restricted to outcomes in the revised design, a clear anticipation of the outcomes orientation of the NVQs. They were originally intended to underpin the work-based nature of the YTS as a general training programme, and to provide a method for developing the potential of work experience beyond narrow or overspecialised and inflexible vocational training. The interrelated concepts of a content-free core and of transferability are fundamental to the whole YTS strategy and its programme design. Shorn of the concept of transferable core skills, the YTS, particularly when provided increasingly by employers rather than in further education (FE) colleges, would offer only what might be quite limited job experience and a range of narrow skills, that is, no real improvement on the old order. The core skills concept therefore had to bear much of the weight of the aspirations for fundamental reform in and through the YTS.

While core skills were essential to the original concept of the YTS, there were two major difficulties in putting them into operation. First, not enough work, either conceptual or empirical, had been done on them when the YTS was rapidly assembled. Thus in the first formative period of the YTS, schemes had to be devised before the core skills were available as a published list with guidance. Many managing agents, not sufficiently understanding core skills and their purpose, or frankly bewildered by the language in which they were described and the multiplicity of aims attributed to them, either overtly or tacitly ignored them. Therefore there were only a few local schemes – and mostly those closely associated with MSC Regional Centres – which genuinely tried to realise their training potential. A good part of the new national youth training scheme started off without one of its supposedly essential components, and kept going. This tended not only to undermine the role of core skills from the start but also to bring into question just what it was that was 'new' about the new philosophy of training, as distinct from the money and the administrative structures.

The second difficulty was in the new form or concept and hence in ways of assessing performance in core skills. They were not conceived as abstract skills, because work-based skills seemed more likely to motivate the trainee and attract the employer. But they were deliberately general rather than occupationally specific; this was essential to realising the idea of skill transfer. An unresolved contradiction lay at their heart. In spite of this, the MSC planned to assess core skills to national standards, which inevitably led to the problems both of contextualising them in occupation terms and giving them an absolute quality prior to any attempt to standardise or even to trial and evaluate them in any serious and controlled fashion. There was, from the beginning, a major difficulty in attaching standards and accreditable levels to core skills, although levels of performance could be inferred from the context in which the skills were demonstrated. They were, however, essentially intended to be free of any specific context so as to be transferable. The real difficulties in the way of making judgements about levels hindered progress on incorporating core skills into schemes, and on assessment.

The difficulty of producing a convincing system for assessing core skills to national standards jeopardised the central position of core skills in the YTS, at the stage when MSC attention focused sharply on the acquisition in the YTS of measurable attainments and nationally recognised qualifications. The line from awareness of this difficulty to the structures of assessment adopted subsequently by the NCVQ is clear to see. The timing of different elements in the rapidly evolving YTS lacked coherence and the overall planning can therefore be criticised for lacking rigour and foresight. No easy resolution can be found to these dilemmas and commendable efforts were made to address them. It is clear that the pace of change was too rapid for the necessary empirical, analytical critical studies to be conducted and the no less necessary reflective interchanges to occur among practitioners, researchers, theoreticians and policy-makers. How far these difficulties have been addressed and are being overcome is a question that must be posed to those responsible for the new national vocational qualifications.

THE TWO-YEAR YOUTH TRAINING SCHEME

In April 1985 the White Paper *Education and Training for Young People* outlined the main elements of an expanded and developed two-year YTS which would, it said, become a permanent feature of vocational education and training provision. This was the third definable refinement in YTS content and design:

> Work continues to improve the Scheme further. The great majority of those schemes and opportunities which do not currently meet the minimum criteria will do so by the end of the year. Better methods to chart training performance and achievement are being developed. The YTS certificate is being improved, with recognition for achievement in mind. Work is in hand to enable trainees to secure credit towards the award of CPVE [Certificate of Pre-vocational Education].
>
> (DES, 1985b, p.4)

Scarcely had one set of design problems been clarified, let alone resolved, when a further set emerged. Everything was in the category of 'work in hand – problem being addressed'. It is difficult to escape the impression that the policy-makers and developers in the first five years of the YTS were working hard into a fierce wind on a lee shore, constantly changing tack to better position themselves in order to keep off the rocks.

176

Figure 7.3 shows the two-year YTS design framework recommended by the MSC Working Group on Training Objectives and Content (MSC, 1985c, p.16) in response to the White Paper (DES, 1985b).

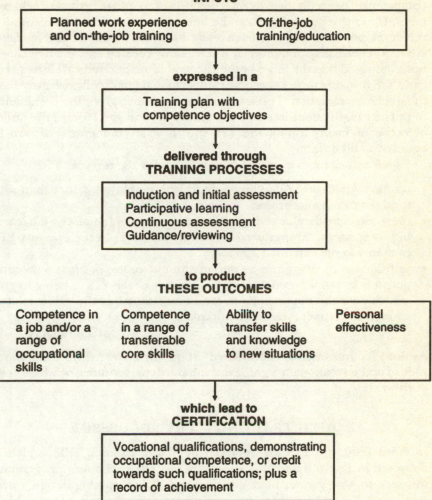

Training content to be delivered through integrated
INPUTS

| Planned work experience and on-the-job training | Off-the-job training/education |

expressed in a

Training plan with competence objectives

delivered through
TRAINING PROCESSES

Induction and initial assessment
Participative learning
Continuous assessment
Guidance/reviewing

to product
THESE OUTCOMES

| Competence in a job and/or a range of occupational skills | Competence in a range of transferable core skills | Ability to transfer skills and knowledge to new situations | Personal effectiveness |

which lead to
CERTIFICATION

Vocational qualifications, demonstrating occupational competence, or credit towards such qualifications; plus a record of achievement

Figure 7.3 The new design framework for the two-year YTS

Source: MSC (1985c, p.16)

The main difference we see emerging in Figure 7.3 is in the relationship between outcomes and certification. The earlier model, though perhaps deliberately unclear, gave a special emphasis, considerable space and at least symbolic importance to outcomes, while certification was squashed in at the foot of the page. In the two-year YTS design framework, outcomes became harnessed to the objective of certification. The *aim* of the extended YTS was the translation of outcomes (formerly 'learning opportunities') into certification: vocational qualifications, demonstrating occupational competence, or credit towards such qualifications; plus a record of achievement. Up to this point there was the optimistic sense that the outcomes – the development of the competences and abilities – were an end in themselves. Credentialism, however, is not so easily resisted and the new directions indicated that the more optimistic, ambitious and radical elements of early YTS thinking were to become captive to that familiar British guardian: the public examination. This was perhaps inevitable, given the dominance of public examinations in schooling at and beyond age 16, and the policy objective of incorporating the YTS into a wider framework of post-16 education and training.

Significant changes occurred in the design for the two-year YTS:

- training was to take place increasingly with employers rather than with local education authorities;
- there was considerable reduction in importance of the off-the-job learning component, now reduced from thirteen weeks in the one-year YTS to twenty in the extended scheme;
- priority was openly given to one of the outcomes, occupational competence, by publicly redefining the objective of the YTS as being to give 'all trainees the opportunity to seek a vocational qualification related strongly to competence in the workplace'

(MSC, 1985c, p.4)

As the YTS thus became 'normalised', it quietly retreated from the more radical and educationally significant, if hazardous, ventures, of which core skills was one.

YOUTH TRAINING – THE SUCCESSOR

In April 1990, the YTS was replaced by Youth Training (YT), which is delivered in England and Wales through the TECs. The new programme was seen to have greater flexibility than the YTS in training design, duration, eligibility and funding, with, as we have seen, the relaxation of both the fixed two-year training requirement and the mandatory length of off-the-job training. The TEC argument was that 'local solutions to local needs do not need centrally designed and imposed training programmes' (D. Skillen, 1992, personal communication). Indeed, some TECs wish to make a clear break with YT (DoE, n.d.). Considerable variety now exists in the type of training, length of training, amount of on- and off-the-job training offered throughout England and Wales. Provisional figures from the DoE indicate some 260,000 young people were in training with YT in England and Wales in March 1992 (DoE, 1992, p.33).

While there is no formal link between apprenticeships and YT, about 52,000 of those on YT (that is, about one in five) may be termed 'apprentices'. In practice YT is increasingly being used as the vehicle for apprenticeship training in areas such as construction and hairdressing. Money from YT added to the employer's contribution gives the trainee two years' training leading to an NVQ, often with off-the-job training in an FE college. After completing the two-year YT, trainees not uncommonly continue their training at their own or their employers' expense. This link in practice between apprenticeship and the earlier YTS also existed, but was not so widespread, partly because YTS training did not necessarily lead to recognised qualifications (D. Short, personal communication).

Objectives for YT include a minimum attainment level for young people on the programme of NVQ level 2, with a strong emphasis to be given to achieving higher-level skills, particularly at craft and technician level. It appears that with the increased diversity of provision through the different TECs, direct concern for matters such as core skills is now mediated through whatever arrangements or requirements exist within those NVQs undertaken by individual trainees. In other words, the NCVQ, rather than the YT authorities, have effectively assumed the running on core skills matters.

In 1990/1, YT saw the piloting of a system of training credits – essentially a system whereby 16- and 17-year-old school-leavers are given a voucher entitling them to a credit specifying a certain monetary value (typically £1,000) which can be exchanged for vocational education and training.

All credit arrangements will need to have, as their objectives, increases in the extent of training and in the attainment of skills. Each scheme will need to include quality careers advice and guidance so that young people make the best choices about use of their credits. In all cases, the training will have to be: to approved standards and skill levels through recognised qualifications (e.g. National Vocational Qualifications); approved by the TEC; and relevant to the needs of employers. Arrangements should build on the processes developed under TVEI and other initiatives that support the National Record of Achievement.

(DoE, 1991a, p.5)

Credits are seen as a way of strengthening the motivation of young people to train, and to train to higher standards, to bring greater efficiency into the training market, and to make training which is relevant to employers' needs an accepted part of normal working life. Whether these aims are achieved, or whether training credits will prove yet another costly diversionary episode (both in direct and opportunity cost terms) in the history of the new vocationalism remains to be seen. The intent among policy-makers is to extend training credits to all areas by 1996 (IFAPLAN/ITS, 1992).

Although terms like 'credit' and 'voucher' suggest a new direction, how different in principle are the credits from old-style scholarships to fee-charging institutions? The main difference seems to be the notion of entitlement, a credit is not so much a privilege gained through achievement as a right conferred on school-leavers. But, it may be asked, why is such a right not also available to those staying on in school? The answer lies not only in the motivational point but also in the determination of policy-makers to continue some form of training, parallel to but separate from schooling.

Following the increasing emphasis on assessed achievement we have noted over the history of the new vocationalism, it is not entirely surprising to note a further change in 1992/3, whereby – ostensibly to increase the effectiveness of the scheme – 25 per cent of the TECs' funding from the Employment Department was made conditional on their meeting the targets set for qualification levels for each TEC, through negotiation with the Employment Department (IFAPLAN/ITS, 1992). There is considerable potential for conflict between the Employment Department, with its emphasis on training outcomes, employment linked, and the TECs, with their more diverse, local development interests.

TRENDS WITHIN THE YOUTH TRAINING SCHEME

Towards accrediting achievement

To return to the development of the YTS, if core skills suffered displacement before the necessary conceptual analysis and field testing had been conducted, there were other significant innovations which could be more readily accommodated within traditional structures and practices. 'Modularisation' is one of these, and it has indeed taken hold.

A visible result of the pressure for quality and clear standards, accreditation and nationally recognised qualifications, and increased priority for the occupational competence objective in the two-year YTS, was the introduction by the MSC of a policy for a modular framework of accrediting achievement. This represented a major shift, from curriculum analysis (pushing) to examinations (pulling); it also signified a determination to break some of the classical rigidities of vocational training: time on task; prescribed sequences and groupings of content; and the inability or unwillingness to formalise experiential learning. On the other hand, it symbolised a retreat towards the convention of credentialling.

A module was defined as a unit of achievement which could be independently assessed and accredited. As acquired by an average trainee, it might be defined in terms of criteria or standards, and eventually be seen as evidence of certain demonstrable skills (like a driving test) which no longer had a specific timescale attached to it. Trainees would obtain a number of modules which would constitute a block of achievement. The scope of a module might be a group of related tasks and activities which occur together in the workplace (that is, within a job) or which are related sequentially for the purposes of training but which may be of a variable time duration. Modules could be delivered either through learning in the workplace or through task-based learning off-the-job. Requirements for knowledge, principles and theory, beyond those needed for the performance of the tasks, can be built into the modules. Alternatively, they can be pushed to one side. The standards of achievement upon which the modules are based should be criterion-referenced to meet the requirements of the *NTI*. The *NTI* also demanded that accreditation of skills and knowledge should be open to everyone by whatever route and at whatever age competence is achieved. And so standards of achievement in modules could be demonstrated without having undergone a prescribed course of training, and could take into account prior learning, learning from experience and so on (Jessup, 1985). This separation of curriculum and institution from attained and ascertained competence has proved to be an important precursor of the NVQ system.

There were many innovative features in this proposal but, their significance notwithstanding, the separate elements of criterion-referencing and time-free mastery learning are not to be numbered among them. Both were familiar in the domain of educational assessment and learning theory well before the YTS was established. It is the whole package, with its distinctive mode of delivery in the workplace, not the single elements, that differentiated the YTS in this, the third design phase, from other forms of education and training. As occupational competence became the dominant motif, and assessed outcomes came to be seen as a major target, the package itself, however, began to resemble well-established practice in the training and further education fields. The work-based learning element then became its most distinctive feature, together with modularisation. The module idea, although not new, represented a fundamental break with the tradition of a sequential and integrated training curriculum incorporating a craft- or occupation-based principle of coherence. A modular system which is competency-based provides the opportunity for assembling quite diverse units into a multiplicity of programmes, and for substantially varying these programmes should the need arise. What must also be noted is that the work-based learning, notwithstanding the emphasis given to it in this design phase, bears no logical relationship to the insistence on outcome-defined competence. Indeed, logically such competences are the ultimate test – not the work or any other context in which they are, supposedly, best acquired.

Scotland had led the way with modularisation. Reporting in 1985, the MSC Working Group on Training Objectives and Content were 'impressed by the speed of progress made in the Scottish Education system with the 16+ Action Plan' (MSC, 1985c, p.10), a momentum, as we have seen, subsequently maintained (Tuck, 1992).

While likely to be occupationally based, the modular system as such, like the outcomes focus, need not be tied to particular occupations or indeed to countries. The way is opened for international as well as national co-ordination. The original feature of the YTS was indeed a broad-based training, to which the modular system lent itself. Its progressive acceptance of performance outcomes cut it free of any particular learning experiences or settings.

For technical reasons, the modules seemed unlikely to cover achievement in the other three YTS objectives – core skills, transfer and personal effectiveness – although this is not ruled out in principle. Modules of transferable skills could perhaps be developed which reflect achievement in more than one context. Modules of personal effectiveness present more difficulties, since they are seldom if ever the subject of stringent measurement; likewise there are difficulties for core skills because of the perceived problems of attaching levels to them. The principal point we want to make, however, is that, whatever direction the contingencies of the work situation or training preferences might take the YTS, and the specific difficulties in operationalising concepts, the fundamental structure of 'modules and competency' is highly flexible and, ultimately, context and curriculum free. Modular structures are not, however, without their weaknesses, the principal ones being their tendency on the one hand to fragment learning and, on the other, to generate massive regulatory procedures and attendant bureaucracies.

As we have seen, the revised design produced after the first year of operation of the YTS increased emphasis on trainee achievement, on recording, assessment and certification procedures. Certification was to be directly related to the four outcomes and achievement recorded in a new instrument – the Record of Achievement. There were signs that one outcome – the acquisition of occupational skills and job competence through planned work experience – was to be given priority.

By the end of 1985, the YTS was taking a recognisable shape, familiar in its compromises and inconsistencies to educators and trainers. The new two-year YTS emerged as primarily employer-based with increased emphasis on ensuring the relevance of off-the-job training, and its integration with the remainder of the programme. The two-year framework for training in occupational competence – envisaging a broad-based foundation training in the first year leading to a more specialised vocational training in the second – and an undertaking that all trainees should have the opportunity to seek recognised vocational qualifications, brought the YTS much closer to established education and training procedures. Emphasis on certification and qualification leading to the formulation of a policy of modules of achievement, in an attempt to reconcile objectives stated in terms of outputs with operations in terms of level of performance, is a direction that has been increasingly followed as the national assessment structure has emerged.

In the space of its first few years of life, the YTS changed from a *one-year generic course* in work-based learning with quite radical curricular and pedagogical aspirations, to a permanent *two-year programme for basic occupational competence*, incorporating a more general foundation year and an occupation-specific second year, expressed in assessable learning units which loomed ever larger as the scheme progressed. What the scheme gained in acceptability and credibility in practice it lost in innovativeness and radical thinking. According to some students of educational innovation, such 'domestication' is necessary if the new idea is to take root (Cuban, 1990). However, adaptation to the exigencies of time and place can mean a loss to the extent that the opportunity for continuing the search for new pathways is prematurely forgone.

By the beginning of 1989, the government seemed to retreat from the *NTI* aim it had supported for several years so vigorously, namely getting all of the under 18-year-olds not in regular employment to stay in education or training. The government told the Training Agency to cease insisting that a full two-year YTS programme be offered by employers and agencies to school-leavers, though not the unemployed. Also, the twenty weeks off-the-job training would no longer be compulsory for school-leavers.

This left the only mandatory element in the YTS as leading to an acceptable qualification, preferably one endorsed by the NCQV. This decision effectively meant that three of the four original YTS outcomes – personal effectiveness, core skills and transferability – had, by the end of the decade, been dropped or relegated.

The relaxing of these requirements by the government was widely, at the time and correctly as events proved, seen as preparing the YTS for hand-over, a pre-semi-privatisation exercise (making it more attractive), to the Training and Enterprise Councils, and anticipating the ending of the YTS and the commencement of YT. The government has reduced both its financial and administrative commitment through this change and in so doing covered its retreat from many of the principles which informed the earlier stages of this innovative programme.

The tendency for the YTS to become assimilated into recognisable educational and training patterns through a process of accommodation to the environment in which it operates is nowhere more evident than in the area of assessment and qualifications. With the establishment of the NCVQ and the growth of qualification-led planning in both youth training and school curriculum policies, the assessment issue has emerged as a dominant motif in the government strategies for the 1990s. From another perspective, the YTS may be seen as the progenitor of major structural changes including national assessment of training.

Towards assessment and qualifications

Thus the pressure for quality and measurable standards, accreditation and nationally recognised qualifications grew with the initial viability and vitality of the YTS. Expounding what he termed 'the qualifications business', George Tolley all too tellingly remarked: 'There is much in the process of education that can be described, simply and profoundly, as labelling' (Tolley, 1986, p.708). The characteristics of the new vocationalism were evolving in the early years of the YTS. The same White Paper which confirmed the existence of the YTS and invited the MSC to advise on its two-year form, also called upon the MSC to review the overall structure of vocational qualifications in England and Wales. The picture of government intentions for the YTS shifted into focus at this stage. As we have seen in Chapter 5, the MSC was asked to recommend a system of vocational qualifications and concentrate initially on the vocational qualification aspects of the YTS. The next stage in the development of the YTS was linked closely with the Review of Vocational Qualifications (RVQ) and, as we saw in the developing programme of the NCVQ in Chapter 5, this conceptual link has taken its place as an important part of the new vocationalism philosophy.

The government drive to rationalise the national vocational qualification system was activated by the growing demand in the YTS for a system of assessment yielding credible accreditation and nationally recognised qualifications. Reform was much needed; not surprisingly, the campaign has gathered its own momentum. Paradoxically, it now looks like overwhelming the innovations it was principally designed to serve, a feature which again links this programme with what has become the educational and training mainstream. The obsession with an *a priori* concept of 'levels' of performance and with measurable behaviours is a reminder that the British tradition combines, with robust common sense, a fondness for calculation almost regardless of the consequences. A reduction of the multiple forms of human action and attainment to a single system of 'levels', wherein the subtleties and interrelationships of knowledge and capability are subject to a single measure, is an extreme form of scientism which presents an easy target to sceptics and critics. Although it appeared to be part of the fundamental logic of the new vocationalism as it was formulated through the policies and programmes of the MSC, this signifies yet another avoidable wrong turn in the new vocationalism, a tendency to go to extremes: too much diversity replaced by too much uniformity.

The YTS Certification Board was set up in April 1986, following the report of the RVQ. Its main task was to obtain qualifications for the YTS based on employers' standards of competence. These should record not only knowledge but the application of skills and of knowledge. Until the appropriate examining and validating bodies had devised qualifications which met these requirements, the Certification Board would make do with existing ones: those mainly of the Business and Technician Education Council (BTEC), City and Guilds of London Institute (CGLI), the Royal Society of Arts (RSA) and the Scottish Vocational Education Council (SCOTVEC), whose representatives made up the membership of the Board. Because the NCVQ was being set up to reform vocational qualifications generally, the members of the YTS Certification Board were initially only appointed for one year; but its life was subsequently extended.

These new outcomes of the YTS are a far cry from the contents of the first YTS design of only four years previously. An enormous amount of rationalisation of activity had taken place, as shown in this perhaps over-confident statement:

> At the heart of the work of the YTS Certification Board lies the concept of workplace competence which comprises three important elements: skill, knowledge and the application of both these in the performance of relevant tasks.
>
> (McFall, 1987, p.20)

The frenetic activity which followed the announcement of the two-year YTS included also the introduction of Approved Training Organisation (ATO) status, designed to ensure that the YTS was 'delivered only by professional and proficient providers of quality training' (YTS, 1987, p.vi). The MSC was to move progressively towards a position where training was provided only by approved bodies, by means of an interim stage (April 1987) at which all organisations offering training would have been given full approval, provisional approval or rejection.

Towards competence and standards

'At the heart of this initiative lie standards of a new kind' (MSC, 1981b, p.6). This *NTI* statement was implemented through YTS activities culminating in the establishment of the YTS Certification Board, and the NCVQ. The catalytic role of the MSC was decisive. Preoccupied with quality and standards since the introduction of the YTS, MSC-backed developments have wrought a remarkable change. Jessup put the MSC view disarmingly in this way:

> Underlying the moves towards new forms of qualifications is the belief that VET [vocational education and training] needs to pay more attention to preparing people for employment. The sets of objectives for education and vocational training are both, of course, legitimate and desirable but we should be clear within any programme of learning what our objectives are.
>
> The recent white paper 'Education and Training – Working Together' clearly shifted to industry and employers the responsibility

for setting the standards for education and training. It is now up to industry to indicate the needs of employment.

(Jessup, 1987, p.1)

Industry, however, is far from homogeneous. Its signals are varied, uneven and often vague. Many parts of industry lack long-term strategies or a clear sense of responsibility for the training of the workforce. Industry is not the only significant interest to be considered in determining standards for education and training.

Industry and commerce were in a weak position to indicate the needs of employment when much of their energy in the 1980s was devoted to shedding employees and engaging in financial manoeuvres unrelated to either the needs of the workforce or of the national economy.

The influence of the new vocationalism can be detected in activating welcome moves within some sectors of industry and commerce and among the examining bodies to define competence and standards; but it is also responsible in part for less welcome results – principally the continuing divide between education and training. Perhaps deliberately, little effort has been made to define the overlap and differences between the two terms.

In the early stages, the historically separate cultures of education and training seemed to some observers to be reconcilable within the YTS, but some developments, and particularly the emphasis on a set of employer-based standards of competence, revealed a considerable divide, and possibly narrowed the potential of work-based learning. If this divide is assimilated as part of its philosophy, the new vocationalism should be viewed with some suspicion. The loss of off-the-job training as a compulsory component was not an encouraging omen in the YTS.

It is therefore appropriate to ask the question, whose standards are setting the benchmarks? Which interests are being served? A true partnership between education, training, industry (and employment generally), the wider community and – not least – the trainees is ultimately required. Each has a perception of standards and a contribution to make to their delineation. A practical way of creating this partnership in the sphere of training has yet to be determined. The politicisation of the process, including a generally negative attitude towards full trade union and wider education agency participation and involvement in evolving education and training policies, has been unhelpful in achieving the much needed national approach.

THE FOUR YOUTH TRAINING SCHEME OUTCOMES IN REVIEW

We suggested earlier in this chapter that in the course of its rapid evolution, the YTS progressively narrowed its focus. This is illustrated in the paring down of the projected outcomes which, taken together and fully developed, might have provided a broad-based national training scheme.

Achieving competence in a range of occupational skills

Competence in skills broadly defined for their occupational relevance is the most concrete of the YTS outcomes, the most accessible and most easily accredited. But it was never the sole objective and it is evident that, as originally planned, the YTS wanted to avoid the restrictions of a narrow vocational training. But since the MSC used in the YTS the devices of inputs, outputs and criteria rather than a fully worked out curriculum framework, the sort of learning which was provided within it depended a lot on the relative weight given to each of the four outcomes by managing agents, and on how the acquisition of occupational skills interacted with the other three outcomes. Trainees on the YTS learnt occupational skills and, presumably, became increasingly employable. (The latter, however, is relative to labour market demands, and 'employable' is a predisposing condition not to be confused with 'to be employed'.) There is equally little doubt that the YTS went some way towards reducing the *NTI* figure of 40 per cent of school-leavers unqualified. What is not clear, though, is either the contribution made by much wider changes in labour market conditions and the impact of demography, or the longer-term formative value of an innovation that has never been thoroughly evaluated.

It is not easy to assess the range of occupational skills covered by trainees and how far a YTS training would achieve a broad preparation for working life, as distinct from short-term competence in a specific field, and employment either in that field or some other. Some experimental work has been done on the relationship of the skills needed in similar or associated jobs. Jobs can be linked in groups and the trainee taught a skill in one job which is relevant to others. This is the concept of grouping related occupations particularly by identifying process factors common to a number of categories of jobs which may also generally be related in substantive terms. Work on occupational training families has continued over the years and is relevant to the attempt to construct a system of interrelated vocational qualifications. What is learnt in one job is relevant to other, similar and associated, jobs when the trainee is made conscious both of having mastered tasks and competences and of their appearance and application in other jobs. We have seen that the acquisition of occupational skills has to be combined with particular types of teaching to achieve the declared generic objectives. The incorporation, among the four outcomes of the YTS, of transferable core skills provides some potential for this, as do required inputs to the training process such as participatory learning, coursework assessment and trainee reviewing of progress. Even if the acquisition of core skills within training had been reduced in importance as an end in itself, its confirmed existence seems likely to lead to a type of teaching/training which encourages mastery learning and consciousness of the transferable qualities of what is learnt.

Achieving competence in a range of transferable core skills

The second outcome – competence in a range of transferable core skills – was included in the YTS in response to the drive for competence generally, and because it was intended to develop flexibility, adaptability and mobility of the workforce along with the learning/training potential in work experience as the key input in a national training scheme. The focus on competence meant that across the spectrum of the education, training, world of work and validating bodies there was a common recognition that skills or competence were needed from school-leavers for their sake and for improved economic performance. It is necessary to point out that there was absolutely nothing new in this idea; where it differed from common-sense understanding of the outcomes of schooling was in the emphasis, first on a deficiency model (assuming poor levels of attainment, low motivation, etc.) and, second, on renewed efforts to identify work-defined needs. Competence in the core skills was to take young people a step beyond what the schools had achieved and, as some argued, would achieve. It was upgraded in the YTS to an important constituent of preparation for life. The attention given to competence in another sense did represent a departure – from the tradition of low expectations of adolescents and the lazy acceptance of a system wherein the large majority of youth 'completed' schooling by simply leaving at the earliest possible age regardless of what had been learnt.

The YTS aimed to deliver for its target population all that is connoted by the term 'competence' and thereby set itself a most demanding challenge. Competence was seen as dispositional – an attitude, a frame of mind or state of the will – as well as an achievement which could be defined in terms of both learning processes and learning outcomes.

The first YTS outcome had prominence in offering evident occupational competence and the opportunity to acquire specific vocational qualifications. This was an important step, but something broader was needed to engender competence as envisaged and to prepare young people for the future labour market and industrial requirements. This need was recognised by *NTI*, and the MSC came up with the – at that stage – loose concept of core skills which was intended to provide the missing ingredient that would, like yeast, transform the dough. While the core skills outcome in principle had the potential to meet this requirement, it was included in the scheme with, as we have seen, insufficiently defined objectives, and too diverse a range of functions.

The core skills, being conceived as compulsory, as part of the minimum criteria of the YTS, were intended to underpin the work-based nature of the YTS, hence the concept of skill transfer (Levy, 1986). The MSC conceived core skills as an innovatory means of operationalising one of the key requirements of a foundation training envisaged by the *NTI*:

number and its application, communication, problem-solving and planning, practical skills and computer literacy/information technology – these are skills that are needed to a greater or lesser extent in all jobs. Schemes should aim to cover these skills through work-related activities during both the planned work experience and off-the-job training.

(YTS, 1984a, p.4)

Work-based rather than abstract, because that seemed more likely to motivate the trainee and prove welcome to the employer, this linkage, as we have seen, was no sooner made than broken in the preoccupation with context-free 'outcomes' or levels of attainment. Thus, core skills were to be assessed to national standards. Although said to be workplace-derived, as presented they became context-free. The completion of this cycle is the NVQ, which is a hypothetically 'pure' attainment or competence independent of any context. Given the virtual disappearance of the youth labour market and the minimal opportunities for youth to gain meaningful work experience, this may be considered as some kind of practical adaptation of thinking to labour market realities. On the other hand, it calls into question the very foundation of the YTS and the context (work) for which the core skills idea was promulgated. The skills as a core were intended as a 'common language' to assist the learning process and the broader reforms of training. The range of anticipated functions for core skills proved over-ambitious, and their very multiplicity threatened their position within the YTS. Not sufficiently clearly associated in the design of the YTS with one important and concrete objective, they suffered in relation to the other outcomes, and the position of core skills was scaled down to the limited task of giving work-based learning a generic aspect. The future for core skills as conceived in the YTS framework seems bleak, as training has moved increasingly towards the enterprises themselves. The underlying concepts, however, are well worth considering as part of a longer-term strategy, even within specific occupational areas.

Achieving ability to transfer

It has always been clear that the success of the four outcomes in achieving all that the MSC demanded of the YTS depended to a large extent on the positive interaction between them. The acquisition of occupational competence on the level possible for the average 16-year-old leaving school with few educational qualifications and initially only a year of training, and the acquisition of core skills defined in basic terms, might not in practice add up to much more than work experience plus remedial instruction unless the necessarily limited learnings could be infused with the magic ingredient of transferability. The claim that the learning of quite ordinary and mundane skills provides an adequate preparation for life is tied up not just with the skills learnt but also – and quite crucially – with the way the learning is offered by the trainer and seen and used by the trainee.

Some of those responsible for training have taken up the challenge but it is impossible to assess results. Nor is it easy to check to what extent on- and off-the-job learning are linked to enhance transfer. As illustrated in our discussion on transfer in Chapter 3, the teaching of the ability to transfer requires more analytical, developmental and evaluative work than it ever received under YTS auspices. Nor have sophisticated means as yet been devised to assess, accredit and award qualifications for the ability to transfer, although this is a challenge that the NCVQ might regard as highly appropriate. The problem the YTS encountered in this respect was that the nuances of learning processes were submerged beneath over-generalised statements of outcomes which were quickly translated into measurable performances. Inadequate attention was given to the ability to transfer skills learnt in any one context to others, whether from school to work, from family life to work, etc. There has been an excessive preoccupation with defining as 'occupational' or 'core' the skills suitable for transfer and producing catalogues which are then turned into testable performances.

Achieving personal effectiveness

The idea of personal effectiveness, the fourth YTS outcome, in practice suffered from two central difficulties: the first is the question of who should define the acquisition of personal effectiveness, a value-laden concept, and the second, the difficulty of assessing and accrediting progress achieved towards the target. In the first case there is a danger that what constitutes personal effectiveness in the work context could be very narrowly defined on the basis of the self-interest of the controlling parties. In the 'package' of outcomes, the YTS can be seen very broadly as a preparation for life. In this context personal effectiveness could be demonstrated in the development of maturity, of capacity for further, self-directed growth, of individual autonomy; the trainers responsible for using teaching methods needed to enable students to take advantage of skills learnt to transfer them to new situations. This would have built into the YTS inputs and processes a genuine attempt to teach something like the meta-cognitive structures required to enable pupils to exploit and transfer what they have learnt (Biggs, 1985). In curriculum development terms this sort of interpretation would have made the YTS creative. However, personal effectiveness could easily be defined both by the trainer and trainee as becoming more employable and amenable.

The interpretation of personal effectiveness, as so much in the YTS, was naturally influenced by MSC policy generally. In the early form of the YTS, while the scheme was more evenly balanced between the values and loci of the education and training worlds, it seemed likely that personal effectiveness might have the sort of flavour found in comparable educational initiatives – with distinct emphasis on the pupil's own individual growth. But the YTS became much more employer-based, aiming for employer standards of competence. This could mean that personal effectiveness is viewed in terms of positive motivation, punctuality and amenableness (characteristics which it is sought to encourage also through the school–industry compacts discussed in Chapter 8). The MSC emphasis on accreditation of particular kinds of learning and acquisition of recognised vocational qualifications to some extent devalued the outcomes less readily accredited.

Comments on the 'increased maturity' of YTS trainees compared with their age group still in school have come from a number of sources. Welcome as some sort of evidence of attaining the goal, it is difficult to evaluate the implications. It could mean nothing more than the demonstration of an appreciation of the world of work, or increased personal control of progress and performance. Again, it is difficult to reach conclusions about the learning likely to come from this outcome. Provisionally it seems reasonable to see personal effectiveness as one of the areas not accorded the highest priority (reserved for the occupational competence outcome) but which has potential. The retention of personal effectiveness as a distinct outcome, and of training processes which require both participatory learning and individual guidance, meant that there was room in every scheme for an imaginative and creative element of learning for the trainee. In many cases this potential in both the YTS and YT has been ignored or wasted, but it was never ruled out in principle. As the acquisition of core skills outcomes has been progressively denuded of its learning potential by being shackled to competence and vocational qualifications, the personal effectiveness outcome might be seen as carrying on the element of curricular flexibility and educational potential. There is no doubt that for the YTS genuinely to realise its ambitious objectives, both trainers and trainees would have had to develop a broad vision of personal effectiveness.

THE YOUTH TRAINING SCHEME AND ITS SETTING

The Manpower Services Commission

Because the YTS was innovative and experimental, the most comprehensive and large-scale practical endeavour yet in Britain's long struggle to reorient training towards the real conditions of working life, it is scarcely surprising that the MSC, through whose agency practically the whole of the government's new vocational drive occurred, from its inception until its absorption into the Department of Employment, underwent major changes in its own role and structure. Part of this has been the result of managing the disbursement of large sums of government money. To financial responsibility for the scheme was added the assumption of responsibility for a large slice of financing of non-advanced further education and a series of parcels of funds for a range of activities sired by the YTS.

If the MSC's financial responsibilities were far-reaching, its possibilities for direct influence in its relatively short life proved even more so. At all levels, the MSC branches influenced standards setting: through the RVQ (by MSC); the establishment of the NCVQ (advised by MSC); the establishment of the YTS Certification Board to which the submissions for acceptance were made through the MSC, which also offered advice and pump-priming funds; the designation of ATO status; the establishment of Accredited Training Centres where the MSC offered training to those staff involved in the YTS whose training needs were not being met by their organisations; the established role of MSC Regional Centres in advising on training; and an expanding network of publications acting as the mouthpiece of MSC, such as the *Youth Training News* and *Competence and Assessment*. In these and other ways, the MSC dominated the British training scene during the few short years of its life.

Enterprise training in the Youth Training Scheme

In December 1986 Lord Young, then Employment Secretary, announced the introduction of a new initiative to pilot 'enterprise training' in the YTS. The then MSC Director, Geoffrey Holland, said:

> An enterprising young person is one who makes and takes opportunities. YTS aims to develop just such skills, we want all young people to be enterprising in whatever setting they find themselves. This means using their imagination, taking responsibilities for ideas and seeing them through to reality. Enterprise training is a natural part of the personal development of young people on YTS.
>
> (Holland, 1987, p.13)

He added, with echoes of *NTI*, that:

> It is also an economic imperative, British Industry needs more enterprising, risk-taking and adventurous people if we are to compete effectively against our trading rivals. The structure of YTS, which puts emphasis on learning processes and outcomes, is tailor-made to include enterprise training.
>
> (Holland, 1987, p.13)

'Enterprise' has been defined, in terms of skills and abilities, as: to take the initiative; to make decisions; to manage resources; to influence others; to show drive and determination; and to monitor progress. As we see in more detail in Chapter 8, interest in 'enterprise education' grew during the 1980s in both education and training circles, encapsulating a move away from traditional training practices which were criticised for suppressing enterprise and encouraging indifference to work at an early formative stage

192

in the development of young people entering the workforce. The YTS requirement for participatory learning processes, the emphasis on learning how to learn and work-based, activity-centred learning were among the elements of the YTS that fitted well with this new emphasis.

The MSC's development of enterprise training modules of achievement in the YTS perhaps represented a kind of peak of the new vocationalism. A place for creative training existed in the YTS because it did not contain a strictly delineated syllabus; because individual schemes were to be formulated from criteria, inputs and outcomes; because the requirements included participatory learning and review of individual performance. It is noteworthy that this initiative appeared to insist that personal effectiveness be given a spirited rather than an apathetic interpretation, to confound the critics of the YTS who predicted the emergence of a cowed, subdued, robotic, young workforce.

Interest in developing entrepreneurship among youth in the UK had, since the 1970s, developed particularly in areas where youth unemployment was markedly higher than the national norm. Those responsible for youth training there were seeking productive alternatives to a merely 'better trained body of unemployed people', and this strand of concern underpinned the subsequent 'personal effectiveness' objective of the YTS (Ball, 1988, p.85).

Entrain was established as a new organisation, formed by a consortium of training, employment and enterprise development agencies, with an initial three-year brief (1987–90) to develop resources – enterprise modules – and practical assistance required by training schemes to introduce this new form of training within the YTS. The approach taken was for trainees, with the help of supervisors, to identify, plan, run and evaluate enterprise projects, which varied in nature from adventure-focused (for example, an expedition of some kind), community service (for example, environmental improvement project), a business (for example, making goods for sale) to improvements in the scheme in which the young people were being trained (for example, establishing a 'quality circle').

In a review of enterprise activities in some thirteen OECD countries, Ball (1988) saw Entrain as undoubtedly the most ambitious of the post-compulsory initiatives he studied, both in terms of its scale and its scope. He noted:

– Firstly, the essential change required among teachers/trainers is methodological. It says to them that they must change *how* they teach or train.
– Secondly, it shows how very general 'cultural' statements of underlying rationale, as stated by Ministers, can be 'boiled down' to identifying particular 'skills', small in number and clear in nature, and quite simple means of developing them.

(Ball, 1988, p.91)

JUDGING THE SUCCESS OF TRAINING IN THE YOUTH TRAINING SCHEME

The success of the YTS has at one level been judged mainly on the proportion of trainees who got jobs. Department of Employment figures indicate that between April 1989 and March 1990, between 56 per cent (YTS 1985/86 trainees) and 67 per cent (YTS 1988/89 trainees) of YTS leavers were in employment, with approximately half of these remaining with the same employer. Of the balance, between 14 per cent (YTS 1988/89 and 1989/90 trainees) and 28 per cent (YTS 1985/86 trainees) were unemployed, while up to 12 per cent were on another YTS scheme and up to 4 per cent on a full-time course (DoE, 1991b, p.33). It is not possible, however, without more fine-grained analysis to say whether these figures establish a causal link between YTS training and employability.

For obvious reasons, and largely indifferent to the research issues involved, trainees, parents, supervisors and government tended to use the fact of success (or otherwise) in obtaining jobs as a measure of quality of individual schemes, even though this was evidently unfair to schemes situated in areas of disproportionately high unemployment. More important, this predominant indicator of success was of quite limited value in assessing the complex issue of quality; it had no link with the stated objectives of the YTS, nor did it indicate whether trainees were well trained for continuing employment in diverse situations. The government and MSC have been guilty of simplistic thinking when they chose, however understandably, and however much in line with the expectations of trainees themselves, to equate success in getting jobs with successful training. Desirable as was the acquisition of a job (when jobs were available), the government undermined its own broad economic and manpower objectives for the YTS by failing to adopt criteria independent of, or rather supplementary to, short-term success in the job market. Political mileage can be, of course, gained from the judicious publication of employment statistics. Is it being unduly cynical to suggest that particular employment targets were never set as YTS objectives in case the gap between target and achievement proved too wide for political comfort?

Not surprisingly, the participants themselves have taken a hard-nosed view of this purpose of the YTS. Eraut and Burke reported that:

> For the trainees themselves, with exceptions . . . the prime purpose of YTS is enhancing their individual employability, and their perception of the merits of the scheme is dominated by this one consideration. . . . Moreover, their expectations are channelled towards jobs identical or very similar to those encountered on the scheme. Their concept of employability, and that of their supervisors as well, is highly occupationally specific. In so far as any wider concept of employability exists, it centres around the notion of personal effectiveness. . . . The notions of general vocational education and trans-

ferable skills, so central to thinking about manpower development for the future, are totally absent from their minds.

(Eraut and Burke, 1986, p.10)

The construction industry – whose early YTS had a high profile, was very popular and virtually guaranteed jobs – almost wholly overlooked the broad interpretation of occupational competence and transferable core skills, believing that:

There is no way you can have an overall YTS scheme, the Building Industry requires its own. All these core skills are not what Building is about.

(Quoted in Eraut and Burke, 1986, p.60)

Eraut and Burke studied the YTS before the introduction of the extended course and the structures set up to approve and recognise the training provided. It is doubtful, however, whether those developments would significantly affect trainee motives.

In the initial schemes training varied immensely in quality, which depended on the existence and calibre of training officers in individual schemes, and on the work placement. Studies such as that of Eraut and Burke (1986) bear witness to the fact that in many places core skills, and any aspect of the YTS which appeared to involve paperwork and theory rather than practical skills, were misunderstood or ignored. However the MSC's relentless drive for quality, for an appreciation by those involved of the opportunities for broader learning in the workplace, filtered through. Trainers, too, have been motivated to analyse and rethink the role of training and the meaning of competence. If the YTS, in its first few years, had achieved only this, it would have added something of real value.

SUMMARY: THE NEW VOCATIONALISM IN THE YOUTH TRAINING SCHEME

The YTS within a very few years grew into a lusty MSC child. It represented in the clearest form the characteristics of the new vocationalism, which might be summarised as:

- a government training policy to promote the interests of the economy and the individual, where reconcilable, the economy having priority;
- a government policy to promote the extension of opportunities for acquiring vocational qualifications;
- a government policy to introduce industry-based, defined standards of competence underpinning all training;
- the promotion, financially and by transformation of '16-plus' education and training structures, of workplace 'practical' learning in competition with school-based 'theoretical' learning;

195

- the idea that competence involves the application of knowledge and skills and is demonstrated through practical activity;
- an emphasis on the concrete and the measurable and testable, the idea of identifiable skills;
- the belief that by specifying learning process outcomes rather than areas covered, a development potential normally associated with educational institutions can be retained;
- a shift in the locus of policy and decision-making from educational providers and institutions to a combination of industry, commerce and the employment/industry areas of government;
- the triumph of commitment, speed, instantaneous feedback, single-mindedness and self-confidence over doubt, reflection and long-term research.

Several areas for concern remain. The first is whether the energetic identification of certain pupils as suitable for the type of training provided in the YTS and YT will have long-term segregational effects, socially and educationally, of the kind that we identified in Chapter 6 in reviewing features of the nineteenth century, when preparation for life was stratified mainly by social level, with repercussions for industrial development.

The second is whether a national training scheme to prepare a sizeable proportion of an age group for both mobility and a rapidly changing employment future should be serviced by as directive a piece of machinery as the MSC, its successor bodies or their parent ministry. Is there to be a constant watcher at the centre for the need for change, to establish a new set of structures, bodies and qualifications to deal with new needs? Will the very thoroughness and proportions of its activities in the first few years of the YTS (and YT) not militate against the requirement for training receptive to changing national needs? The concentration of authority and power in national training policy that the government achieved through the YTS is no different in principle from what it has sought and largely won in the schools sector through the 1988 Education Act. It seems highly likely, therefore, that a strong central drive will remain a dominant feature of the new vocationalism. The present decentralisation of management through the local TECs is a source of potential conflict (national directives versus local action).

The third and probably most significant concern relates to the trainees. In spite of all the work-based learning, the measuring of performance, the acquisition of nationally recognised qualifications, what do they get? Are they, will they be, competent? Competence is not just skills, and certainly is not achieved by defining in aggregate specific, discrete skills. It implies a combination of skills, knowledge, attitudes and dispositions, and values integrated through experience. The YTS proponents have not, of course, been unaware of this. The question is, first, whether the framework has proved robust enough for the purpose. Second, whether to the value that is added by the best training schemes there is a comparable benefit across the country. Competent employees are required because they are expected to perform well in work situations. Know-how or technical capability are not enough. Work-based learning is not in itself enough. Peters reminds us that:

> We do not call a person 'educated' who has simply mastered a skill even though the skill may be very highly prized. . . . For a man to be educated it is insufficient that he should possess a mere know-how or knack. He must have also some body of knowledge and some kind of conceptual scheme to raise this above the level of a collection of disjointed facts.
>
> (Peters, 1966, p.30)

The MSC, through the YTS, clearly aimed for a transformation of the traditional, narrow image of training. But it does glorify training, however imbued with enterprise or personal effectiveness, at the expense of wider education processes. Will the average products of the new vocationalism have a 'conceptual scheme' in which to place their learning and training, or will the work-based learning and training be their only conceptual scheme?

Perhaps the most fundamental question, however, is whether a training scheme directed at relatively low achievers, the school early leavers, could have a long-term future. The collapse of the youth labour market and the pressures resulting in extended participation in schooling may prove more decisive for the future of youth training schemes than any amount of debate or the proliferation of specific training schemes for 16-year-olds.

From the outset, it was clear that neither the declared outcomes nor inputs of the YTS and its design could serve as more than the most general guide to the ultimate character of the YTS until they were given concrete form – for example, through curriculum design and assessment. These inputs and outcomes are capable of being translated into a wide range and variety of curriculum frameworks and syllabuses. The process of such translation, however, given the analyses made in the *NTI* and the industry-partner approach adopted by the MSC, entails complex and politically difficult negotiations. It would be unfair and misleading to pretend otherwise. Criticism of the scheme must be tempered by full acknowledgement of the precipitous nature of the heights being scaled.

In the years in which the YTS and YT have been operating there have already been quite substantial and frequent changes in major design features of the scheme. These changes have not been worked out carefully – they have often been made 'on the run'. Many different curricula in fact operate in the schemes and are taken up in different workplace settings. There has also been a move towards creating recognisable syllabuses, inevitably, as some would say, as a consequence of the attempts now being made to define standards and to attach qualifications of some kind to successful performance in the two-year YTS. These syllabuses are intended to incorporate fundamental principles and learning strategies – for example, the generic concept of core skills – but it is not evident that this intention has been realised except incidentally.

The original approach in the YTS resembled that of mastery learning or performance-specified objectives in that the contents were not stated as ground to be covered but as capabilities to be displayed. Hence the interest in criterion-referenced assessment, and the necessity felt by the MSC to produce criteria for the approval of schemes. Usually, however, far too little time has been given to working out details or implications and this in part explains the bewildering rapidity of adjustments and adaptations. It should also be noted that the MSC enjoyed the luxury of very large-scale funding, at a time when other parts of the national educational system were enduring substantial cuts.

The developing YTS and its successor YT perhaps displayed qualities also detectable in the TVEI and predictable in City Technology Colleges, characteristic of the MSC and perhaps the new vocationalism itself, of a directive financial structure encasing a curriculum defined only by criteria. That distinctive and potentially creative feature of the TVEI (discussed in the next chapter) may have been lost in the YTS as it has been progressively whittled away by the drive for employer-based standards of competence and for opportunities for acquisition of nationally recognised vocational qualifications. How far, then, has the massive investment really turned around vocational preparation, as distinct from manipulating the youth (un)employment market? This is not so much a leading question as a question on notice, to be answered in the years ahead.

8

VOCATIONAL INITIATIVES FOR SCHOOLS AND COLLEGES

Enterprise and partnership culture

It is high time that the confusion and shortcomings that have characterised qualifications in England and Wales were finally removed.
(National Commission on Education, 1993, p. 67)

INTRODUCTION

Although the Youth Training Scheme (YTS) has been the spearhead of much of the employment-led rethinking of pre-vocational and vocational education, it was part of a larger and wider reappraisal, as we saw in Chapter 5. The more far-sighted, and not only among the vocational educators, had for decades recognised the inadequacies of provision and its increasing disjunction with the changing needs of young people and society at large. Having discussed this provision and its historical background in earlier chapters, and in Chapter 7 examined the major single initiative, the YTS, we turn now to other major initiatives of this period. It was not only the Manpower Services Commission (MSC) which identified the need and took action. Ideas and proposals for the reform of curricula and examinations for upper secondary and further education (FE) have been abundant. Likewise in the latter part of the compulsory period of schooling the vocational thrust has been a powerful force for change at the level of the schools themselves.

Starting with the activities of the Further Education Unit (FEU), which has been the leader of the further education as distinct from the industry–employment wing of the reform movement, we consider next a series of initiatives and proposals for strengthening the vocational role of the school and further education systems. These and other developments demonstrate the scale and diversity of activity proceeding under the banner of new vocationalism. Whether, taken together, they constitute the coherent and adequately comprehensive reform that is needed is, however, questionable. The outstanding, unresolved issue is the future of a system of secondary education, the pinnacle of which is the unreconstructed A level examination.

199

A BASIS FOR CHOICE

The FEU brought considerable influence to bear on the new vocationalism, as the MSC freely acknowledged. Its ideas were, however, based on rather different presuppositions from those of the MSC. The FEU, established in 1977 by the Secretary of State for Education and Science, was charged with the task of making possible a more co-ordinated and cohesive approach to curriculum development in further education. It soon began to publish documents designed to stimulate discussion and policy and to participate in a number of demonstration projects. Clearly identified with the established further education sector (schooling model), although lacking power or resources to commission pilot projects or national schemes on the scale needed, its impact on policy, strategic thinking and practice has been considerable.

In June 1979 the FEU published its influential and often reprinted report, *A Basis for Choice* (FEU, 1979). This seminal work surveyed the range of full-time pre-employment courses available for 16-plus pupils who were entering further education after leaving school but without specific vocational or academic commitments. The FEU concluded that the existing provision lacked both co-ordination and a nationally recognised framework, an observation which, while it caused no great surprise, was widely endorsed as highlighting a major weakness in the national system. In order to promote the rationalisation and effectiveness of the numerous existing and proposed courses, the report recommended a unifying curriculum structure in the new form of a set of criteria which present and future schemes might satisfy. The objectives were defined as flexibility, transferability and currency, themes that were to recur throughout the 1980s. The real importance of *A Basis for Choice* is that, in quite simple terms, it provided policy-makers and practitioners alike with a clear sense of the directions that should be pursued to overcome the widely agreed deficiencies.

Many of the ideas it advanced were taken up in the design of the YTS. Its weakness, or rather that of the system of which it was a part, lay in the inadequate policy and power structure for effective decision-making in post-16 education in Britain.

The schemes envisaged by the FEU were, like the YTS, intended for a wide range of ability but the FEU had in mind a distinct, school/college-based target group. It recommended provision

> for young people who enter further education after leaving school and who need something other than GCE studies or programmes preparing them for specific occupations. These mainly one-year courses are intended for young people of average ability and attainment (but not those with special learning difficulties) who may be vocationally uncommitted at the start but who wish to develop an informed orientation while keeping their employment and further education options open.
>
> (FEU, 1979, p.1)

The FEU astutely pointed straight towards one of the principal weaknesses in national policy and provision. This target group might be thought of as a parallel to the YTS trainees, but with this major difference: that they could continue a form of general education, within the environment of the formal education institution (for example, the tertiary education college). These were among the students the authors of the Newsom Report, *Half Our Future* (Central Advisory Council for Education (England), 1963), had in mind when, in the 1960s, the effects of longer periods of full-time schooling for all were being debated nationally. They were to be the target of numerous proposals and initiatives to reform the middle and upper years of secondary schooling and curriculum and assessment procedures for use by schools and colleges.

The FEU objective, if a tacit one, was to counteract underachievement and apathy among pupils with some potential for staying on in school. These were likely to be

> intending to enter employment in the reasonably short term, and probably had a disinclination to embark on a full-time course of more than a year's duration, at least initially.

(FEU, 1979, p.7)

One purpose of the proposed new course was to offer provision positively designed for the needs of the target group. The authors of *A Basis for Choice* drew attention to the number of post-16 one-year O level courses which, in spite of an apparently high failure rate, continued to attract pupils without a definite job or job destination, presumably because of the perceived usefulness or 'currency' of the General Certificate of Education (GCE). While the then prospective substitution of the General Certificate of Secondary Education (GCSE) for the GCE promised to reduce wastage in the form of outright failure, it was seen as likely to render one-year repeat courses an even less fulfilling activity. As Pauline Green put it in 'A new curriculum at 17?', the concept of a new course could be

> seen as an exciting opportunity to provide educationally worthwhile experiences to students in forms expressly designed to meet their needs, rather than:
> - their repeating earlier 'failure' (re-take CSEs)
> - attempting academically unsuitable courses which had never been designed for 'them' (O level) or:
> - being 'dumped' into low-level, unrespected courses which delimited future opportunities (CGLI 365).

(Green, 1987, p.4)

The FEU report does not, in any global way, examine an age group, or deal with national provision. It puts under a microscope the existing arrangements for a defined clientele – that is, non-specific vocational preparation

201

for 16-plus students with limited but varying academic success and inclination. This is a clientele that has always fallen into the interstices between the categories and differentiated schemes that have formed the staple of national policy and provision. A merit of the FEU thinking is the recognition of a specific target group whose needs command attention by virtue of past failures of policy and yet can be clearly addressed. By way of caution, however, it should be recalled that the aim of the post-Second-World-War reformers in implementing the 1944 Act was to provide, through separate secondary modern and technical schools, an alternative of equal value to the grammar schools. Eventually, this system of separate and supposedly equal strands was abandoned in favour of comprehensive schools. We have already said, but it bears repeating in this context, that one of the crucial, unresolved issues in the 16-plus debate is the quality and acceptability of the several alternatives now offered to those (the majority) not proceeding through the GCSE to A levels. Due in very large part to the legacy of separate elements and the status monopoly enjoyed by an A level system which is quite explicitly tailored to meet the needs of a small minority, Britain as yet lacks a coherent framework of education for those aged 16 and over. Especially in relation to the A level issue, policy, while clear enough, is inadequate in relation to requirements for the majority (Mathieson, 1992).

To return to the endeavours of the FEU, we can, with them, acknowledge the undesirability of simply adding to a plethora of existing courses. The FEU objective has been to substitute something more useful (functional) in the eyes of students, parents and employers. In view of this objective it was necessary to provide a balance between something general (because uncommitted to a vocation) and something regarded as useful in a future job; and between something nationally recognisable as a qualification and locally appropriate, and which took into account labour market characteristics. This sensible approach required a combination of national criteria and local flexibility, not easy in practice to achieve. Most important for the longer term, the FEU, unlike the MSC, accepted that the existing structure of further education institutions should be the starting point and provide the framework for action. This is a fundamental point. The MSC in advancing the YTS, started with a deficiency model – deficient content and pedagogy, deficient structures – and sought to remedy both by setting up its own, new programmes which would be (largely) independent of the existing school/college system. The FEU, however, took as its starting point the experience and potential of the existing system and argued for evolutionary change with that system as the base of operations. Acknowledging its limitations and defects, the FEU nevertheless has consistently taken the view that reform from within was the more desirable course to follow.

In many ways, the FEU's assumptions were more realistic and cost effective, and better grounded in the deep structure of assumptions about what is appropriate provision, than the grand strategy of the MSC. On the other hand, without that grand strategy, neither the penetrating critique nor the necessary mobilisation of resources that have characterised the new vocationalism would have occurred.

In the FEU proposals, colleges would determine the curriculum on a local basis with the help of agencies such as the Careers Service, MSC Area Boards (and their heirs) and local education authorities. The need for focus would be met by a common area of studies; to be too job-specific would be inappropriate, so various combinations of common core, vocational and optional studies would be made available. They could be achieved in a number of ways. Colleges might group courses around their existing departments such as 'hotel and catering', 'building and construction' or 'the caring professions'; or around groupings of skills cutting across these divisions; or around local industries.

While the FEU was not concerned with a full-blown national plan, it stressed the advantages to be gained from rationalisation of courses and in particular from national validation. Mention was made of the argument contained in the report by Garnett College, *One Year Pre-employment Courses for Students Aged 16-Plus: A Survey of Provision in Colleges of Further Education* (Bailey, 1978), that the proliferation of courses is one of the major factors working against their recognition and perceived usefulness to students. Emphasis was to be placed upon assessment and the provision of a nationally recognised award available to students who successfully complete a validated course. This is a sign of the spread of the determination, already discernible in the MSC and the Department of Education and Science (DES), for clarification, rationalisation, centralisation and hence control of qualifications, which appears to be an essential feature of the new vocationalism. The important issue, still unresolved, is whether this will result in sterile tidying up, a further large concentration of power at the national level, or in increasing recognition and currency for a range of useful qualifications.

THE QUEST FOR NEW 16-PLUS QUALIFICATIONS

This is not the place to recount the long, frustrating and still inconclusive saga of proposals and attempted reform of curricula and examinations for 16- to 18/19-year-olds remaining in full- or part-time school or college education. There have been many studies of and commentaries on this unedifying episode of contemporary educational history (Gipps, 1992; Mathieson, 1992). The continued dominance of the GCE A level examinations, designed for a small minority of the age group and geared towards the single subject and joint honours degree programmes of the British universities, have been one factor but not the only one, militating against a fundamental restructuring. The Schools Council for Curriculum and

Examinations, the Committee of Vice-Chancellors and Principals, the DES and the examining bodies have been among those essaying major reforms. The successful combination, at 16-plus, of the previously separate routes of GCE O levels and Certificate of Secondary Education (CSE), in the form of the GCSE, is one of the few examples of a major reform in this arena that was carried through to successful implementation and even it has been under attack for allegedly 'jeopardising standards'.

Among the key reference points in the establishment of new 16-plus qualifications is the construction by the National Council for Vocational Qualifications (NCVQ) of the frameworks of National Vocational Qualifications (NVQs) and General National Vocational Qualifications (GNVQs), which we discussed in Chapters 3 and 5. The NVQs and GNVQs are the source or expression of criteria for accrediting qualifications to pre-determined levels. Although not in themselves qualifications, the NVQ/GNVQ frameworks are designed to have a powerful impact on courses and qualifications. The cases of the Certificate of Pre-vocational Education and its successor, the Diploma of Vocational Education, are interesting in this respect.

CERTIFICATE OF PRE-VOCATIONAL EDUCATION AND ITS SUCCESSOR

The FEU has not been without influence in the quest for new qualifications that respond to changing realities. In response to *A Basis for Choice* the DES took a decision in favour of a new 17-plus qualification, the Certificate of Pre-vocational Education (CPVE), thereby declaring its intention to make headway in one of the most intractable areas of British educational policy, namely the territory that lies between O level (now GCSE) and A level. This qualification, as it emerged from the thickets of educational practices, policies and politics, soon took on a form both narrower and more instrumental than the FEU seems to have envisaged in its consideration of alternatives. It, and its proposed successor, the Diploma of Vocational Education, are part of a lengthy, inconclusive saga dating to the Crowther Report (Central Advisory Council for Education (England), 1959) which enshrined the specialist, academic subject as the key to post-16 school curriculum and examinations.

In May 1983 the Joint Board for Pre-vocational Education was set up by the Business and Technician Education Council (BTEC) and City and Guilds of London Institute (CGLI) at the request of the Secretary of State for Education in England and Wales. The Board was 'to establish a system of pre-vocational education on a national basis including a 17+ qualification' and to have new schemes introduced in schools and colleges from September 1985. The proposals, circulated to all those concerned as *The Certificate of Pre-vocational Education: Consultative Document* (May 1984), aimed to meet the needs of about 100,000

16 year olds of all abilities who would benefit from a further year of full-time education but who require a programme of learning and development neither conventionally academic nor purely vocational to help them prepare for adult life and work.

(Joint Board for Pre-vocational Education, 1984, p.4)

The courses should be 'demonstrably relevant to the needs of young people as emerging adults and prospective employees' and the curriculum should facilitate

not only the acquisition of knowledge and analytical and critical skills, but also constructive and creative activity which involves putting ideas into practice, making, doing and organizing.

(ibid., p.4)

The CPVE programmes, as described in the document, should incorporate features which by then were becoming staple inputs in school and work-based vocational innovations:

- a balance of core, vocational and additional studies;
- learning through practical experience;
- planned work experience;
- provision for careers education, guidance and support;
- involvement of young people in the planning, organising and assessment of their learning.

(ibid., p.4)

The framework for the certificate contained three major components: the common core; the vocational studies; and the additional studies. Intended to take up 60 per cent of course time, the ten defined core areas were: personal and career development; communication; numeracy; science and technology; industrial, social and economic studies; information technology; skills for learning, decision-making and adaptability; practical skills; social skills; and creative development.

The vocational studies were to be based upon clusters of activities which have a common purpose and related learning objectives and were included because they:

(i) are relevant to young people and may therefore enhance motivation;

(ii) provide the focus for the development of the required core skills;

(iii) provide for development of broad vocational skills to appropriate standards;

(iv) provide an important basis for progression into employment, further education and training.

(ibid., p.10)

Standards of attainment were to be linked with those nationally agreed for entry into employment and initial and continuing training, with assessment based on a variety of performances.

The additional studies 'provide encouragement and opportunity for young people to complement their core and vocational studies with other activities relevant to their own particular interests, capabilities and aspirations' (ibid., p.5). The additional studies were an optional element, to use up to 25 per cent of course time, designed to meet individual needs and interests within the curriculum and might lead to additional qualifications.

The first CPVE programmes started in 1985 and the first certificates were awarded in 1986. The envisaged character of CPVE as a curriculum development can be explored in intentions expressed in various public documents. In government White Papers *Training for Jobs* (DoE/DES, 1984) and *Education and Training for Young People* (DES, 1985b), it is referred to in passing under the heading of developments within education which play a part in equipping young people for work. *Better Schools* (DES, 1985a) stresses the tidying up role of the CPVE, which

> is intended to replace a range of existing courses including the pre-vocational courses of the CGLI, BTEC and the Royal Society of Arts, and the Certificate of Extended Education offered by most CSE and GCE Boards.
>
> (DES 1985a, pp.35–36)

To think of CPVE merely as 'tidying up' is, however, to overlook its relationship with the principles outlined in *A Basis for Choice*. Taken together, the CPVE and *A Basis for Choice* are a reminder of the strong conviction, during the period when the YTS was attracting substantial resources and publicity, that education and training, general and specific preparation for working life and adult roles can and should be combined within comprehensive post-16 programmes in which formal education can collaborate closely with the workplace. As school participation rates rise, the impetus for a separate, YT type of training diminishes and the A level system retains its hold, the need for the thinking and planning that resulted in the CPVE will become ever greater, but it will need to be considerably developed beyond the rather circumscribed limits of the initial formulation.

A Basis for Choice did not attempt to address the full range of educational opportunities available to all 16- or 17-year-olds and the CPVE was limited in its potential audience. Neither was part of an explicit, overarching policy designed to clarify structures and co-ordinate provision.

The authors of *A Basis for Choice* considered that a common core of learning was an important ingredient for courses and recommended a core which it described as 'not new but . . . derived from knowledge of existing good practice'. Recognition of the value of courses would, in their view, require an identifiable core of learning in and between courses, which was nationally validated, recognised as educationally sound, and which guaranteed certain levels of competence in basic skills in those who gained a certificate. The criterion of transferability carries implications for the nature of these core studies, as does the need for flexibility and the desirability of a vocational focus.

(FEU, 1979, p.18)

The claim for a link between the acquisition of competences needed for survival in an increasingly technological but ill-defined work context and a broad framework of common core learnings is exhibited in the Technical and Vocational Education Initiative (TVEI), YTS and CPVE alike. In the CPVE, the common core contribution is described in terms of objectives, learning opportunities and methods of approach to teaching and learning. It is based mainly on the apparent advantages of blurring subject boundaries and avoiding jerky transitions and/or unnecessary repetitions and on the much stressed integration of core and vocational studies. At its inception, the CPVE as a whole – core and vocational studies (additional studies being optional) – was intended, among other things, to 'assist the transition from school to adulthood by further equipping young people with the basic skills, experiences, attitudes, knowledge and personal and social competencies required for success in adult life including work' (Joint Board for Pre-vocational Education, 1984, p.9).

As in the YTS, it was also expected to promote the acquisition of 'process skills' such as 'those of analysis and problem-solving, social skills, personal qualities such as resilience, autonomy and responsibility'; and the capacity to transfer competences from one situation to another (ibid., p.22). Again, as in YTS core skills, the common core was intended to be used as a checklist against which the performance of individual young people must be matched in order for starting points and learning programmes to be agreed.

Throughout the Consultation Document, emphasis was placed on personal attainment recorded in individual *profiles* together with certification for all who completed the course and combined with validation to national criteria. Thus the award aspired to embody achievements in 'core and vocational studies with an indication of their highest levels reached where appropriate, together with a statement of the context within which the skills were demonstrated' (ibid., p.14). The blueprint contained all the then 'acceptable' elements – reflection of individual needs, recording of achievement, certification for all who complete – yet it promised to offer levels of achievement, quality control and recognition and currency for the award.

From this overview of aims and structural features, it is clear that the plan for the CPVE, while locating it firmly in the heartland of the new vocational thinking, envisaged a broad range of educational values and procedures. It was to be, in a sense, the education system's vocational showpiece for the

16-plus age group. It is not our purpose to attempt to assess the efforts made to implement the CPVE and the various kinds of resistance, both direct and indirect that it encountered. Despite proving popular with staff (who found the new teaching methods challenging and progressive) and students (who found it extremely motivating) (Nicholls, 1992b), less than a decade after its introduction it had suffered the fate of many other initiatives: lack of significant uptake and lack of credibility among employers and the academic community. Moreover, its alleged lack of rigour and limited screening functions ('too high' a pass rate) have made it appear in some quarters as unduly accommodating to educational values that rest uneasily with the more recent approaches through highly stratified, output-based assessments.

In 1990, the Minister of State for Education announced that from September 1991 schools could offer BTEC First courses – effectively providing direct competition to the CPVE from one of its existing joint sponsors. Subsequently, the CGLI was given sole responsibility for the CPVE, with a brief to bring greater rigour into its assessment and ensure clearer progression routes for students. The CGLI proceeded to produce a new qualification, the Diploma of Vocational Education (DVE) to replace both the CPVE and foundation programmes (Nicholls, 1992b). Yet again, a new qualification containing valuable ideas seems to have vanished beneath 'structural reform', in part no doubt because of inadequate preparation and lack of consensus between the several parties involved or likely to be affected.

The DVE, in the line of descent from the CPVE but with close linkages with the new structures for general and vocational education, will cater for a wider age range (14–19 years) and be taken at three different levels (to correspond to key stage 4 in the national curriculum, and levels 2 and 3 of GNVQs). Like the CPVE, the DVE will have a hybrid quality. The genuine educational objective of putting form and purpose into what has been called a 'pot-pourri' of 16-plus activities will continue to be combined with a sweep of the new vocational influences – the world of work, emphasis on qualifications, short-term employer versions of personal development. A fairly prescriptive curriculum including a common core of the familiar studies (communication, numeracy, problem-solving, etc.) and studies with 'vocational clusters' will be a feature of the DVE. Thus, the DVE will, like the CPVE, maintain a strong orientation towards further, vocational specific training or employment (Nicholls, 1992a).

Alongside the DVE is to be another new qualification, the Technological Baccalaureate, launched in 1991 and piloted, significantly, in several City Technology Colleges (CTCs) and schools and other colleges. The Technology Bac is tailored to the framework of key stages (national curriculum) and levels (NVQs) to permit successful candidates, according to the degree standard attained, to proceed to higher education (NVQ5, first-degree), advanced further education (NVQ4), or further education and training (NVQ3). It is thus a typical case of the adaptiveness – or opportunism – of the examining authorities.

ORIENTING THE SECONDARY CURRICULUM TOWARDS WORK

The general educational foundation of preparation for work and adult life have long been recognised and claimed by the schools, but the meaning of vocational education in the current 'new vocationalism' context involves certain ideas which embody or imply criticism of schools and general, liberal education. The challenge to schools has been: first, to establish closer links with the workplace – that is, work experience, simulated work experience, learning more relevant to the pupils' future lives, links between teachers and local industry, etc.; second, to deploy more practical, problem-solving, initiative-building teaching methods; and third, to give greater attention to the acquisition of concrete, measurable, testable skills and competences.

This functionalist strand of educational philosophy has been evident in policy-making and in practice in some schools for many years, certainly since before the establishment of the MSC or the FEU, though it has been strengthened and accelerated in the 1980s. It can be clearly identified in the literature, appearing from time to time over the last 150 years or so of English education. Moreover, the functionalist and instrumentalist elements do not tell the whole story, since the progressive movement in education in the late nineteenth century and well into the twentieth provides many antecedents to the current emphasis on student-centred education, practical and experiential learning and so on.

Government policy for schools throughout the 1980s was increasingly influenced by the new vocationalism. The *New Training Initiative* (DoE/DES, 1981) which, as we have seen in Chapter 5, outlined proposals for a better trained and more flexible workforce and introduced the YTS, also stressed the need for better preparation in schools for working life.

The last two years of compulsory education are particularly important in forming an approach to the world of work. Every pupil needs to be helped to reach his or her full potential, not only for personal development but to prepare for the whole range of demands which employment will make. The Government is seeking to ensure that the school curriculum develops the personal skills and qualities as well as the knowledge needed for working life, and that links between schools and employers help pupils and teachers to gain a closer understanding of the industrial, commercial and economic base of our society.

(DoE/DES, 1981, p.5)

This is noteworthy as a clear statement, at the beginning of a decade which witnessed more changes in educational policy than any previous decade, of the responsibility of schools for economic performance. What is interesting is not so much that government wished to stress these objectives – what government faced with declining economic fortunes would not? – but that it was felt necessary to adopt a strongly interventionist stance to do so.

In 1984 another White Paper, *Training for Jobs* (DoE/DES, 1984), again primarily concerned with developments in the YTS, stressed the contribution of the schools. It itemised arrangements for the CPVE; for increasing links between employers and schools and colleges, and for introducing the TVEI. But the first item was the school:

> **The school curriculum is being developed for this purpose.** Objectives have been set for mathematics and will shortly be set for science teaching. National criteria are being established for the improvement of the 16-plus examinations and their syllabuses. New programmes are in operation for micro-electronics education and for pupils for whom the 16-plus examinations are not designed.
>
> (DoE/DES, 1984, p.6)

Many other statements aimed at fostering close links between the secondary curriculum and work appeared throughout the 1980s. However, perhaps the most decisive action was that taken by the MSC in launching the TVEI.

THE TECHNICAL AND VOCATIONAL EDUCATION INITIATIVE (TVEI)

The MSC's involvement in preparing young people for working life was taken a step further when the government diverted money from the DES to the MSC and that organisation embarked upon youth training and entered the school system. This was with the acquiescence of the DES and resulted in the introduction of the TVEI into the curriculum for 14–18-year-olds. It was a momentous decision, signifying the largest ever curriculum development project funded and administered by central government with consequential developments in schooling in all parts of the country. The aim was simple, direct and audacious: to change the curriculum for the 14–18 age group by giving it a more practical and applied character and drawing out its function as a bridge to the world of work (MSC, 1985b).

On 12 November 1982 the Prime Minister announced the government's intention to launch an initiative to stimulate the provision of technical and vocational education in the schools, beginning at age 14. The MSC was invited to establish some ten pilot projects of full-time general, technical and vocational education in England and Wales in association with the DES and through local education authorities (LEAs).

Programmes, although broadly work-oriented, were to be within the education system with LEAs bidding and being bound by the contracts awarded to deliver specified programmes. The lessons from the early, pilot projects were intended from the start to provide a basis for lasting educational developments for 14–18-year-olds (MSC, 1984c). At the same time, like the YTS, the TVEI had no established syllabus; aims and objectives were not narrowly defined and through pilot projects, evaluations and a great deal of debate and discussion, a considerable variety of practice and approach emerged across the country. As with the YTS, the TVEI was to be directed by national guidelines allowing considerable local flexibility. In order to obtain MSC support, programmes (in the case of the TVEI devised by LEAs) had to fulfil criteria defined by a National Steering Group. Although there was no overt mention of a core of skills as such to be learnt, all programmes had to include a common or 'core' element; and the characteristics identified for the content of the programmes, as we see below, included areas common to other vocational innovations. The TVEI includes general, technical and vocational elements; '"vocational education" is to be interpreted as education in which the students are concerned to acquire generic or specific skills with a view to employment' (MSC, 1984c, Annex B Criteria).

Since the purpose of each project, and the TVEI as a whole, was to explore and test programmes of general, technical and vocational education for 14–18-year-olds, suitable for replication, a series of very different projects was deliberately launched. Within the overall framework, the goals of the individual projects were numerous and varied, ranging from the introduction and development of new practical/vocational courses, through building links with work and adult life to improving examination performance. What those projects had in common was a definite content orientation:

Each project should comprise one or more sets of full-time programmes with the following characteristics:
(1) Equal opportunities should be available to young people of both sexes and they should normally be educated together on courses within each project. Care should be taken to avoid sex stereotyping.
(2) They should provide four year curricula, with progression from year to year, designed to prepare the student for particular aspects of employment and for adult life in a society liable to rapid change.
(3) They should have clear and specific objectives, including the objective of encouraging initiative, problem-solving abilities, and other aspects of personal development.
(4) The balance between the general, technical and vocational elements of programmes should vary according to students' individual needs

and the stage of the course, but throughout the programme there should be both a general and a technical/vocational element.

(5) The technical and vocational elements should be broadly related to potential employment opportunities within and outside the geographical area for the young people concerned.

(6) There should be appropriate planned work experience as an integral part of the programmes, from the age of 15 onwards, bearing in mind the provisions of the Education (Work Experience) Act 1973.

(7) Courses offered should be capable of being linked effectively with subsequent training/educational opportunities.

(8) Arrangements should be made for regular assessment and for students and tutors to discuss students' performance/progress. Each student, and his or her parents, should also receive a periodic written assessment, and have an opportunity to discuss this assessment with the relevant project teachers. Good careers and educational counselling will be essential.

(MSC, 1984c, Annex B 2)

Students would normally be expected to obtain one or more nationally recognised qualifications, according to ability; and they would be issued with a record of achievement. Industry and commerce were to be involved, as partners in design and delivery and not merely as recipients of the finished 'product'. All of this has a most familiar ring: the TVEI has been part of the wider strategy whose assumptions and major elements we have seen in the different settings of the new vocationalism.

In September 1983, fourteen LEAs started the first year of TVEI programmes. This involved 4,315 pupils in 100 schools. A further forty-eight LEA pilot projects began in 1984. Scotland joined, but later; the reason offered by one commentator is interesting:

'Caledonian caution', a concern to ensure that participation in the initiative would not compromise Scottish educational developments, or breach educational principles which had been established in Scotland as a result of the experiences gained in attempting to introduce vocational elements into the curriculum of Scottish schools during the 1960s.

(Pignatelli, 1987, p.52)

These experiences led the Scots to abandon the idea that the school curriculum might be built around 'the vocational perspective'; rather, a balance was required between the vocational emphasis and the broader curriculum of the schools.

In its first phase, the TVEI catered for a small percentage of the relevant age group. But in the light of initial experience, and the willingness of most local authorities to co-operate (not least because of the much needed financial resources on offer), plans were announced in the summer of 1986 to extend the TVEI as an option for the entire 14–18 age group by 1997. Funding per school was to be lower than during the expensive pilot phase. Twelve LEA projects began in 1985, twenty-one in 1986, eleven in 1987 and the remainder in 1988 (HMI, 1991e, p.2). In 1990, budgetary cuts meant new schools would have less than half their anticipated funding, leading a number to threaten to withdraw from the scheme. Nonetheless by 1992, the TVEI had become available UK-wide with, for 1992–93, over 1,000,000 students involved, 5,000 schools participating, and all LEAs involved (DoE official figures, personal communication). Responsibility for the TVEI has remained with the MSC and its successor agencies (now within the Department of Employment), although the Training and Enterprise Councils (TECs) have shown strong interest in the now £900 million/year activity, as indeed has the DES/DfE.

The TVEI, like the YTS, was a favoured child of the new vocationalism movement. Viewed in one light, it is at the cutting edge, a leader among a series of national initiatives to improve preparation for working life through education and training; in another light, it is part of a series of arrangements devised to impose central government policies on education and training organisations by cash and directive. Its introduction implied dissatisfaction with the existing curriculum in the schools. Like the YTS, it appeared to be designed to meet a specific utilitarian objective – to provide for employers' needs.

The DES in *Better Schools* gave a lengthy resume of what the TVEI, at that time, was seen to offer:

> The TVEI embodies the Government's policy that education should better equip young people for working life. The courses are designed to cater equally for boys and girls across the whole ability range and with technical or vocational aspirations, and to offer in the compulsory years a broad general education with a strong technical element followed, post-16, by increasing vocational specialisation. The course content and teaching methods adopted are intended to develop personal qualities and positive attitudes towards work as well as a wide range of competence, and more generally to develop a practical approach throughout the curriculum. The projects are innovative and break new ground in many ways, being designed to explore curriculum organisation and development, teaching approaches and learning styles, co-operation between participating institutions, and enhanced careers guidance supported by work experience, in order to test the feasibility of sustaining a broad vocational commitment in full-time education for 14–18 year olds.
>
> (DES, 1985a, pp.16–17)

The form and content of TVEI pilot schemes during the early, creative phases recognised the need for more active learning methods, to meet the challenges posed by changes in industry and the rapid development of technology. Assuming the need for pupils to learn through experience, and to solve practical problems requiring the use of initiative, team work, etc., as a preparation for work, the TVEI's objectives were:

> first to widen and enrich the curriculum in a way that will help young people to prepare for the world of work, and to develop skills and interests, including creative abilities, that will help them to lead a fuller life and to contribute more to the life of the community; and second, to help students to learn to learn, to enable them to adapt to the changing occupational environment.
>
> (MSC, 1984c, p.11)

Specific guidance on how to achieve these methods of learning was not given at this time.

The TVEI did not define a core, list core studies or identify essential core skills, though all the first fourteen TVEI pilot projects included some core elements which can be seen as, in practice, constituting a 'TVEI core': for example, careers education and planned work experience, incorporating preparation and follow-up in school. The balance between 'core' and 'options' depended very much on local decision, but the first projects, either through core or options, tended to offer a broadly similar set of learning opportunities – for example, variety of vocational experience, technology, design, computers, business studies and science. Given the provenance of the TVEI and the purposes it was intended to serve, matters could hardly be otherwise.

The administrative and financial arrangements for the TVEI were innovatory. While in some ways they were more directive and inflexible than the financing methods used by the MSC and its heirs in the YTS, they at the same time offered schools a certain freedom to experiment. Local education authorities were responsible for the formulation and delivery of project proposals. These needed, however, to satisfy centrally determined criteria. The TVEI as a whole was initially administered through a small unit in the MSC, in liaison with the DES over major policy matters. Elaborate arrangements for accountability, auditing, evaluating and monitoring involved the MSC, Her Majesty's Inspectorate (HMI) in the DES and the LEAs themselves. Funds available to support the TVEI were normally allocated to meet costs of additional staffing, premises and equipment. In principle, teachers with TVEI allowances might be required to justify receipt of them by their performance, while the percentage of pupil time on the TVEI and the content of activity differed considerably from project to project. In practice the MSC funds potentially offered much needed encouragement and momentum for schools and teachers confidently to explore what they may already have been striving to offer or trying to develop piecemeal. In the words of the *TVEI Review* of 1984, MSC funding

> enables LEAs to broaden and enrich their existing provision, so as to explore and develop technical and vocational education within a framework of general education for each student involved. . . . In general terms, TVEI activities are broadly based in order to prepare students for a rapidly changing world and to avoid premature special-isation. Thus the changes in the curriculum as a result of TVEI go beyond only narrow definition of technical and vocational education.
>
> (MSC, 1984c, pp.8, 9)

At the same time LEAs operating TVEI were instructed that

> Each programme should be part of the total provision of the institu-tion(s) in which it takes place so that the students may take part with others in the life of the institution(s). (The education offered in the institution(s) to those not on the programme should continue to contain technical or vocational elements as appropriate, and those not on the programme should not be adversely affected by the con-duct of the programme.)
>
> (ibid., p.26)

The exploration, innovation, and experimentation supported by TVEI and MSC money were from the outset intended to be set firmly in a broad general education context. In terms both of the national structure support-ing it and its thematic orientation, the TVEI suggests a strategy that posited age 14 as the terminus of serious endeavours to sustain a fully compre-hensive education for all. With the apparent move in many 'extension' schools, however, away from seeing the TVEI as a separate course and towards a broader enhancement of many existing curriculum areas for all pupils, this object may not be achieved.

As Roger Dale (1985) points out, the early outlines of the TVEI explain little about why it was set up in the way it was; in order to reach conclusions about its real intentions it is necessary to examine the problem it was created to solve. This is not, however, so difficult. Government statements, as we have seen, have tended to define the problem mainly in terms of making good the schools' lack of preparation for successful acquisition of, and performance in, a job. Indeed, David (now Lord) Young, as Chairman of MSC in 1982, believed when introducing the TVEI, that it would lead to young people becoming 'highly employable' by the time they left school. But the TVEI as it has come to be organised in practice need not be viewed only in more functional vocational terms. It is equally possible to emphasise its role in developing communication between schools and industry (Sadler, 1989) and its potential as a catalyst in the 14-plus curriculum. Much depends on three factors: local circumstances, including pre-existing school–industry links; how it is introduced and managed in individual schools; and the qualifications with which it is associated. The strategy that envisages a parting of the educational ways at age 14 would be aborted were the schools themselves to build the TVEI into the heartland of the curriculum for all.

The effect of the TVEI in any school and its power to attract and keep pupils over a wide ability range depend at least in part on each school's interpretation of the guidelines, but most of all on what Dale describes as 'the salience' of the scheme within the school. This in turn depends on a number of factors: how the scheme is publicised to staff, pupils and parents when selecting options for 14-plus; whether it is developed through existing subjects taught with a new approach or through a series of new subjects and courses; whether it is offered openly to a targeted group, defined by ability, or implicitly by the subject options which it is associated with; the calibre of the teachers and so on.

Early studies of the TVEI suggested that it soon attracted some A level students and boosted staying-on rates at school. In 1986 in Solihull, for example, the percentage of the age group staying on in school after 16 was 10 per cent; but among TVEI students entering their third year, the retention rate was 50 per cent. Moreover, the TVEI began to infiltrate A level courses. Sixth-form college A level students getting experience of the TVEI for the obligatory non-GCE work found it a challenging option (Nash, 1987).

These assessments refer to the early, more innovative phases in the development of the TVEI, when it attracted a good deal of positive interest notwithstanding anxieties about the inroads being made by an essentially employment-based agency (MSC) into the school system (Gleeson, 1987). Extension, following the joint DoE/DES White Paper (1986), inevitably meant greater consistency and an attempt to sift from the diverse experiments of the pilot phase approaches that seemed to hold greater promise for a national policy. The national curriculum was being developed concurrently. From one point of view the prescriptive character of the national curriculum undermined the diversity inherent in the TVEI and together with other (mainly financial) factors weakened its impact: 'The status of TVEI was gradually being undermined and marginalised by displacement by other educational reforms and the diminution of its funding' (Merson, 1992, p.16). From another standpoint, however (HMI, 1991e), the TVEI succeeded precisely because of its incorporation into the new curriculum policies and structures. The frequency of change is not, however, justified by such incorporation. Is the TVEI yet another vocational initiative introduced without due thought being given to its implications and likely consequences for the system as a whole?

For schools, the TVEI has been a central strand of the new vocationalism, because of its aims, its explicit work orientation, its method of introduction, and financial arrangements. It has the familiar form of compulsory criteria coupled with curricular flexibility, itself a curious if increasingly accepted combination. Unlike the YTS, its pilot and evolutionary stages have not been rapidly followed by greater prescription and reduced flexibility; however, in the extension phase, the TVEI was broadened to the whole curriculum and linked with other initiatives, inevitably with the national curriculum for schools (HMI, 1991e). It is still the individual interpretations of local authorities and the freedom of teachers, if they care to exercise it creatively in whatever they teach, which will decide the shape of the programmes. What the TVEI has to offer for replication nationally is its individual approach to curriculum planning, grounded in the work orientation stated in its first set of aims, rather than a standard package, together with potential as a catalyst for the 14-plus curriculum. The initiative has had a number of positive results, the method of financing has ensured the establishment and not only the design of new courses; more practical and applied work is observable in classrooms; links with local employers have been established (HMI, 1991e).

The advent of the national curriculum posed a real challenge for successful expansion of the TVEI to all schools, not because it would of necessity exclude it but because of the need for teachers and authorities to recast their approaches in the new curriculum framework. As yet it is not clear how it will fare, given that the TVEI is still a programme for some, not all students. However, the TVEI has been credited, by HMI, with a role in the development of GCSE and in the evolution of cross-curriculum themes in the national curriculum (HMI, 1991e).

While specific studies of the TVEI, such as those by researchers at Newcastle and Leeds Universities (Barnes *et al.*, 1987; Fitz-Gibbon *et al.*, 1988), and more general appraisals of policy and direction including those cited above, give rise to rather diverse conclusions, two points are clear. First, the TVEI has been a highly innovative and dynamic national programme which quickly made visible several of the main themes in the government's commitment to and understanding of the new vocationalism. Second, as a funded initiative designed to draw attention to one of the elements in a shifting, evolving set of national policies and programmes, the TVEI would eventually be assimilated or closely related to the emerging foci of concern in those policies and be subject to the common pattern of innovation funding whereby start-up expenditures are progressively reduced. With the reservations noted above – that is, the too rapid succession of new initiatives – the TVEI legacy will be the impetus and reinforcement it has given to the central vocationalist idea that schooling should, among other functions, orient young people towards work and actively assist them to prepare for working life.

ENTERPRISE CULTURE AND PARTNERSHIP

While the most obvious features of the new vocationalism in the developments and specific programme innovations discussed in this chapter are summed up in the terms 'vocational' or 'work orientation', direct work preparation or vocational training have to be put in a much broader context. On the one hand, the foreshadowed distinctive vocational culture and separate administrative structure have gradually been assimilated to the general education system specifically of schools and further education colleges. On the other hand, the urgency of the youth unemployment problem has diminished: it is an acceptable and 'politically bearable' problem; the youth labour market has virtually evaporated except for part-time and certain low paid jobs and the informal labour market. For these reasons, changes in the formal educational structure, in curriculum, teaching and learning and relations with the wider environment, must become the central concern of policy-makers and developers, whether specifically identified as 'vocational' or 'general', 'training' or 'education'. Attention must, once again, be focused on the fundamental challenges to schooling – broadly defined, and away from specific, particularly non-school-based, preparatory courses for adolescents with employment in mind.

Many of the ideas and practices which emerged in the more specific work preparation programmes have become of recognised value in schooling – as we saw in discussing the TVEI. One of them, school–industry partnerships, has long been a feature of vocational and technical education institutions and programmes. Another, enterprise skills, is closely associated with changing practice in work organisation (as we saw in Chapter 1) and with the attention labour market and employment policy-makers have been giving to the skills needed by people who will gain employment by setting up their own businesses or in small-scale enterprises. 'Partnerships' and 'enterprise skills' are likely to gain considerable support in schooling, at all levels, since they coincide with long-established educational ideals and practices: school–community relations and the fostering in schools of initiative, creativity, independence and the ability to work with others.

A large number of projects and programmes under the banners of 'partnership' and 'enterprise education' have sprung up within the orbit of the new vocationalism with, on the ground locally, often considerable interaction between the projects and programmes. The most common forms of school–industry links in English secondary schools have been: work experience placements (in 91 per cent – schools with pupils in their final compulsory year), visits to industry (in 72 per cent – all secondary schools), curriculum development involving industry (in 52 per cent), mini-enterprises as part of the curriculum (in 40 per cent) and problem-solving projects specifically with industry (in 32 per cent) (OECD, 1992g, p.12). The development of such school–industry partnerships has also been widespread since the 1980s among other industrialised countries, with the key emerging pattern being that 'the vast majority of partnerships are small, local and basic' (OECD, 1992g, p.13).

The focus on 'enterprise', which we discussed with reference to the YTS in Chapter 7, has also been within the context of considerable international activity. After reviewing practical initiatives in various countries, Ball concluded that:

> there are, in effect, two definitions of, or approaches to, the word 'enterprise' and the practice of it. One approach, which can be termed a 'narrow' one, regards enterprise as business entrepreneurialism, and sees its promotion and development within education and training systems as an issue of curriculum development which enables young people to learn, usually on an experiential basis, about business start-up and management. The second approach, which can be termed the 'broad' one, regards enterprise as a group of qualities and competences which enable individuals, organisations, communities, societies and cultures to be flexible, creative and adaptable in the face of, and as contributors to, rapid social and economic change. . . . What is significant about the implications of the broad approach for educationalists is that it requires changes in education methods and pedagogy towards what is termed 'enterprise learning' rather than (as in the case of the narrow approach) changes in the curriculum.
>
> (Ball, 1988, p.3)

SCHOOL–INDUSTRY PARTNERSHIPS AND COMPACTS

The recent activity in school–industry partnerships in the UK is traced by Lawlor and Miller (1991) to the Schools Council Industry Project (SCIP), established in 1978 soon after James Callaghan's Ruskin College speech (see Chapter 5). Involving the Confederation of British Industry (CBI), it emphasised from the beginning local solutions to local problems, work experience, the development of simulations and case studies, and has pioneered mini-enterprise in schools. The launch of the TVEI in 1982, as we have seen, gave a strong impetus to a variety of school–industry contacts, during both its pilot and extension phases. Industry Year, designated in 1986 by the Royal Society of Arts, proved a concerted attempt to raise the esteem in which industry was held, through bringing together into local committees people from education and industry, to organise at least one activity or event in every school and college during the year.

In September 1988, the Enterprise and Education Initiative was launched by the Secretaries of State for Trade and Industry, Employment, and Education and Science. The initiative was to encourage

> more employers to become involved with their local schools. In particular, a network of advisers on enterprise and education, mainly

based in the private sector, is being established to help employers link up with schools in their area. They will work closely with all those involved in business and education link activities in their areas and will contribute to better co-ordination at the local level. Specific objectives include ensuring that enough employers are involved so as to provide work experience for every pupil before leaving school and for 10 per cent of teachers a year.

(DoE, 1988a, p.45)

Initiatives in the higher and further education sectors were also outlined at the same time (Enterprise in Higher Education Initiative and Work-related Further Education Programme).

In 1990, another grand initiative, the Education Business Partnership Initiative, was announced by the Secretaries of State for Employment, Education and Science, and Trade and Industry.

Partnerships between education and business offer opportunities to make education more relevant to life and work; to raise standards and levels of attainment, to raise enterprise awareness and industrial understanding amongst teachers and students, and to inform and develop advice and counselling so that individuals are better placed to build and use their skills.

(DoE, 1990a, p.1)

A number of demonstrable outcomes were expected from partnership activities, including:

* increased business involvement with, and support for, primary and secondary education;
* improved opportunities to assist students in school and college in the transition to work;
* increased volume, relevance and breadth of information and guidance offered to students by careers teachers and the Careers Service;
* increased numbers of young people staying in relevant and appropriate full-time and part-time education;
* improved access to, and participation in, further and higher education.

The partnership, which was to be developed locally by the then newly established TECs, thus had very ambitious and wide-ranging goals, with the expectations that activities in each locality would vary.

Of particular note among the plethora of school–industry link activities has been the development of compacts, modelled on the Boston, USA, compact of the early 1980s. The 'London Compact', launched in March 1987, was essentially an agreement between schools and employers in an area of high social and economic deprivation, with a history of mistrust and hostility between employers and educators. The agreement guaranteed offers of local jobs to pupils at participating inner-city schools if they fulfilled their side of the compact. This meant students attending 85 per cent of lessons, meeting nine out of ten deadlines for all assignments, completing a school record of achievement (the London Record of Achievement) and satisfactorily completing two weeks of work experience (Hargreaves, 1984; Nuttall, 1989; OECD, 1992g). Ainley notes that in reality,

> while they do not explicitly guarantee employment, employers under-take to give priority in job offers to those school-leavers who achieve the educational targets. This can mean a guaranteed interview or a reserved place on a company-run Youth Training scheme. Partici-pating employers also support school–industry links with the schools involved, by offering work experience, work shadowing, holiday jobs and teacher–industry exchanges.
>
> (Ainley, 1990, p.49)

Run by the London Education Business Partnership, the scheme initially involved the now defunct Inner London Education Authority and a consor-tium of companies, among them Whitbread, whose community pro-gramme director, Richard Martineau, was the moving force behind the initiative. One of the compact's main initial objectives was to encourage continued education in schools and colleges and increase the level of training at work. Employers would give day-release for school-leavers to continue studies and improve their qualifications. In the London pilot schools, teachers reported a dramatic growth in pupil retention at school after 16, where the compact's guarantee of a job held good until pupils were aged 18. Other effects to do with positive orientation towards work and becoming better qualified were reported.

The first year of the London Compact was seen as so successful that in 1988 the government adopted the idea and launched the compact initia-tive nationally, in the context of its Action for Cities Programme. For the national initiative,

> A Compact is an agreement between employers, young people, schools and colleges. Employers guarantee a job with training, or training leading to a job, to at least YTS standards, for every partici-pating young person who has achieved a set of agreed personal goals and objectives. And every school and college involved undertakes to support and encourage young people in the achievement of stand-ards and competences. Eventually, employers may wish to encourage young people to go on to further and higher education in order to meet their skills shortages at professional, managerial and technical level. This encouragement could include individual sponsorship, work experience and either full-time or part-time release.
>
> (DoE, 1988a, p.47)

In the first year of the programme, the government funded compacts in thirty areas of the country, and by 1989 it had become a £17 million programme of the Department of Employment. Subsequently, new forms of compacts were initiated in which higher and further education institutions guaranteed places on programmes to local students if they met previously agreed criteria. In at least Birmingham and London, there has been considerable productive interplay between compacts and the TVEI in local schools (OECD, 1992g, pp.90–93).

The interest of the compact initiative is in the positive – and formal – support seen to be given by local industries and employers to the mainstream education system; expensive new initiatives of the CTC variety, discussed below, are not part of the approach. Compacts are practical, unostentatious and something which could feasibly be – and indeed have already been – generalised to many areas of the country. Experience of compacts has shown that the idea of a deal between schools and businesses linked to student performance and recruitment can indeed help generate enthusiasm, but needs to be handled with care (OECD, 1992g, p.33). Inevitably, comparisons are drawn between the CTC and compact initiatives and employers have generally had to choose which to support, given the limitation on resources.

NEW KINDS OF SCHOOL

Consistent with its intention to reintroduce into a putative comprehensive system firm distinctions between different routes, whether to higher education or to a restructured technical – vocational system, late in 1986 the government announced plans to establish, as part of its Action for Cities Programme, twenty independent City Technology Colleges in selected inner-city locations. Each was to take between 750 and 1,000 11–18-year-old students across the full ability range. It was intended that the first colleges would open in 1988, and the full twenty be in operation by 1990. While progress has been less rapid than anticipated in these optimistic forecasts, the CTCs are yet another manifestation of the national endeavour to build bridges between education and employment.

> Their purpose will be to provide a broadly-based secondary education with a strong technological element thereby offering a wider choice of secondary school to parents in certain cities and a surer preparation for adult and working life to their children.
>
> (DES, 1986b, p.2)

To be established first on a pilot basis (as were the TVEI and CPVE), with the hope that their influence would spread, they were expected to adopt the best practices of the TVEI and successful secondary schools generally. Their status was to be that of registered independent schools, subject to inspection by HMI but charging no fees, and functioning alongside existing secondary schools. While they would obtain financial assistance from the DES, a substantial part of their cost was to be met by 'promoters', a return to the voluntary principle, but a pious hope as subsequent events proved.

The CTCs, despite the moderate success thus far in attaining the targets set by government, are of significance at this stage insofar as they signal strategies that go far beyond the institutions themselves. Behind the fundamental policy objective of government to interest the private sector in funding, and thereby to revive the dormant tradition of voluntary provision, lay another purpose, namely the weakening of the power of local education authorities, a policy since pursued with great vigour and on a number of fronts.

It was initially intended that CTCs would be established in twenty-seven designated inner-city areas, either purpose built on vacant sites or through purchasing redundant schools. A shortage of suitable sites bedevilled the scheme from the start, and, despite the initial intention of their serving deprived inner-city areas, there has instead been a first come first served approach to their approval, depending on available sites and sponsors being found. There appears, now, to be no geographic plan behind identifying potential CTCs, with three of the first fifteen close to each other in the outer London (Croydon) area (Ainley, 1990).

Sponsorship was much slower than anticipated, with the government by 1991 moving from the position that 'the principle of funding will be that the promoters will meet all or a substantial part of the capital costs' (DES, 1986b, p.8) to one which saw 'private business and industry . . . providing a substantial [sic] proportion – at least 20 per cent – of the capital funding for each of the colleges' (DES, 1991, p.1). Recurrent funding is provided by the state. Because of the high-tech approach to resourcing the schools, individual school set-up costs have been very high, leading to situations such as that in Nottingham where some £9 million was spent on building the new CTC as against the city's entire annual capital expenditure on all its schools of less than £2.5 million. It is thus hardly surprising that the CTC programme has engendered resentment among many working in the less resource favoured state sector, especially at a time when parents are being encouraged to choose schools. While CTCs officially have a non-selective intake, the government-stipulated criteria are seen to be unworkable and there appears no doubt about their taking a disproportionate percentage of the more motivated students, if only because of their preferring those who agree to remain until age 18 (Ainley, 1990; Murphy et al., 1990).

City Technology Colleges are certainly now under way, although the bold plans of twenty CTCs by 1990 was rather drastically revised downwards, with some fifteen to be operational by 1993 (Gillmon, 1992). Even when the ultimate goal of twenty pilot schools is reached, however, they constitute a very small group in relation to the nation's 4,000 secondary schools and their impact must be awaited. With a few exceptions, industry has been relatively slow in supporting them, reportedly in many cases because of jeopardising existing links with local schools where productive school–industry partnerships exist (McCullogh, 1991). They are more substantially government-supported than anticipated and also in some instances have generated considerable local parent and community antagonisms, especially where existing schools have been closed down to be sold as CTCs. Disquiet over the impact of CTCs on the offerings, morale and intake in neighbouring schools has been of concern to many education authorities (AMA, 1987). The role of CTCs as models for plans for specialist 'magnet' schools and for opting out by mainstream schools has been mentioned by some commentators; this point could be more persuasively made if the government's growth targets for CTCs had proved in any way realistic.

Plans for a new network of voluntary-aided CTCs – utilising part of the 1944 Education Act compromise on the then dominant religious question – were announced in 1990. These plans would enable an existing LEA school to apply to become a voluntary-aided CTC – as long as the school could raise £500,000 from sponsors. The government would provide further funds for refurbishment. The CTC Trust hopes also to find a way of enabling grant-maintained schools to gain CTC status.

The CTCs are to be treated as independent schools with no statutory requirement for them to comply with the national curriculum. National curriculum goals are, even so, expected to be influential in the different schools developing 'characteristic identities', and early indications support this.

Early indications, again, suggest that the learning programmes CTCs offer their pupils are innovative, and potentially challenging, drawing on much of the TVEI curriculum development of recent years – hardly surprising in a well-resourced, high profile new endeavour. Keeping up the momentum and establishing a well-structured 11–18 programme will prove a considerable challenge in years to come.

The form and content of the CTC curriculum as originally proposed by the DES put equal emphasis on technological content and on standards and attitudes: 'There will be a large technical and practical element within the broad and balanced curriculum . . . up to the age of 16. The importance of doing and understanding as well as knowing will be emphasised throughout' (DES, 1986b, p.7). Indeed, cross-curricular approaches based on projects and themes, mixed ability teaching and an emphasis on 'open' learning, backed by good investment in information technology have become the early trend.

Jones argues that

Increasingly, in CTCs, as elsewhere in secondary education, the emphasis is shifting from the discrete post-16 curriculum to planning for 14–19 education and training. For the majority of young people

224

this will mean a continuum rather than a cut-off point at 16, guided vocational choices beyond 14 leading to increased specialization towards 18 or 19, and a culture which takes for granted that education and training will continue throughout life.

(Jones, 1992, p.43)

In particular, CTCs are contributing to developments in: integrating post-16 education and the world of work (by working closely with local industry, encouraging a business-like culture in CTCs, emphasising vocationally oriented awards); broadening the curriculum (by offering a broad range of vocational options in addition to academic awards, developing strategies to allow students choice of accreditation, exploring possibilities for a coherent common curriculum for the post-16 age group); developing new vocational routes which have parity of status with academic progression routes to higher education (by their involvement in new awards, such as the Technological Baccalaureate); developing new curriculum methodologies (by piloting credit transfer schemes, developing modular curricula) (Jones, 1992, p.3).

Following the Continental pattern, CTCs operate longer school days, and on more days in the year, than most state-maintained schools. This is to allow for more enrichment activities and a more varied curriculum, and appears to have strong student, parent and teacher support (Hagedorn, 1992).

It seems probable that CTCs and other schools which take the opt-out/specialist route, with favoured treatment financially and selected pupils, will have sufficient vitality to generate their own values and learning patterns. This is to assume that the whole scheme continues to make progress, a subject upon which there has been much debate. We are still at the stage where policies have been declared and initial progress made but not to the point where it is clear that the lines set in the early stages will become embedded in the educational and training system.

The establishment of independent CTCs takes a stage further the administrative device introduced by the intervention of the MSC into the secondary schools with the launch of the TVEI. In November 1982, the then Chairman of the MSC, David Young, observed:

Much has been made in the media . . . that the MSC has the power and the authority to open its own establishments, so let me say at the outset that we have no intention of doing that as I believe and hope we can work as partners with the local education authorities. If that did not prove possible, then we might have to think again.

(Young, 1982, p.4)

In practice, local authorities have been willing to bid for resources with which to experiment with the TVEI. We have seen some LEAs willing to bear the brunt of parent and community opposition to closing existing schools, then selling them to open as CTCs. But we have also seen only a handful of major sponsors coming forward to endow CTCs, and the government needfully committing vastly greater funding than initially planned to the project.

In common with most of the initiatives under the new vocationalism, for the CTCs there is a variety of ostensible objectives: to prepare children for jobs with a high technological content (economic policy); to give parents greater choice of school and show responsiveness to criticism of existing schooling (education/consumerism policy); and to help fight inner-city decay (social/economic policy). As with other new vocationalism policies, it is important to examine very carefully the real, sometimes hidden, objectives. The published material about the CTCs makes it clear that although the organising principles and pedagogy of the education likely to be offered in CTCs bear marked similarities to the YTS and TVEI, the real point of CTCs, as far as government is concerned, lies in their broader new vocationalism characteristics and in the potential of CTCs, in consort with the other developments, to weaken the ideology and to restructure the framework of all-through comprehensive education. The CTC initiative, like its forebears, increases central government power, at the expense of the local authorities. This is the DES/DfE version of the instruments used effectively by the MSC for rapid construction and change – mainly the disposal of substantial sums of government money.

The CTCs also form part of the government strategy of offering choice to the parent – the shopping basket of schools. Parents, keen to choose new publicity-conscious schools which appear likely to increase the pupils' job prospects, could well be attracted by the standards of discipline, the emphasis on attitudes and the acquisition of qualifications. But many parents appear reluctant to do this at the expense of losing existing schools.

The most likely pattern of development is the establishment and successful operation of a relatively small number of CTCs. These will act as development and demonstration sites for both official and unofficial ideas about more practical, applied, work/industry-related education. Their influence on the national system is likely to be quite moderate overall, but on specific topics – for example, project-based teaching, school–industry partnerships, advanced technology teaching – some of them may serve a lighthouse role. It is for these reasons, not the scale of the innovation, that the CTC project deserves closer scrutiny and its development will be watched with considerable interest by the whole education community and not only those with a particular vocational bent.

A not unrelated development is the Technology Schools Initiative (TSI) which was launched in December 1991 by the then Minister of State Tim Eggar. It aims at establishing a network of secondary schools committed to providing technology and associated courses of a strongly vocational nature. Eventually the experience of these TSI schools should be disseminated system-wide. The initiative allocated capital funding for equipment and building work, totalling some £50 million, to 222 schools over the first two years (D. Short, personal communication).

SUMMARY

For the past two decades new thinking and programmes for strengthening the vocational dimension of schooling have called into question long-established policies and practices in the worlds of both education and work. It has been an era of fast-moving innovation, with more evidence of a determination to design and implement new programmes than of carefully planned and evaluated experiments or overall policy coherence.

The MSC has been a leader but not the only one. At the national level, the DES and agencies such as the FEU have played a major part, steadily regaining the policy-dominant role that seemed to be slipping away from them in the early 1980s. In the background the long-established school and further education sectors and the examining and accrediting bodies have themselves adapted to the policy changes, responded to the resource opportunities and repositioned themselves to absorb the new thinking and, in due course, to reaffirm their roles as the primary deliverers of education, both general and vocational.

This chapter has illustrated the quest for new 16-plus qualifications, the move to orient the secondary curriculum towards work, new kinds of schools and school–industry links and partnerships, and the unresolved dilemmas in the continuing 16-plus jungle. With the increasing numbers staying on post-16 – and the prospect of the effective universalisation of upper secondary schooling – the case for a comprehensive and searching reform strategy for 16-plus becomes overwhelming, the A level obstacles notwithstanding.

Although remarkably fruitful in ideas and energetic as never before, the new vocationalism, as expressed through these developments, has still been somewhat to the side, in terms of impact upon mainstream educational thinking, with many of the old problems remaining. While there have been many specific innovations, it is far from clear whether the system as a whole has learned the lessons the reformers have been urging upon the country.

9

EDUCATION AND TRAINING
FOR ALL YOUTH

The idea still prevails that a truly cultural or liberal education cannot have anything in common, directly at least, with industrial affairs, and that education which is fit for the masses must be a useful or practical education in a sense which opposes useful and practical to nurture of appreciation and liberation of thought.

(Dewey, 1916, p.301)

The upsurge of interest in the vocational dimension of education in the world's industrialised and industrialising countries has as its root cause two of the central objects of modern public policy, namely, creating basic conditions for sustained economic growth, and ensuring that the workforce is both quantitatively and qualitatively adequate in the face of changing demands. Other considerations include concern over the social and personal consequences of large pools of low-skilled, unemployed young people, rigidities in the established education and training systems and the need to establish new kinds of roles and relationships among the several partners in the education and training enterprises.

These policy concerns, both economic and social, in turn are the manifestation, in the public sphere, of that interplay of scientific, technological and productive forces which, together with democratisation, have created the modern state. Not merely a piece of remedial action to correct certain deficiencies and imbalances in education and training, the new vocationalism is itself an aspect or dimension of that 'rationality' which, from Max Weber to Jürgen Habermas, has been treated as the defining characteristic of the market-based bourgeois, capitalist state. It was in the 1960s that this model of the state received its most severe challenge in the post-war era – in the form of the large-scale protest movements in Western Europe, the United States and Australasia, and in the 1970s that the market-based societies mounted a serious 'counter-reformation' which included a resurgence of neo-liberal ideologies. The 1960s' challenge, which was a crisis that passed, was more fundamental in that the target was the capitalist system itself. The chronic condition that supervened – large-scale unemployment with attendant skills–employment mismatches – although less fundamental, in that the society itself was not a direct object of attack, was just as threatening. It suggested that the system was, for large numbers of its members and especially the young, unable to provide the conditions (work and income) that were necessary for full social participation and to enjoy the principal benefit offered by the system, namely a high and increasing standard of material well-being.

For this and for other reasons, which in Britain include a succession of economic crises on the one hand and, on the other, the steady rise of knowledge-based industry, education and training, have rapidly become among the foremost objects of national policy. The belief that investment in and reform of any main area of education and training can significantly affect economic growth and ameliorate social deprivation demonstrates that there has been a fundamental change in economic and social thinking. The classical factor of labour has been transformed into trained intelligence and high levels of education throughout the community, and there has been a restoration of confidence in the social consequences of educational improvements – both the avoidance of 'harm' to the foundation of the socio-economic system, and the maintenance of stability and steady growth of that system. While this may still be a debatable point in economic and social theory, and while the precise role of particular forms of intelligence and education cannot be equated with specific economic or social outcomes, it is easy to understand the renewal of interest in education and training as key factors in public policy. A very clear case, but not the only one, is the substantial decline in the demand for untrained and unskilled labour. Another illustration is provided by the expansion of the professions and of the service sector of commerce and industry which, unlike traditional agriculture and manufacturing, provide few opportunities for poorly educated people. Yet again, the scale of social problems, of poverty amidst plenty, of crime, urban decay and social and economic disadvantage, has occasioned a fresh interest in the potential of public intervention, including education and training programmes, to succeed in preventative measures where remediation is often a costly failure.

Thus countries facing major economic and social challenges, whether in the form of declining productivity and competitiveness, shortages of key personnel required for new developments or social disorder and deprivation, have turned to education as a major instrument of economic as well as social reform. Britain provides a striking example of this tendency, since it is a country in which, until relatively recently in historical terms, there existed neither public structures nor public policies for universal education extending from early childhood into adulthood. The extraordinary scale and scope of educational reform measures in Britain during the past two decades is a measure of recognition that a restructuring of the system is an essential prerequisite for the new directions for social and economic policies that have been sought.

The vocational dimension of education even in its broader definition is not, of course, the only one which has been addressed during this period of unprecedented upheaval. The restructuring of the school curriculum and assessment of student performance, the conversion of higher education from a binary to a unitary system, the changes in governance, accountability and control, are among the indicators of a determination by central government to play a much more decisive and strategic role in educational policy than at any previous period in the country's history.

Vocational education, or rather the vocationalising of education, is, in this process, one of several key elements in the government's and the wider community's interest in educational reform. As we have seen, the initial approach was to erect or to reinforce a separate and distinctive 'vocational' system. This was to be separate in two senses. First, new structures and forms of organisation, finance and control, independent of and often in competition with those that existed for the formal education system, whether through the Department of Education and Science or through the local education authorities. Second, the vocational system was to be separate in the sense that it was defined as a form or type of training that was work-based or very closely work-focused and distinctly different from that typically provided by schools and colleges, whether part of the general education system or indeed within the older tradition of vocational education. It was soon realised both that a wholly separate vocational system was not attainable and that as much effort was needed in the reorientation of school and college education in general as in the development of work-based, targeted employment preparation schemes.

Among the several endeavours to achieve a distinctive and separate form of training, the Youth Training Scheme (YTS) stands out as both a symbol of the new vocationalism, and, for the decade of the 1980s at least, a very considerable part of its substance. It started on something of a triumphalist note as an employer-led, work-based Department of Employment/ Manpower Services Commission (MSC)-financed scheme. Its meteoric career was witness to changes of policy and control to the point where the YTS has been largely reabsorbed into a wide and varied landscape of vocational initiatives. In reviewing the YTS, and in particular the highly innovatory strategy of core skills, we have drawn attention alike to its achievements and to its weaknesses. That scheme was accompanied and followed by other initiatives, of which the Technical and Vocational Education Initiative (TVEI) within the school system is not only of most relevance to the themes and issues we have discussed but also perhaps of most significance in terms of effect on thinking about the place of the vocational element within the educational mainstream.

The new vocationalism has been a most substantial response, to serious, deep-seated problems and to fundamental challenges which faced Britain. Yet, notwithstanding the evidence of major transformations in thinking and the structures and instruments of state action, and the innovatory nature of programmes such as the YTS, TVEI and others that we have addressed, there has been only a slow evolution in the understanding of what the new vocationalism is really about. In the years between the establishment of the MSC in 1973 and the beginning of the last decade of the twentieth century, profound changes in the British economy and society have brought about a realisation that the concept of the vocational and the structures to support it including those recently put in place must themselves change.

The orthodox view of vocational education is and has for long been that it is the form of education – often termed training – that is oriented towards a single point, namely work in the restricted sense of that term – that is, regular, paid employment. Vocational education or training is that which makes people more useful as workers and more employable. General education, on the other hand, serves a much wider range of intellectual, moral, social, civic, aesthetic and personal concerns. The distinction is commonly made, but it is a false one, based on an unreflective traditionalism which is a correlate of obsolete forms of social stratification. For reasons that we shall now consider, its utility – to the extent that it was ever useful – is greatly diminished by dramatic changes in the world of employment and in our understanding of what work entails over and above the performance of a job, in the progress of knowledge and in the democratisation of the social order.

Two basic considerations affect the analysis. First, a very large and varied array of educational experiences, not merely those labelled 'vocational' or 'training', may properly be regarded as fitting people – ultimately – for work and employment. This has always been so and is obvious if one considers the role of so-called general or academic education in preparing personnel for the professions and the Civil Service, for example. Now, as industry and commerce, the professions and other fields of employment become increasingly knowledge-dependent, education that is preparatory for them must, for the typical worker, incorporate more powerful concepts, intellectual strategies, advanced structures of knowledge, stronger theories and other qualitative improvements. Basic skills training is necessary but very far from sufficient. The increased holding power of the school or college is another consideration: youth is being largely removed from the labour market and is instead being increasingly schooled. This means greater not lesser attention to the educative role of the school, including the vocational dimension as a part of general education.

Second, important as work in the economic sense is, it occupies a decreasing proportion of the lifespan and the role of worker must be interrelated with many other roles, personal, social and cultural, that are part of the lifeworld of all people in democratic societies. Preparation for paid employment must be treated as one of several, interrelated dimensions of the educational process. 'Training' can be separated out but only on the condition that it is subsequently reintegrated into this wider process of 'life formation'. The time for building a large-scale separate system of work-based or work-focused vocational training in Britain was the latter part of the nineteenth and first half of the twentieth centuries. Serious losses resulted from failure to do so then, but they are not a reason, now, to try to build what would indeed be an anachronistic system.

The strategies, vocationally oriented programmes and innovations of various kinds that we have discussed represent attempts that have been made, especially but not exclusively in Britain, to achieve greater clarity and focus in both thinking and practice. Initially, these attempts consisted of an undesirably sharp separation of the vocational from other forms of education. That separation, although it continues in certain structures and attitudes, has become increasingly irrelevant in policy and practice. What, then, is distinctive of the new vocationalism, and to what extent can it be regarded as a fundamental transformation or rehabilitation of the vocational education system in Britain, a basis for the future rather than a tardy attempt to overcome past deficiencies? That a kind of rehabilitation, indeed reconstruction and creation, has taken place is undeniable, but one of the consequences, a welcome if perhaps an unexpected one, is that the distinctiveness of the vocational, at least as far as youth education is concerned, has begun to disappear. The objective of notable thinkers earlier in the century, such as Dewey and Whitehead, has been achieved, if unintentionally, in that the classical distinction between separate vocational and general kinds of education no longer makes sense in the education of children and youth.

The new vocationalism is nevertheless still too often presented as if it had an existence, a reality independent of the theory and practice of education in general. Yet, from the activities and the analysis of the past two decades, no clear or obvious way of distinguishing general from vocational education and separating vocational as a distinct domain of the overall educational enterprise has emerged, unless it be the contingent controlling mechanisms, or the instrumentalist assumptions and values. The vocational is said to be distinguished by its practicality. But writing an essay, carrying out a laboratory experiment, conducting a field survey and undertaking a simulation on a computer – all common features of the curriculum of schools and higher education – are also practical. The vocational is said to be responsive to well-defined social and economic need and indeed to be defined as a deduction from such need.

Such responsiveness is now a common feature of statements of major educational reform strategies for all levels and forms of education – where it is no less problematic or value-laden than is the case with the differentiated vocational tendency. A new science syllabus for upper secondary education or a programme of drug awareness in lower secondary schools, or schools undertaking local waste-recycling activities as part of an environmental awareness programme, are examples of direct response to a defined social need, to say nothing of the functions of formal education in laying the foundation for economic activity of all kinds.

The vocational is sometimes defined as a programme or course created through a close partnership between employers and training institutions. Such partnerships are neither novel, in that they are a long-established feature of the technical and further education sectors, nor is the theme of partnership in any way distinctive of particular courses given its growing significance in schools and higher education. Vocational education and training is said to be characterised by its grounding in the working world – often it is provided in the workplace itself. This is a significant consideration, but the settings of the formal education system have become increasingly diverse and often include work experience. Moreover, we must look beyond the setting ('school', 'workplace') to see what kind of teaching and learning processes are in use: their similarities may be as great as their differences. In these and other ways the lines between vocational and general education have become blurred.

Is the vocational to be defined by virtue of its direct relevance, in content, procedures and institutional linkages, with paid, regular employment? Is vocational that which is a direct preparation for paid employment? The link with employment is the strongest and clearest point in the argument that vocational education is to be understood as a distinctive and in important senses a separate field of endeavour. This argument has been, historically, a most persuasive one. The historical evolution of vocational education is a story of ideas and practices which directly relate education to employment. Vocational education for young people has most often been a separate stream or system of institutions whose objectives, content and ways of teaching and learning have all been shaped by perceived employment needs and demands. It should be noted, however, that traditionally these needs and demands relate primarily to the blue-collar worker: there was, as we saw in reviewing the work of the great nineteenth-century commissions, a very definite social class bias in the concept of the vocational. This bias has long existed in practice and helps to explain both the low status of much of what is defined as vocational training and the difficulty of achieving in practice a unitary concept of general and vocational education.

Structural change in society, however, does occur and it profoundly affects established relationships and understandings. Such changes can destroy the basis of long-standing patterns and alter the meanings and the systems of thought to which they give rise. The direct link between vocational education and employment depends upon the availability of employment and the nature of tasks to be performed in the workplace as much as it does upon the specific content and organisation of the educational regime. Change the employment factor and the educational regime must itself change. Conversely the advancement of knowledge and educational changes, especially in the field of advanced science and technology and the social sciences, have profound effects on the nature of employment – as in new ideas about the service sector or such sunrise industries as computing and genetic engineering. Changes in employment (which reciprocate with higher education and research), such as the apparent inability of societies like Britain to generate a sufficient quantity of jobs and the demands for improved competence, have rendered obsolete traditional notions of vocational training. What we have witnessed during the past two decades is a series of endeavours to find alternatives, to resolve both quantitative and qualitative issues.

The major contribution of the MSC was to initiate a powerful critique of established educational and training policies and practices in Britain and to follow this with alternatives in the form of experimental training strategies for the young whether in work or school or unemployed. These initiatives, at first pointing towards a separate system of vocational training, have themselves contributed to the new understanding of just what a modern system of vocational education and training entails. The new vocationalism of the MSC was to be new in the sense that it was to be redefined and restructured in accordance with the dramatically changed economic and labour market conditions facing Britain in the aftermath of the Second World War. New strategies and programmes were developed with immense effort, vast resources, and varying degrees of uptake and impact. The most profound structural change in the period we have been examining, however, is not to be found in the design and development of new programmes and organisations to deliver them but in the decline, temporary revival, and now, it seems, final collapse of the youth labour market. A form of education in early to mid adolescence which has as its immediate objective and organising principle preparation for employment is fundamentally flawed if employment ceases to be an option or becomes such a distant and remote prospect as to render the claims for employment relevance and preparation hollow. The demise of the MSC, and the waning influence of its successor bodies, whatever specific politico-bureaucratic factors were at work, symbolises the collapse of the strategy of training the mass of youth for immediate employment in the adolescent years.

While there may be a case for treating employment of a very special kind as a continuing option for youth, it can no longer be regarded as a primary objective and target in education and training at that stage. In a segmented labour market, there will no doubt remain limited opportunities for full-time, paid youth employment, but these are likely to be in jobs which are short term or of limited significance for purposes of long-term career development. Even jobs such as these can – and ought to – be combined with systematic education. Requiring either relatively low levels of competence or highly specialised knowledge, and often being of a temporary or transient nature, such jobs do not warrant the elaborate and expensive apparatus of national policy frameworks, except that they should be included in a national policy of full-/part-time education for all youth up to and beyond the age of 18 or 19 years.

Employment in the sense of a full-time, paid occupation which provides the chief source of income for the individual and is a major factor in the economic production of the country, no longer makes sense as a serious option for young people or a youth policy objective for government. In recognition of this, there is a growing consensus that the employment of youth should not be a significant policy objective of the advanced industrialised countries in the future. This is not to suggest that opportunities for work have evaporated in the broad sense that we have discussed, a point to which we return below, but rather that policy thinking needs to be directed at a lifestyle for young people which will involve continuing education, leisure and recreation, physical activities and the performance of socially useful, but not necessarily economically productive, tasks. As 'employment' recedes as a major objective of youth policy, so does the concept of 'work' become more salient as a dimension or quality of each of these elements of the lifestyle. It is 'work' that must be severed from its traditional identification with paid employment and brought into a dynamic relationship with education to replace that which has been so earnestly and unsuccessfully sought for, 'paid employment'.

Education for work or work-oriented education should thus become the object of our concern and 'vocational' should revert to its earlier connotation, namely as a chosen form of life, a means of achieving fulfilment and the development of full human potential in some broadly defined field of human endeavour. Training of a highly specific kind should become increasingly an employer responsibility and be seen in a context of lifetime skill formation and re-formation according to changing employment needs and personal interest.

Unfortunately, the deflection of the more profound insights that have emerged from the new vocationalism experience into a new qualifications industry means that a critical reappraisal of work, education and training in the context of lifelong learning is receiving scant attention.

While these reflections might suggest a revival of utopian thinking, it must be reiterated that their source is not the gospel of Saint-Simon, John Ruskin or William Morris but the changed conditions of the modern economy and the circumstances in the modern society where large segments of the youth population find too few opportunities for personal fulfilment and worthwhile action. The development of human potential during the years of adolescence and of outlets for its expression in socially worthwhile activities, are proper objects of national policy but that policy is still not rising sufficiently to the challenge. It is only a hundred years since on both economic and political grounds efforts to extend full-time schooling from the elementary into the secondary years were successfully resisted. Child labour was eventually proscribed in advanced countries for very good reasons; adolescent labour is now similarly anachronistic, even though the conditions of that labour have vastly improved by comparison with the exploitative conditions of the Victorian age. What, then, are young people to do?

When the new vocationalism began to gather strength in Britain in the 1960s, it was quite reasonably, for the time, presented as a long overdue response to structural weaknesses and failures of practice in the national approach to preparing young people for work. There was then a long-established tradition of young people leaving school and taking up paid employment in the early to middle years of adolescence. Indeed, that seemed to the average young person and her or his family to be in the nature of things, continuing full-time education being the natural order for those who were destined for higher occupations and social prominence. At that time there were severe mismatches between the competences required in the employment sector and those possessed by many young people. The economy was in need of a better and differently trained young labour force, and unemployment, by contrast with more recent years, was of modest proportions. Although, in some countries the beginnings of universal participation in a full secondary education were already apparent, in Britain participation rates beyond the age of 15 and then, when the leaving age was raised, to 16, were extremely low. Of the three principal options available to youth: paid employment, continued full-time education and unemployment, the first was, for a variety of understandable reasons, preferred for and by a majority of young people. The schooling option was, in the memorable words of one young school-leaver as quoted in the Newsom Report, decidedly unattractive: 'It might all be marble, sir, but it would still be a bloody school.'

Unemployment, a spectre from the 1920s and 1930s for large parts of the population, the enemy that Keynes and Beveridge from their different perspectives set themselves to put down, and a frightening economic and social prospect for governments, was a major driving force in the efforts to restructure and reform education along vocational lines. The dangerously over-simplified argument ran then in some official circles: unemployment is a significant function of the low skill levels of youth; those in employment have higher skills than those not; raise the skill levels, and thereby reduce unemployment. What this formulation lacked in logic and empirical foundations, it made up in rhetorical power. Bitter disputes took place between education and labour market people, the one group feeling they were being unfairly and inappropriately blamed for rising youth unemployment; the latter perplexed and frustrated by the inadequacies of the educational system.

While the origins of the new vocationalism in the employment situation and the economic difficulties of the 1960s and early 1970s are understandable and explain both the urgency and the scale of the reform efforts, it is necessary now to take a very different view of the matter. The case for the school option, as distinct from the work option, for youth has become stronger not only by virtue of the structural changes in the labour market that we have referred to but also as a result of changes that have occurred and are occurring in schooling itself. These changes are in part an outcome of the new vocationalism movement itself. The sustained critique of education from a vocational standpoint, which we have considered in previous chapters, has not been without its effects. In particular, the introduction of a vocational strategy through the TVEI has major implications, still being worked out, for the curriculum and ways of teaching and learning throughout secondary education. Despite the difficulties of achieving substantial changes in schooling, to many of which we have already alluded, change is possible and is occurring. Through dialogue, closer co-operation and partnerships between the various interest groups, through continuing review of the contents of education, through new orientations in teacher education and through changes in monitoring and assessment, it is certainly possible to implement major reform strategies. Such changes require sustained effort, nationally and locally, in both the public and private sectors, and a continuity of purpose and approach, all of which have been lacking in the past in British education, but are now much more in evidence. Still needed, however, are a more concerted quest for consensus and a replacement of the rapid succession of new programmes and structures by a steadier, longer-term, research-based strategy where changes become inbuilt rather than abandoned because of their unworkability.

The challenge that the new vocationalism has presented is essentially one no longer to vocational education as a distinct and separate entity for youth, but to education as a whole. The specific, job-related training function traditionally associated with vocational education is better seen as a responsibility of employers, to be carried out both within enterprises and in the transition period between formal education and work which, as we have argued, for the large majority of young people in the future will be a function of early adulthood. The lessons of training learnt from the new vocationalism will also be highly relevant in adult training and retraining, for which there is a growing need, thus there is a legacy of fertile ideas and innovations with a high degree of relevance, both to the general education system and to the specialised system of adult training and retraining. The latter is not our concern in this book, but for the former, several tasks not yet completed might be mentioned.

In the construction of the new national curriculum, there has been undue reliance on the traditional, subject-centred models which have long dominated secondary education in Britain. Work done on core skills and on learning processes more generally within the new vocationalism is a valuable and under-used resource for strengthening and diversifying the subject requirements of the national curriculum. If indeed all young people are to stay on throughout the years of secondary schooling, beyond the GCSE, up to and beyond the sixth form, further thought, beyond the orthodoxies of the national curriculum and its associated testing regime, must be given to curriculum structures and assessment tasks. They are still too much modelled on the expectations and requirements of the minority or a bare majority of the population, too much an embodiment of the interests of academic professionalisation and its social correlates. The sixth form and the A level examination represent icons of a system which, whatever its values – and they are certainly high – is no longer adequate for the impending age of universal schooling to age 18 or so. The first requirement is to recognise that all youth have an entitlement to full-time education or combined education and work-based training which, whatever its particular character, is formally acknowledged as of equal worth and value in society. The persistence of a highly selective and socially stratified system beyond the age of 16 has been the major weakness in British policy and should be resolutely addressed.

Whether the device of National Vocational Qualifications (NVQs) will prove to be of great value is a question to pose. Its emphasis on employment-related competences misses the point of the changes to which we have drawn attention on the one hand, and, on the other, over-emphasises outcomes at the expense of the processes and the settings in and through which these outcomes have been expressed and developed.

However, a reconstructed national qualifications framework has considerable potential in achieving the unified structures that are necessary if the historically deeply divided system of education and training in Britain is to be replaced by a more coherent set of clearly defined, sequential and well-linked learning pathways.

Of the other themes which have been prominent in the new vocationalism two of the most pervasive may be summed up in the expressions 'work-based' and 'enterprise' learning. The idea of work-based learning is not at all inconsistent with the school-based model. On the contrary, as we have outlined it, the concept of work has no necessary relationship with paid employment, but refers to attributes and characteristics which need to be expressed in a wide variety of activities. Such ideas as a clear sense of purpose, a commitment to tasks which have a discernible result, continuity and perseverance of activity, readiness to address and solve problems, willingness and ability to work co-operatively with others, a commitment to completing tasks to a high standard and a keen interest in the products and consequences of one's activities are of great importance in the education of all people. The idea of a work base is that the need for such characteristics is more visible and opportunities for operationalising them more readily available in the workplace. In the school or college setting, which can be thought of as a base for education and not merely a place in which people are educated, such qualities and opportunities can and should be developed, in close association not only with employers but also other community interest groups.

The continuing interest in analysing and developing enterprise skills and more broadly in competence has been one of the principal strengths of the new vocationalism. Schooling which confirms and registers failure, which fails to elicit the interest and active engagement of all students, which creates dependencies, and rewards low levels of information recall needs to be challenged and replaced by the kinds of qualities that have been to the fore in the discussions of enterprise culture. Indeed we should be looking to the schools to transform a traditional academic culture which has certainly benefited and rewarded those who experience success in it by a culture which, perhaps under the name of enterprise, projects an image of achievement, performance, competence and successful effort. It is such a culture that the new vocationalism has played a significant part in defining: it constitutes a large part of its legacy to the educational system, and provides a profound challenge to the whole educational community.

For the future, it seems clear that the policy agenda of the past two to three decades will be continued, with such remaining gaps and weaknesses in the national structures that have been erected attended to according to the underlying assumptions that have been such a consistent feature of the new vocationalism. The challenge that all of this represents to older traditions and established ways is a worthy one, but there are dangers. The first is the persistence of an unreflective, uncritical confidence in a systems approach that has been manifested in the successive schemes and structures. There is an over-reliance on models (for example, of skill formation and of assessment), the pre-specification (in an uncertain world) of 'outputs', which is combined with weak or inadequate analysis of aims, values and purposes and a studied neglect of curriculum structures.

This problem is exacerbated by a second issue, which is the growing acceptance of unemployment or, more precisely, lack of job opportunities for the young, as an artifact of the system which can be tolerated and to which the system can adjust – for example, through income support and training schemes which are not so much a preparation for gainful employment as a substitute for it. If indeed full employment is not an object of policy, why so much emphasis on training for employment unless that training is of a highly specific kind for high-level jobs? To put the matter differently, tolerance of a high level of unemployment is an argument for less rather than more mass vocational training and for such training as is provided to be much more targeted than has been the case in the new vocationalism. There needs to be a rethinking of the employment issue, since ambivalence of employment policy is creating unnecessary confusion and uncertainty in the goals for education and training.

A third concern is that just as there is a risk that a permanent accommodation will be reached with unemployment, so will the confusion and discontinuities of the present pattern of post-16 education be tolerated indefinitely on the grounds that a national system of qualifications will provide something for everyone. One of the achievements of the new vocationalism is its challenge to some of the ancient hierarchies. In the post-16 arena, the hierarchy that has not been sufficiently or effectively challenged is that which has the single subject A level system at its peak. For as long as this continues there will remain a status stratification that contradicts one of the fundamental objectives of the new vocationalism, which was to gain parity of esteem for a wide range of competences beyond those associated with theoretical knowledge defined according to the conventions of academic subjects. We have argued for a common core curriculum approach extending into the upper years of secondary education. From this perspective, the A level strand would be an option, of critical importance, yes, but not the dominant force it now is, not only in the upper secondary stage but in the influence it extends lower down. Clearly the universities, and perhaps especially the newer ones, could play a very significant role in the needed reconstruction of the upper secondary years.

A final concern is that the welcome development of dialogue, partnerships and other forms of communication between formal education and training and the wider community may come to be seen, not as a genuine interchange from which all will learn and through which all will modify their actions, but as one-sided domination of education by the employment interest. Much has been said to alleviate this concern. However, good intentions may be undermined by social structures and social dynamics. A powerful apparatus for the control and direction of decision-making has been established in part as a function of the new vocationalism. This apparatus has substantially diminished the authority and direct influence of the education profession. It is the prospect of dominance by particular sets of technical and political interests that has caused many educators to question the increasing integration of education and employment. Yet one of the achievements of the new vocationalism has been to show the way in developing new forms of dialogue and communication. What is needed is a restoration of the ideal of consensus and a sharing of values which will not be those exclusive to any one of the partners but a new creation of them all.

BIBLIOGRAPHY

Abramovitz, M. (1988) *Thinking About Growth*. Cambridge. Cambridge University Press.

Achtenhagen, F. (1992) 'How should research on vocational and professional education react to new challenges in life and in the worksite'. Paper presented at the European Conference on Educational Research, University of Twente. Mimeo.

Adamski, W. and Grootings, P. (eds) (1989) *Youth, Education and Work in Europe*. London. Routledge.

Adler, M. (1982) *The Paideia Proposal*. New York. Macmillan.

Ailes, C.P. and Rushing, F.W. (1980), *A Summary Report on the Educational Systems of the United States and the Soviet Union: Comparative Analysis*. Washington, DC. Department of Education.

Ainley, P. (1988) *From School to YTS: Education and Training in England and Wales, 1944–1987*. Milton Keynes. Open University Press.

Ainley, P. (1990) *Vocational Education and Training*. London. Cassell Education.

Aitken, J. (1946) Letter from the Duke of Wellington to Mr Croker, 6 March 1833 in *English Letters of the XIX Century*. Harmondsworth, Middlesex. Penguin.

Alberty, H. (1947) *Reorganizing the High School Curriculum*. New York. Macmillan.

Aldcroft, D.H. and Richardson, H.W. (1969) *The British Economy 1870–1939*. London. Macmillan.

AMA (Association of Metropolitan Authorities) (1987) *City Technology Colleges: A Speculative Investment*. London. AMA.

Amaya, T. (1990) *Recent Trends in Human Resource Development*. Tokyo. Japan Institute of Labour.

American Association for the Advancement of Science (1989) *Science for All Americans*. Washington, DC. AAAS.

Annett, J. and Sparrow, J. (1986) 'Transfer of training: a review of research and practical implications'. *PLET* 22(2), pp.116–124.

Anthony, P.D. (1977) *The Ideology of Work*. London. Tavistock.

Appay, B. (1989) *Social Control and Training: A Comparative Study of Recent Developments in Training in France and England*. European Perspectives No. 3. Post-16 Education Centre. London. Institute of Education, University of London.

Araujo e Oliveira, J.B. (1992) 'The Business of Learning'. Geneva. ILO. Mimeo.

Arendt, H. (1959) *The Human Condition*. New York. Doubleday Anchor Books.

Armytage, W.H.G. (1955) *Civic Universities*. London. Benn.

Armytage, W.H.G. (1970) *Four Hundred Years of English Education*. London. Cambridge University Press.

241

Ashmore, C. (1987) 'Vocational education in the USA as a vehicle for the entre-preneurial spirit' in Twining, J., Nisbet, S. and Megarry, J. (eds) *Vocational Education*. World Yearbook of Education 1987. London. Kogan Page.

Ashton, D., Maguire, M. and Spilsbury, M. (1990) *Restructuring the Labour Market: The Implications for Youth*. Cambridge Studies in Sociology. London. Macmillan.

Australian Education Council (1991) *Young People's Participation in Post-compulsory Education and Training*. AEC Review Committee. Canberra. AGPS.

Australian Education Council (1992) *National Report on Schooling in Australia 1991*. Melbourne. Curriculum Corporation.

Australian Education Council and Ministers for Vocational Education, Employ-ment and Training (1992) *Putting General Education to Work: The Key Competencies Report*. Sydney. Sands and McDougall.

Bailey, W. (1978) *One Year Pre-employment Courses for Students Aged 16 Plus: A Survey of Provision in Colleges of Further Education*. London. Garnett College.

Baker, K. (1989) 'Further education: A New Strategy'. Speech by Secretary of State for Education and Science to Annual Conference of the Association of Colleges of Further and Higher Education. London. Department of Education and Science.

Ball, C. (1988) 'Towards an "Enterprising" Culture'. The Social and Economic Integration of Young People project. Paris. OECD. Mimeo.

Ball, C. (1991) *Learning Pays: The Role of Post-Compulsory Education and Training*. Interim Report. London. Royal Society of Arts.

Barnabo, L. (1985) 'Adolescents in Italy' in Skilbeck, M., Lowe, N. and Tait, K. (eds) *A Question of Quality: the core skills project of the Youth Training Scheme in international perspective*. London. MSC/London University, Institute of Education.

Barnes, D., Johnson, G., Jordan, S., Layton, D., Medway, P. and Yeomans, D. (1987) *The TVEI Curriculum 14–16: A Second Report Based on Case Studies in 26 Schools*. Leeds. University of Leeds.

Barnett, C. (1986) *The Audit of War: Illusion and Reality of Great Britain as a Great Nation*. London. Macmillan.

Bates, I. (1989) 'Versions of vocationalism: an analysis of some social and political influences on curriculum policy and practice'. *British Journal of Sociology of Education* 10(2), p.215.

Bayliss, S. and Jackson, M. (1982) 'MSC threatens l.e.a.'s with rival technical school system'. *Times Educational Supplement*, 19 November, pp. 1, 3.

Bell, G.H. (1981) 'Industrial culture and the school: some conceptual and practical issues in the schools–industry debate'. *Journal of Philosophy of Education* 15(2), pp.175-189.

Benner, H., Krekeler, N. and Pampus, K. (1985) 'Core curriculum and vocational learning: information and remarks from the German standpoint' in Skilbeck, M., Lowe, N. and Tait, K. (eds) *A Question of Quality: the core skills project of the Youth Training Scheme in international perspective*. London. MSC/London Univer-sity, Institute of Education.

Bennett, W.J. (1987) *James Madison High School: A Curriculum for American Students*. Washington, DC. US Department of Education.

Bennett, W.J. (1988) *American Education: Making it Work*. Washington, DC. US Department of Education.

Benson, C. and Silver, H. (1991) 'Vocationalism in the United Kingdom and the United States'. Working Paper No. 10. Post-16 Education Centre. London. Insti-tute of Education, University of London.

Benson, J. and Lloyd, J. (1983) *New Technology and Industrial Change: The Impact of the Scientific–Technical Revolution on Labour and Industry*. London. Routledge & Kegan Paul.

Berton, F., Podevin, G. and Verdier, E. (1991) 'Continuing vocational training in France: review and perspectives'. *Training and Employment: French Dimensions* No. 2, winter. Paris. CEREQ.

Bertrand, O. (1992) 'Assessment, certification and recognition of occupational skills and competences: comparability and recognition of qualifications: European experiences'. Paper for conference on The Changing Role of Vocational and Technical Education and Training, Porto. Paris. OECD. Mimeo.

Best, J.H. (ed.) (1962) *Benjamin Franklin on Education*. New York. Teachers College, Columbia University.

BIAC/TUAC Committee to the OECD (Business and Industry Advisory Committee to the OECD/Trade Union Advisory Committee to the OECD) (1991) *Education and Training: A Joint Statement by BIAC and TUAC*. Paris. BIAC/TUAC.

Biggs, J. (1985) 'Core skills and the curriculum' in Skilbeck, M., Lowe, N. and Tait, K. (eds) *A Question of Quality: the core skills project of the Youth Training Scheme in international perspective*. London. MSC/London University, Institute of Education.

Bishop, J. (1991) *Academic Learning and National Productivity*. Ithaca, NY. Center for Advanced Human Resource Studies, New York State School of Industrial Relations, Cornell University.

Blackmore, J. (1990) 'The text and context of vocationalism: issues in post-compulsory curriculum in Australia since 1970'. *Journal of Curriculum Studies* 22(2), p.177.

Blakers, C. (1990) *Youth to Adult in a Changing Society: An Annotated Bibliography*. Canberra. AGPS.

Blakers, C. (1992) *Is Anyone Listening? Young People Speak About Work and Unemployment*. Hawthorn, Victoria. Australian Council for Educational Research.

Borges, J.L. (1979) 'The Gold of Tigers' in *The Book of Sand*. Harmondsworth, Middlesex. Penguin Books.

Bourdieu, P. and Passeron, J.C. (1977) *Reproduction in Education, Society and Culture*. London. Sage.

Bowles, S. and Gintis, H. (1976) *Schooling in Capitalist America*. London. Routledge & Kegan Paul.

Bowman, M.J. (1988) 'Links between general and vocational education: does one enhance the other?' *International Review of Education* 34(2), pp.149–171.

Bridges, D. (1993) 'Transferable skills: a philosophical perspective'. *Studies in Higher Education* 18(1), pp.43–52.

Broadfoot, P. (1992) 'France' in Nisbet, J. (ed.) 'Assessment and curriculum reform'. Draft manuscript. Aberdeen. University of Aberdeen. Mimeo.

Brosio, R.A. (1992) 'Reconstructions: schooling in capitalist America by Samuel Bowles and Herbert Gintis'. *Educational Studies* 23(4), pp. 423–38.

Bryce Report – see Royal Commission on Secondary Education (1895).

Brynner, J. (1992) 'Experiencing vocational preparation in England and Germany'. *Education and Training* 34(4), pp.3–8.

Burgess, T. (1986) *Education for Capability*. Windsor. NFER-Nelson.

Bush, G. (1991) *America 2000: An Education Strategy*. Washington, DC. US Department of Education.

Caillods, F. (1984) 'Education and training for work: the need for an integrated overall planning'. Paris. IIEP. Mimeo.

Callaghan, J. (1976) 'Towards a national debate: the Ruskin College speech'. *Education*, 22 October, pp.332–333.

Campinos-Dubernet, M. (1991) 'Training and automation in production activities: a logic of profiles or of levels?' Paper for conference on Technological Innovation and Economic Change: Pedagogical and Organisational Implications for

Vocational and Technical Education and Training, Sainte-Croix. Paris. OECD. Mimeo.

Cantor, L. (1989) *Vocational Education and Training in the Developed World: A Comparative Study*. London. Routledge.

Carnoy, M. and Levin, H. (1985) *Schooling and Work in the Democratic State*. Stanford, California. Stanford University Press.

Carr Report – see Ministry of Labour and National Service (1958).

Carton, M. (1984) *Education and the World of Work*. Paris. Unesco/IBE.

Cassels, J. (1990) *Britain's Real Skill Shortage and What To Do About It*. London. Policy Studies Institute.

Castro, C.M., Wilson, D.N., Oliveira, J.B. and Nettleton, G. (eds) (1991) *Innovations in Educational and Training Technologies*. Turin. ILO International Training Centre.

CEDEFOP (Centre Européen pour le développement de la formation professionelle) (1981) *Youth Unemployment and Alternance Training in the EEC*. Conference Report. Berlin. CEDEFOP.

Central Advisory Council for Education (England) (1959) *15 to 18*. Crowther Report. London. HMSO.

Central Advisory Council for Education (England) (1963) *Half Our Future*. Newsom Report. London. HMSO.

CEREQ (Centre d'études et de recherches sur les qualifications) (1980) *Recherches sur les compétences professionelles à developper dans les enseignements: analyses du travail dans les systèmes énergétiques-thermiques*. Paris. CEREQ.

CEREQ (1982) *L'informatisation des activités de gestion: mutations en cours et perspectives*. Paris. CEREQ.

CEREQ (1991a) 'Continuing vocational training in France: review and perspectives'. *Training and Employment: French Dimensions* No. 2, winter. Paris. CEREQ.

CEREQ (1991b) 'Initial training and labour-market entry among French youth'. *Training and Employment: French Dimensions* No. 3, spring. Paris. CEREQ.

CERI (Centre for Educational Development and Innovation) (1992) *Adult Illiteracy and Economic Performance*. Paris. OECD/CERI.

Chapman, A. (1985), 'Employment and unemployment in the community'. *Social Europe* No. 2/85, July, p.34.

Chion-Kenney, L. (1992) 'Overview: making school work for all students' in *Hands and Minds: Redefining Success in Vocational Technical Education*. Washington, DC. Education Writers Association.

Chitty, C. (1985) *TVEI: A Perspective for PSEC*. Viewpoints no. 1. Post-16 Education Centre. London. Institute of Education, University of London.

Chitty, C. (1987), 'The commodification of education'. *Forum* 29(3), p.66.

Clarendon Commission (1864) *Report of Her Majesty's Commissioners appointed to inquire into revenues and management of certain colleges and schools, and the studies pursued and instructions given therein; with an Appendix and Evidence*. 4 vols. London. Eyre & Spottiswoode for HMSO.

Colardyn, D. (1990) 'Further education and training of the labour force. Assessment and recognition of skills and competences: developments in France'. Paris. OECD. Mimeo.

Coleman, J.S. (1979) *Equality of Educational Opportunity*. New York. Arno Press.

Coleman, J.S. and Husen, T. (1985) *Becoming Adult in a Changing Society*. Paris. OECD.

Commission of the European Communities (1982) *The Young Europeans*. Brussels. CEC.

Commission of the European Communities (1991a) *Employment in Europe – 1991*. Directorate-General Employment, Industrial Relations and Social Affairs. Luxembourg. CEC.

Commission of the European Communities (1991b) *Vocational Training in the European Community in the 1990s*. Commission Memorandum. Brussels. CEC.

Commission of the European Communities (1992) *From the Single Act to Maastricht and Beyond: The Means to Match Our Ambitions.* Bulletin of the European Communities, Supplement 1/92. Brussels. CEC.

Commission on the Skills of the American Workforce (1990) *America's Choice: High Skills or Low Wages!* Rochester, NY National Center on Education and the Economy.

Commonwealth Secretariat (1987) *Jobs for Young People: A Way to a Better Future.* Report of a Commonwealth Expert Group. London. Commonwealth Secretariat.

Confederation of British Industry (1989) *Towards a Skills Revolution.* Report of the Vocational Education and Training Task Force. London. CBI.

Confederation of British Industry (1993) *Routes for Success. Careership: A Strategy for All 16–19-year-old Learning.* London. CBI.

Connell, W.F. (1980) *A History of Education in the Twentieth Century World.* Canberra. Curriculum Development Centre New York. Teachers' College Columbia University.

Conseil Régionale Poitou-Charentes (1992) *Education, formation et emploi.* Actes du colloque européen en Poitou-Charentes, Poitiers, 15–20 April 1991. Poitiers. Conseil Régionale Poitou-Charentes.

Conseil Supérieur de l'Education (Quebec) (1992) *Le Travail rémunéré des jeunes: vigilance et accompagnement éducatif.* Avis au Ministre de l'Education, Quebec. Sainte-Foy, Quebec. Conseil Supérieur de l'Education.

Coombe, C. (1988) *Survey of Vocationally-Oriented Education in the Commonwealth.* Commonwealth Secretariat Human Resource Development Group Education Programme. London. Commonwealth Secretariat.

COSTAC (Commonwealth/State Training Advisory Committee, Australia) (1990) *A Strategic Framework for the Implementation of a Competency-based Training System.* Report of the COSTAC Working Party on Competency-based Training. Canberra. COSTAC.

Cremin, L.A. (1961) *The Transformation of the School.* New York. Alfred A. Knopf.

Crittenden, B. (1982) *Cultural Pluralism and the Common Curriculum.* Melbourne. Melbourne University Press.

Crowther Report – see Central Advisory Council for Education (1959).

Cuban, L. (1990) 'Reforming again, again, and again'. *Educational Researcher,* No. 19, January–February.

Curtis, S.J. (1967) *History of Education in Great Britain.* London. University Tutorial Press.

Dale, R. (ed.) (1985) *Education, Training and Employment: Towards a New Vocationalism.* Oxford. Pergamon Press.

Dampier, W.C. (1946) *A Shorter History of Science.* Cambridge. Cambridge University Press.

Davie, G.E. (1981) *The Scottish Enlightenment.* London. The Historical Association.

Davis, D. (1988) *School to Work: The EHW Factor.* Melbourne. Nelson.

Dawkins, J.S. (1989) *Improving Australia's Training System.* Canberra. AGPS.

Dean, J. and Steeds, A. (1981) *17 Plus: The New Sixth Form in Schools and FE.* Windsor. NFER-Nelson.

Dearing, R. (1993) *The National Curriculum and its Assessment: Final Report.* London. School Curriculum and Assessment Authority.

Deasy, R. and Penn, I. (1985) 'Implications in the American experience for the assessment of core skills and the credentialling of youth' in Skilbeck, M., Lowe, N. and Tait, K. (eds) *A Question of Quality: the core skills project of the Youth Training Scheme in international perspective.* London. MSC/London University, Institute of Education.

DEET (Department of Employment, Education and Training, Australia) (1991)

Australia's Workforce in the Year 2001. Economic and Policy Analysis Division. Canberra. AGPS.

DEET (1992) *Review 1992.* Canberra. AGPS.

de Leeuw, D., Hertenstein, C., Jackson, M., Lum, B.J., O'Donoghue, S., Rahn, M., Rubin, V., Stern, D. and Whitehurst-Gordon, A. (1992) *Examples of Integrated Academic and Vocational Curriculum from High School Academies in the Oakland School District.* Berkeley. National Center for Research in Vocational Education. University of California.

DENI (1990) *Signposts for the 90s: A Review of Further Education.* Bangor. DENI.

DENI (1991) *Further Education in Northern Ireland: The Road Ahead.* Bangor. DENI.

DENI (1992a) *Aspects of Provision and Response in Education in Northern Ireland 1989–91.* Bangor. DENI.

DENI (1992b) *The Curriculum for 14–19-year-olds: – A Framework for Choice.* Bangor. DENI.

DENI (1992c) *Post-16 Provision in Grammar Schools.* Bangor. DENI.

Department of Labour (1962) *Industrial Training.* Government proposals presented to Parliament. Cmnd 1892. London. HMSO.

DES (1965) *The Organisation of Secondary Education.* Circular 10/65. London. HMSO.

DES (1979) *A View of the Curriculum.* HMI Matters for Discussion Series. London. HMSO.

DES (1981) *Curriculum 11–16: Review of Progress.* London. HMSO.

DES (1982) *17+: A New Qualification.* London. HMSO.

DES (1983) *Curriculum 11–16: Towards a Statement of Entitlement.* London. HMSO.

DES (1985a) *Better Schools.* Cmnd 9469 London. HMSO.

DES (1985b) *Education and Training for Young People.* Cmnd 9482. White Paper. London. HMSO.

DES (1986a) 'Announcing the National Council for Vocational Qualifications'. Press release. London. DES.

DES (1986b) *City Technology Colleges: A New Choice of School.*London. HMSO.

DES (1989) *National Curriculum: From Policy to Practice.* London. DES.

DES (1991) *Educational Design Initiatives in City Technology Colleges.* London. HMSO.

DES/DoE/MSC (1985) *Labour Market Monthly.* London. HMSO.

DES/DoE/Welsh Office (1991) *Education and Training for the Twenty-first Century.* White Paper. Cm 1536. Vol. 1. London. HMSO.

DES/MSC (1985) *Review of Vocational Qualifications in England and Wales.* Interim Report. London. DES.

Dewey, J. (1913) *Vocational Education II.* New York. Teachers College Press.

Dewey, J. (1916) *Democracy and Education.* New York. Macmillan.

DfE (1992) *Choice and Diversity: A New Government Framework for Schools.* Cmnd 2021. London. HMSO.

DfE (1993) 'Patten speeds up new vocational qualifications'. *DfE News,* 5 April, 100/93.

Dickinson, H. and Erben, M. (1983) 'The "technicisation" of morality and culture: a consideration of the work of Claude Grignon and its relevance to further education in Britain' in Gleeson, D. (ed.) *Youth Training and the Search for Work.* London. Routledge & Kegan Paul.

DoE (1988a) *Employment for the 1990s.* White Paper. Cm 540. London. HMSO.

DoE (1988b) *Training for Employment.* White Paper. Cm 316. London. HMSO.

DoE (1990a) *Education Business Partnerships: A Prospectus for TECs and LEAs on the Launch of the Education Business Partnership Initiative.* Sheffield. DoE.

DoE (1990b) *Training Statistics.* Sheffield. DoE.

DoE (1990c) *TVEI Review.* Sheffield. DoE.

DoE (1991a) *Training Credits for Young People: 1991 Prospectus.* Sheffield. DoE.

DoE (1991b) *Training Statistics.* Sheffield. DoE.

DoE (1992) *Training Statistics.* Sheffield. DoE.

DoE (n.d.) *Effective Training Delivery. Youth Training Credits: Learning from Experience.* Developing Good Practice Series. Sheffield. DoE.

DoE/DES (1981) *A New Training Initiative: A Programme for Action.* Cmnd 8455. London. HMSO.

DoE/DES (1984) *Training for Jobs.* Cmnd 9135. London. HMSO.

DoE/DES (1986) *Working Together: Education and Training.* White Paper. London. HMSO.

Dore, R., Bounine-Cabale, J. and Tapiola, K. (1989) *Japan at Work: Markets, Management and Flexibility.* Paris. OECD.

Drake, K. (1991) 'Policy integration and co-operation: a persistent challenge'. Paper for conference on Linkages in Vocational-Technical Education and Training: Challenges – Responses – Actors, Phoenix, Arizona. Paris. OECD. Mimeo.

DTI (1991) *Introducing the Enterprise Initiative.* London. HMSO.

Duncan, R.D. and Kelly, C.J. (1983) *Task Analysis, Learning and the Nature of Transfer.* Manchester. Manpower Services Commission.

Education Writers Association (1992) *Hands and Minds: Redefining Success in Vocational Technical Education.* Washington, DC. Education Writers Association.

Eliasson, G. (1987) *The Knowledge Base of an Industrial Economy.* Stockholm. Almqvist & Wiksell.

Eliasson, G., Fëlster, S., Pousette, T. and Tayman, T. (1990) *The Knowledge Based Information Economy.* Stockholm. Industrial Institute for Economic and Social Research.

Eliasson, R. (1992) *The Changing Role of Vocational and Technical Education and Training (VOTEC): Report from Sweden,* Chapters 1–3. Paris. OECD. Mimeo.

Ellis, P. (1990) *Measures Increasing the Participation of Girls and Women in Technical and Vocational Education and Training: A Caribbean Study.* London. Commonwealth Secretariat.

Employment and Skills Formation Council (1992) *The Australian Vocational Certificate Training System.* Carmichael Report. Canberra. National Board of Employment, Education and Training.

Eraut, M. and Burke, J. (1986) *Improving the Quality of YTS.* University of Sussex Education Area. HMSO.

Ernst, D. and O'Connor, D. (1989) *Technology and Global Competition: The Challenge for Newly Industrialising Economies.* Paris. OECD.

EURYDICE (Education Information Network in the European Community) and CEDEFOP (1991) *Structures of the Education and Initial Training Systems in the Member States of the European Community, 1990.* Brussels. Commission of the European Communities.

Evans, G.T. and Poole, M.E. (n.d.) 'Classifying life skills and implications for the curriculum'. Brisbane. University of Queensland. Mimeo.

Federal Ministry of Education and Science (Germany) (1989a) *Basic and Structural Data: Education Statistics for the Federal Republic of Germany 1989/1990.* Bonn. Federal Ministry of Education and Science.

Federal Ministry of Education and Science (Germany) (1989b) *Report on Vocational Education 1989* No. 3/89, Part 1. Bonn. Federal Ministry of Education and Science.

Feinberg, W. and Horowitz, B. (1990) 'Vocational education and equality of opportunity'. *Journal of Curriculum Studies* 22(2), p.188.

Fensham, P.J. (1986) 'Curriculum for post-compulsory schooling'. *Curriculum Perspectives* 6(1), p.76.

FEU (1979) *A Basis for Choice.* Report of a Study Group on Post-16 Pre-employment Courses. London. HMSO.

FEU (1981) *How Do I Learn?* Project Report PR9. London. FEU.

FEU (1984) *Common Core: Teaching and Learning.* London. FEU.

FEU (1985a) *CPVE in Action: The Evaluation of the 1984/5 Pilot Schemes.* London. FEU.

FEU (1985b) *Signposts.* London. FEU.

FEU (1986) *Aspects of CPVE.* London. DES.

FEU (1993) *Principles for the Development of Core Skills Across the Curriculum.* Dorset. Blackmore Press.

Figueiredo, A. and Steele, R. (1992) 'A trans-European network for education and training'. Conference Paper. The Faro Forum, Portugal. Task Force Recursos Humanos, Educaçao, Formaçao e Juventude. Commission of the European Communities.

Finegold, D (1992) *Breaking Out of the Low-skill Equilibrium.* NCE Briefing No. 5, July. London. National Commission on Education.

Finegold, D., Keep, E., Miliband, D., Raffe, D., Spours, K. and Young, M. (1990) 'A British "baccalauréat": ending the division between education and training'. Education and Training Paper No. 1. London. Institute for Public Policy Research.

Finn, B. (1991) *Young People's Participation in Post Compulsory Education and Training.* Report of the Australian Education Council Review Committee. Canberra. AGPS.

Finn, D. (1987) *Training Without Jobs: New Deals and Broken Promises.* London. Macmillan.

Fitz-Gibbon, C.T., Hazelwood, R.D., Tymms, P.B. and McCabe, C. (1988) 'Performance indicators and the TVEI pilot'. *Evaluation and Research in Education* No. 2, pp.49–60.

Foster, P.J. (1965) 'The vocational school fallacy in development planning' in Anderson, C.A. and Bowman, M.J. (eds) *Education and Economic Development.* Chicago. Aldine.

Freshwater, M.R. (1982) *The Basic Skills Analysis: How a Checklist Can Help Make the Most of Training Opportunities.* Sheffield. MSC Training Services Division, MSC Training Studies.

Further Education Colleges (Scotland) (1990) *Fast Forward with Further Education.* Glasgow. Curriculum Advice and Support Team for Scottish Education Department.

GAO (General Accounting Office, USA) (1991) *Transition from School to Work: Linking Education and Worksite Training.* GAO/HRD-91-105. Washington, DC. GAO.

Gerth, H.H. and Mills, C.W. (1948) *From Max Weber.* London. Routledge & Kegan Paul.

Gibbs, B., Hedge, R. and Clough, E. (eds) (1991) *The Reality of Partnerships: Developing Education Business Partnerships.* Harlow, Essex. Longman.

Gill, C. (1985) *Work, Unemployment and the New Technology.* Cambridge. Polity Press.

Gillmon, E. (1992) *Business Education in the Secondary School: a CTC Response.* London. CTC Trust.

Gipps, C. (1992) 'The United Kingdom' in Nisbet, J. (ed.) 'Assessment and curriculum reform'. Draft manuscript. Aberdeen. University of Aberdeen. Mimeo.

Gleeson, D. (ed.) (1987) *TVEI and Secondary Education: A Critical Appraisal.* Milton Keynes. Open University Press.

Goodlad, J. (1986) 'Core curriculum: what and for whom' in Gorter, R.J. (ed.) *Views on Core Curriculum.* Enschede, Netherlands. National Institute for Curriculum Development.

Gorter, R.J. (ed.) (1986) *Views on Core Curriculum.* Enschede, Netherlands. National Institute for Curriculum Development.

Green, A. (1991) 'The reform of post-16 education and training and the lessons from Europe'. Working Paper No. 11. Post-16 Education Centre. London. Institute of Education, University of London.

BIBLIOGRAPHY

Green, P. (1987) 'A new curriculum at 17? Some issues in the certification of prevocational education'. Occasional Paper No. 1. Post-16 Education Centre. London. Institute of Education, University of London.

Grubb, W.N. (1987) 'Responding to the constancy of change: new technologies and future demands on US education' in Burke, G. and Rumberger, R.W. (eds) *The Future Impact of Technology on Work and Education*. London. Falmer Press.

Grubb, W.N. (1992) 'Postsecondary vocational education and the sub-baccalaureate labor market: new evidence on economic returns'. *Economics of Education Review* 11(3), p.225.

Grubb, W.N. and Lazerson, M. (1982) 'Education and the labour market: recycling the youth problem' in Kantor, H. and Tyack, D.B. (eds) *Work, Youth and Schooling*. Stanford, Calif. Stanford University Press.

Habermas, J. (1989) *The Structural Transformation of the Public Sphere: An Inquiry into a Category of Bourgeois Society*. Cambridge. Polity Press.

Hagedorn, J. (1992) *The Longer School Day and Five Term Year in CTCs: Some Initial Observations*. London. CTC Trust.

Hanley, J. (1993) *Further Education Review Group: Response by Jeremy Hanley, MP, Minister for Education*. Bangor. DENI.

Happ, M.E. (1991) *La Recherche sur l'enseignement secondaire en République Fédérale d'Allemagne*. Colloque de directeurs d'instituts de recherche pédagogique, Saint-Marin, Conseil de la Coopération Culturelle. Strasbourg. Council of Europe. Mimeo.

Hargreaves, D. (1984) *Improving Schools: Report of the Committee on the Curriculum and Organisation of Secondary Schools*. London. ILEA.

Harland, J. (1988) 'Upper secondary curriculum in England and Wales: current developments and emerging structures'. *Journal of Curriculum Studies* 20(5), pp.407–422.

Hayes, F.C. (1985) *Education and Training in Four OECD Countries: A Brief Analysis of Attitudes and Values*. Directorate for Social Affairs, Manpower and Education. Paris. OECD. Mimeo.

Hesketh, B., Andrews, S. and Chandler, P. (n.d.) 'Training for transferable skills: the role of examples and schema'. Sydney. School of Psychology, University of New South Wales. Mimeo.

HMI (1977) *Curriculum 11–16*. London. HMSO.

HMI (1984) *Education for Employees: An HMI Survey of Part-time Release for 16–19-year-olds*. London. HMSO.

HMI (1985) *Report by HM Inspectors on the Youth Training Scheme in Further Education 1983–84*. London. HMSO.

HMI (1987) *Non-Advanced Further Education in Practice*. Department of Education and Science. London. HMSO.

HMI (1989a) *Learning Assignments in Vocational Further Education*. Education Observed 8. Department of Education and Science. London. HMSO.

HMI (1989b) *Post-16 Education and Training: Core Skills*. London. Department of Education and Science.

HMI (1990a) *Aspects of Education in the USA. Vocational and Continuing Education: A Commentary*. Department of Education and Science. London. HMSO.

HMI (1990b) *Work-based Learning in Further Education*. Education Observed. London. HMSO.

HMI (1991a) *Aspects of Upper Secondary and Higher Education in Japan*. Department of Education and Science. London. HMSO.

HMI (1991b) *Aspects of Vocational Education and Training in the Federal Republic of Germany*. Education Observed. Department of Education and Science. London. HMSO.

HMI (1991c) *Mathematics in Vocational Courses in Further Education.* Education Observed. Department of Education and Science. London. HMSO.

HMI (1991d) *National Vocational Qualifications in Further Education 1988–1990.* London. Department of Education and Science.

HMI (1991e) *Technical and Vocational Education Initiative (TVEI) England and Wales 1983–90.* Department of Education and Science. London. HMSO.

Hodges, L. (1987) 'Aptitude tests will sift out CTC high flyers'. *Times Educational Supplement,* 26 June, p.12.

Holland, G. (1987) 'Enterprise in YTS'. *Youth Training News* No. 36, February.

Holmes, E. (1911) *What is and What Might Be.* London. Constable.

Holt, M. (ed.) (1987) *Skills and Vocationalism: The Easy Answer.* Milton Keynes. Open University Press.

Horio, T. (1988) *Educational Thought and Ideology in Modern Japan.* Tokyo. University of Tokyo Press.

Hoyt, K.B. (1976a) *Career Education and the Business–Labor–Industry Communities.* Monographs on Career Education. Washington, DC. Department of Health, Education and Welfare.

Hoyt, K.B. (1976b) *Refining the Career Education Concept: Part I.* Monographs on Career Education. Washington, DC. Department of Health, Education and Welfare.

Hoyt, K.B. (1977) *Refining the Career Education Concept: Part II.* Monographs on Career Education. Washington, DC. Department of Health, Education and Welfare.

Hughes, G. (1991) *Manpower Forecasting: A Review of Methods and Practices in Some OECD Countries.* Report No. 1. Dublin. FAS/ESRI Manpower Forecasting Studies.

Hughes, P. (1992) 'Diversification of secondary education'. Paper for OECD International Education Conference, Hiroshima, October. Paris. OECD. Mimeo.

Hughes, P. (1994) *International Conference on Educational Co-operation in the Asia-Pacific Region.* Paris. OECD.

Hull, D. and Parnell, D. (1991) *Tech Prep Associate Degree: A Win/Win Experience.* Waco, Texas. Center for Occupational Research and Development.

Hultin, M. (1987) *Vocational Education in Developing Countries: A Review of Studies and Project Experience.* Document 34. Stockholm. Swedish International Development Authority. Education Division.

Husén, T. (1982) *A Cross-national Perspective on Assessing the Quality of Learning.* Washington, DC. Department of Education.

Huxley, T.H. (1906) 'On the educational value of the natural history sciences' in his *Man's Place in Nature and Other Essays.* London. J.M. Dent.

Hyland, T. (1993) 'Vocational reconstruction and Dewey's instrumentalism'. *Oxford Review of Education* 19(1), pp. 89–100.

IFAPLAN/ITS (1992) 'Initial training of young people – United Kingdom: an overview of recent developments'. Prepared for the Commission of the European Communities. Brussels. CEC. Mimeo.

ILO (International Labour Office) (1979) *Training Systems in Eastern Europe.* Geneva. ILO.

ILO (1992a) 'Assessment of training aspects of general technical cooperation projects'. Paper for 254th Session of Governing Body. GB.254/OP/2/1. Geneva. ILO. Mimeo.

ILO (1992b) 'Recent events in the United Nations system'. Paper for 252nd Session of Governing Body. GB.252/I0/3/6. Geneva. ILO. Mimeo.

IMS (Institute of Manpower Studies) (1982) *Foundation Training Issues.* Report No. 39. London. IMS.

IMS (1983) *Training for Skill Ownership.* Report No. 68. London. IMS.

IMS (1985) *Competence and Competition: Training and Education in the Federal Republic of Germany, the United States and Japan.* Report by the IMS for the NEDC and the MSC. Hayes Report. London. NEDC/MSC.

Iwaki, H. (1988) 'The organisation and content of studies at the post compulsory level. Country study: Japan'. *Educational Monographs.* Paris. OECD. Mimeo.

Jallade, J.P. (1982) *Alternance Training for Young People: Guidelines for Action.* Berlin. CEDEFOP.

Jallade, J.P. (1985) 'The transition from school to work revisited'. *European Journal of Education* 20(2–3), p.173.

Jarman, T.L. (1963) *Landmarks in the History of Education: English Education as Part of the European Tradition.* London. John Murray.

Jeffrey, A.W. (1985) 'The implications of the core skills and their assessment in Scotland' in Skilbeck, M., Lowe, N. and Tait, K. (eds) *A Question of Quality: the core skills project of the Youth Training Scheme in international perspective.* London. MSC/London University, Institute of Education.

Jencks, C. (1973) *Inequality: A Reassessment of the Effect of Family and Schooling in America.* New York. Harper & Row.

Jessup, G. (1985) *Technical Note on the New Training Initiative: Implications for Standards, Assessment Procedures and Accreditation.* Sheffield. MSC.

Jessup, G. (1987), 'Editorial'. *Competence and Assessment* No. 1.

Jessup, G. (1991) *Outcomes: NVQs and the Emerging Model of Education and Training.* London. Falmer Press.

Johnson, R. (1987) 'Transition from school to work in Western Europe' in Twining, J., Nisbet, S. and Megarry, J. (eds) *Vocational Education.* World Yearbook of Education 1987. London. Kogan Page.

Joint Board for Pre-vocational Education (1984) *The Certificate of Pre-vocational Education: Consultative Document.* London. Joint Board for Pre-vocational Education.

Joint Board for Pre-vocational Education (1985) *The Certificate of Pre-vocational Education. Part A: The CPVE Framework and Criteria for Approval of Schemes.* London. BTEC Publications.

Jonathan, R. (1983) 'The Manpower Service model of education'. *Cambridge Journal of Education* 13(2), pp.3–10.

Jonathan, R. (1987) 'The Youth Training Scheme and core skills: an educational analysis' in Holt, M. (ed.) *Skills and Vocationalism: The Easy Answer.* Milton Keynes. Open University Press.

Jonathan, R. (1990) 'The curriculum and the new vocationalism'. *Journal of Curriculum Studies* 22(2), p.184.

Jones, B. (1982) *Sleepers Wake! Technology and the Future of Work.* Melbourne. Oxford University Press.

Jones, H. and Banks, J. (1985), 'Towards a new form of secondary education for all'. *Social Europe* No. 3/85, p.13.

Jones, R. (1992) *Post-16 Provision in CTCs: Bridging the Divide.* London. CTC Trust.

Kapferer, J.L. (1988) 'Education versus training: youth policy in Britain and Australia'. *Curriculum Perspectives* 8(2), p.1. Australian Curriculum Studies Association.

Kay, C., Fonda, N. and Hayes, C. (1992) 'Growing an innovative workforce: a new approach to vocational education and training'. *Education and Training* 34(3), p.4.

Kennedy, K.J. (1988) 'The policy context of curriculum reform in Australia in the 1980s'. *Australian Journal of Education* 32(3), p.357.

Kilpatrick, W.H. (1929) *The Foundations of Method.* New York. Macmillan.

King, K. (1984) *The Planning of Technical and Vocational Education and Training.* Paris. IIEP/Unesco.

Kirby, P. (1985) *Report of the Committee of Inquiry into Labour Market Programs.* Canberra. AGPS.

Kliebard, H.M. (1986) *The Struggle for the American Curriculum.* London. Routledge & Kegan Paul.

Landes, D.S. (1978) *The Unbound Prometheus: Technological Change and Industrial Development in Western Europe from 1750 to the Present.* Cambridge. Cambridge University Press.

Lantier, F. (1985) 'In the light of the social, cultural and technological changes that are taking place, what is the role of core skills in the training process and what changes would seem to be required in the corresponding curricula?' in Skilbeck, M., Lowe, N. and Tait, K. (eds) *A Question of Quality: the core skills project of the Youth Training Scheme in international perspective.* London. MSC/London University, Institute of Education.

Lauglo, J. (1983), 'Concepts of "general education" and "vocational education" curricula for post-compulsory schooling in western industrialised countries: when shall the twain meet?' *Comparative Education* 19(3), p.285.

Lauglo, J. and Lillis, K. (eds) (1988) *Vocationalising Education: An International Perspective.* Oxford. Pergamon Press.

Lawlor, S. and Miller, A. (1991) 'Partnership issues in the UK' in Gibbs, B., Hedge, R. and Clough, E. (eds) *The Reality of Partnerships: Developing Education Business Partnerships.* Harlow. Longman.

Lawton, D. and Chitty, C. (1987) 'Towards a national curriculum'. *Forum* 30(1), p.4.

Layton, D. (n.d.) 'VET: its changing relations with science and technology education'. Mimeo.

Lee, D., Marsden, D., Rickman, P. and Duncombe, J. (1990) *Scheming for Youth: A Study of YTS in the Enterprise Culture.* Milton Keynes. Open University Press.

Legrand, L. (1983) *Pour un collège démocratique.* Rapport au Ministre de l'Education Nationale. Paris. La Documentation Française.

Levin, H.M. and Rumberger, R.W. (1989) 'Education, work and employment: present issues and future challenges in developed countries'. Paper for 25th Anniversary IIEP Conference. Palo Alto. Stanford University. Mimeo.

Levy, M. (1986) 'Work based learning: tools for transition'. Core Skills Project research report. Blagdon. Further Education Staff College.

Lindauf, H. and Roettig, P.F. (1991) 'Training and development of skilled workers in Austrian industries'. Paper for conference on Technological Innovation and Economic Change: Pedagogical and Organisational Implications for Vocational and Technical Education and Training, Sainte-Croix. Paris. OECD. Mimeo.

Link, F. R. (n.d.) 'Instrumental Enrichment: A Strategy for Cognitive and Academic Improvement' in Link, F.R. (ed.) *Essays on the Intellect.* Alexandria, Va. Association for Supervision and Curriculum Development.

Locke, M. and Bloomfield, J. (1982) *Mapping and Reviewing the Pattern of 16–19 Education: A Working Document for LEAs, Schools and Colleges.* Schools Council Pamphlet 20. London. Schools Council.

Longden, J. (1987) 'School to work in England and Wales' in Twining, J., Nisbet, S. and Megarry, J. (eds) *Vocational Education.* World Yearbook of Education 1987. London. Kogan Page.

Low, G. (1988) 'The MSC: a failure of democracy' in Morris, M. and Griggs, C. (eds) *Education: The Wasted Years? 1973–1985.* Lewes, Sussex. Falmer Press.

Lundgren, U.P. (1980) *The Development of School Curricula as a Context for Work.* Stockholm. Department of Educational Research. Stockholm Institute of Education.

Lundgren, U.P. (1981) *Education as a Context for Work.* Stockholm. Department of Educational Research, Stockholm Institute of Education.

Lynch, J., Modgil, C. and Modgil, S. (eds) (1992) *Education for Cultural Diversity: Convergence and Divergence.* London. Falmer Press.

McClure, A.F., Chrisman, J.R. and Mock, P. (1985) *Education for Work: The Historical Evolution of Vocational and Distributive Education in America*. Cranbury, NJ. Fairleigh Dickinson, Associated University Presses.

Maclure, S. and Davies, P. (eds) (1991) *Learning to Think: Thinking to Learn*. Oxford. Pergamon Press.

McCullogh, G. (1991) *The Secondary Technical School: A Usable Past?* London. Falmer Press.

McDerment, W. (1985) 'Robotics: work organisation and vocational training'. *Vocational Training Bulletin* No. 18, September, 1985/II, p.63.

McFall, J. (1987) 'Summary of vocational qualifications in YTS'. *Youth Training News* No. 39, July.

McMahon, W.W., Jin, H.J. and Boediono (1992) 'Vocational and technical education in development: theoretical analysis of strategic effects on rates of return'. *Economics of Education Review* 11(3), p.181.

McMullen, T. (1985) 'The growing influence of vocational preparation on general education'. *Vocational Training Bulletin* No. 17, July, 1985/I, p.7.

McPhail, T. (1992) 'The role of lead bodies'. *Broadcast* No. 19, pp.20–21.

Mannheim, K. (1943) *Diagnosis of Our Time*. London. Routledge & Kegan Paul.

Mansell, J. and Miller, J. (1987) *The Organisation and Content of Studies at the Post-compulsory Level. Country Study: England and Wales*. Paris. OECD. Mimeo.

Marklund, S. (1988), 'Integration of school and the world of work in Sweden' in Lauglo, J. and Lillis, K. (eds) *Vocationalising Education: An International Perspective*. Oxford. Pergamon Press.

Mathews, J. (1989a) 'From post-industrialism to post-Fordism' *Meanjin* 48(1), p.139.

Mathews, J. (1989b) *Tools of Change: New Technology and the Democratisation of Work*. Sydney. Pluto.

Mathews, J., Hall, G. and Smith, H. (1987) 'Towards flexible skill formation and technological literacy: challenges facing the education system'. Occasional Paper No. 1. Melbourne. Resources Co-ordination Division, Ministry of Education, Victoria.

Mathieson, M. (1992) 'From Crowther to core skills'. *Oxford Review of Education* 18(3), pp.185–199.

Melaville, A.I. and Blank, M.J. (with Gelareh Asayesh) (1993) *Together We Can: A Guide for Crafting a Profamily System of Education and Human Services*. Washington. US Department of Education, Office of Educational Research and Improvement, and US Department of Health and Human Services, Office of the Assistant Secretary for Planning and Evaluation.

Merchier, J. (1991) 'Changing skills in metalworking industries: a review of research'. *Training and Employment: French Dimensions* No. 4, summer. Paris. CEREQ.

Merson, M. (1992) 'The four ages of TVEI: a review of policy'. *British Journal of Education and Work* 5(2), p.5.

Mickel, W. (1982), 'Vocational training systems in the European Community'. *Vocational Training Bulletin* No. 10, December, p.10.

Middleton, J. (1988) 'Changing patterns in vocational education policy planning and research'. Working Paper No. 26. Washington, DC. World Bank.

Ministère de l'Education Nationale (France) (1977) *Savoirs et savoir-faire à l'issue de la scolarité obligatoire*. Paris. Ministère de l'Education Nationale.

Ministère de l'Education Nationale (France) (1992) *L'Etat de l'école: 30 indicateurs sur le système éducatif*. Paris. Ministère de l'Education Nationale.

Ministère de l'Education Nationale (France) (1993) 'Rapport à l'OCDE sur le système éducatif de la France'. Paris. OECD. Mimeo.

Ministry of Education (New Zealand) (1992a) *Mathematics in the National Curriculum: Draft*. Wellington. Ministry of Education.

Ministry of Education (New Zealand) (1992b) *Science in the National Curriculum: Draft.* Wellington. Ministry of Education.

Ministry of Education and Cultural Affairs (Sweden) (1991a) *Growing With Knowledge: A Reform of Upper Secondary and Municipal Adult Education in Sweden.* Government bill and the decisions of Parliament in June 1991. Draft version 2. Stockholm. Ministry of Education and Cultural Affairs. Mimeo.

Ministry of Education and Cultural Affairs (Sweden) (1991b) *The Responsibility for Schools.* Government bill and the decisions of Parliament in December 1990. Draft version 1. Stockholm. Ministry of Education and Cultural Affairs. Mimeo.

Ministry of Education and Science (Sweden) (1992) *The Swedish Way Towards a Learning Society.* Report to the OECD. Stockholm. Ministry of Education and Science.

Ministry of Labour (1982) *Industrial Training: Government Proposals.* Cmnd 1892. London. HMSO.

Ministry of Labour and National Service (1958) *Training for Skill: Recruitment and Training of Young Workers in Industry.* Carr Report. London. HMSO.

Mitter, W. (1987) 'The organisation and content of studies at the post-compulsory level. Country study: Germany'. Educational Monograph. Paris. OECD. Mimeo.

Montagu, A. (1961) *Man in Process.* New York. Mentor Books.

Morris, B. (1972) *Objectives and Perspectives in Education.* London. Routledge & Kegan Paul.

MSC (1977) *Review and Plan.* London. MSC.

MSC (1981a) *A New Training Initiative: A Consultative Document.* London. MSC.

MSC (1981b) *A New Training Initiative: An Agenda for Action.* London. MSC.

MSC (1984a) *Core Skills in YTS, Part 1: Number, Communication, Problem-solving, Practical.* Youth Training Scheme Manual. Sheffield. MSC.

MSC (1984b) *Guide to the Revised Scheme: Design and Content.* YTS. Sheffield. MSC Quality Branch.

MSC (1984c) *TVEI Review 1984: Technical and Vocational Education Initiative.* London. MSC TVEI Unit.

MSC (1985a) *Core Skills in YTS, Part 2: Computer and Information Technology.* Sheffield. MSC.

MSC (1985b) *TVEI Review 85.* Sheffield. MSC.

MSC (1985c) *Working Group on Training Objectives and Content: A Report.* YTS. Sheffield. MSC.

MSC (n.d.) *Pilot YTS Certificate: Part II.* Sheffield. MSC.

MSC/DES (1986) *Review of Vocational Qualifications in England and Wales.* A Report by the Working Group to Review Vocational Qualifications. London. HMSO.

Murata, S., Yamamoto, S. and Ishino, T. (1985) 'Quality in education and training: the role of core skills' in Skilbeck, M., Lowe, N. and Tait, K. (eds) *A Question of Quality: the core skills project of the Youth Training Scheme in international perspective.* London. MSC/London University, Institute of Education.

Murnane, R.J. (1992) 'New challenges for vocational education'. Synthesis Report from an OECD Seminar on the organization and pedagogy of vocational and technical education and training, Sainte-Croix. Paris. OECD. Mimeo.

Murphy, M. (1992) 'Assessment, certification and recognition of occupational skills and competences: Australia'. Paper for conference on The Changing Role of Vocational and Technical Education and Training. Paris. OECD. Mimeo.

Murphy, R., Brown, P. and Partington, J. (1990) *An Evaluation of the Effectiveness of City Technology Colleges' Selection Procedures: A Report of the Department of Education and Science.* Nottingham. School of Education, University of Nottingham.

Murray, M. (1986) 'Recent developments in the school curriculum in France' in Heywood, J. and Matthews, P. (eds) *Technology, Society and the School Curriculum: Practice and Theory in Europe.* Manchester. Roundthorn.

Murray, M. and Heywood, J. (1986) 'Education for work in the Federal Republic of Germany' in Heywood, J. and Matthews, P. (eds) *Technology, Society and the School Curriculum: Practice and Theory in Europe*. Manchester. Roundthorn.

Muthesius, H. (1987) *The English House* [first published in German 1904]. New York. Rizzoli.

Myrberg, M. (1987) 'The organisation and content of studies at the post-compulsory level. Country study: Sweden'. Educational Monographs. Paris. OECD. Mimeo.

Nash, I. (1987), 'Taking the initiative to the most able students'. *Times Educational Supplement*, 4 September, p.14.

National Center for Education Statistics (USA) (1992) *The Condition of Education 1992*. Washington, DC. US Department of Education, Office of Educational Research and Improvement.

National Commission on Education (Paul Hamlyn Foundation) (1993) *Report: Learning to Succeed*. London. Heinemann.

National Commission on Excellence in Education (USA) (1983) *A Nation At Risk*. Washington, DC. Government Printing Office.

National Education Goals Panel (USA) (1992) *Building a Nation of Learners*. Executive Summary: The National Education Goals Report 1992. Washington, DC. National Education Goals Panel.

National Institute of Education (n.d.) *A Comparison of Four Experience-based Career Education Programs*. Washington, DC. US Department of Health, Education and Welfare.

National Training Board (Australia) (1991) *National Competency Standards: Policy and Guidelines*. Canberra. National Training Board.

National Training Task Force (1992) *National Targets for Education and Training*. London. NTTF.

Naylor, F. (1985) *Technical Schools: A Tale of Four Countries*. CPS Policy Study No. 70 London. Centre for Policy Studies.

NCC (1990a) *Annual Report 1989–1990*. York. NCC.

NCC (1990b) *Core Skills 16–19*. York. NCC.

NCC (1990c) *The Whole Curriculum*. Curriculum Guidance Series No. 3. York. NCC.

NCVQ (1987) *National Council for Vocational Qualifications: Its Purposes and Aims*. London. NCVQ.

NCVQ (1990) *Core Skills in NVQs: Response to the Secretary of State*. London. NCVQ.

NCVQ (1992a) 'General NVQs: Draft Information Note', GNVQPG/92/12. 8 April. London. GNVQ Policy Group, NCVQ. Mimeo.

NCVQ (1992b) *National Record of Achievement: Guidance for Schools*. London. NCVQ.

Neave, G. (1984) *The EEC and Education*. Stoke on Trent. Trentham Books/ European Institute of Education and Social Policy.

Neave, G. (1988), 'Policy and response: changing perceptions and priorities in the vocational training policy of the EEC Commission' in Lauglo, J. and Lillis, K. (eds) *Vocationalising Education: An International Perspective*. Oxford. Pergamon Press.

Newcastle Commission (1861) *Elementary Education*. London. HMSO.

Newsom Report – see Central Advisory Council for Education (1963).

New Zealand Qualifications Authority (1991a) *A Qualifications Framework for New Zealand: Developing the National Qualifications Framework*. Wellington. New Zealand Qualifications Authority.

New Zealand Qualifications Authority (1991b) *A Qualifications Framework for New Zealand: The Framework and Schools*. Wellington. New Zealand Qualifications Authority.

Nicholls, A. (1992a) 'Bridging the academic-vocational divide: curriculum developments for the over-16s'. *Education and Training* 34(2), p.18.

Nicholls, A. (1992b) 'Choice with clout'. *Vocational Education and Training*, January, p.8.

Nisbet, J. (ed.) (1992) 'Assessment and curriculum reform'. Draft manuscript. Aberdeen. University of Aberdeen. Mimeo.

Noah, H.J. and Eckstein, M.A. (1988), 'Business and industry involvement with education in Britain, France and Germany' in Lauglo, J. and Lillis, K. (eds) *Vocationalising Education: An International Perspective.* Oxford. Pergamon Press.

Nuttall, D. (1989) 'Measuring social justice in education'. Working Paper No. 4. Melbourne. State Board of Education.

Nuttall, V. (1991) 'Education/industry partnership: past omissions, present progress, future plans'. *Industry Education Links. Developments 14.* Technical and Vocational Education Initiative. Sheffield. Department of Employment.

O'Connor, D. (1987) 'Technological change and the restructuring of the global economy in the post-war period' in Burke, G. and Rumberger, R.W. (eds) *The Future Impact of Technology on Work and Education.* London. Falmer Press.

O'Dell, F. (1988) 'Recent Soviet vocationalisation policies' in Lauglo, J. and Lillis, K. (eds) *Vocationalising Education: An International Perspective.* Oxford. Pergamon Press.

OECD (1979) *Austria: School Policy.* Paris. OECD.

OECD (1981a) *Educational Reforms in Sweden.* Reviews of National Policies for Education. Paris. OECD.

OECD (1981b) *United States: Federal Policies for the Disadvantaged.* Reviews of National Policies for Education. Paris. OECD.

OECD (1982a) *The Challenge of Unemployment.* Report to Labour Ministers. Paris. OECD.

OECD (1982b) 'The competencies needed in working life'. Paris. OECD. Mimeo.

OECD (1982c) 'Towards a guarantee of youth opportunities'. Paper prepared for the OECD by the Education Ministers of Sweden, Norway and Denmark. Paris. OECD. Mimeo.

OECD (1983a) *Compulsory Schooling in a Changing World.* Paris.OECD.

OECD (1983b) *Education and Work: The Views of the Young.* Paris. OECD/CERI.

OECD (1984a) *Improving Youth Employment Opportunities: Policies for Ireland, Portugal.* Paris. OECD.

OECD (1984b) *Youth Employment in France: Recent Strategies.* Paris. OECD.

OECD (1985a) *Comprehensive Education for the Younger Adolescent: Synthesis of Findings of Four Country Review.* Paris. OECD.

OECD (1985b), *Education and Training after Basic Schooling.* Paris. OECD.

OECD (1985c) *Education in Modern Society.* Paris. OECD.

OECD (1985d) *Educational Reforms in Italy.* Reviews of National Policies for Education. Paris. OECD.

OECD (1986a) 'Changing work patterns and the role of education and training'. Paris. OECD/CERI. Mimeo.

OECD (1986b) *Flexibility in the Labour Market: the Current Debate.* Paris. OECD.

OECD (1989a) *Pathways for Learning: Education and Training from 16 to 19.* Paris. OECD.

OECD (1989b) *Schools and Quality: An International Report.* Paris. OECD.

OECD (1991a) *Employment Outlook: July 1991.* Paris. OECD.

OECD (1991b) *Further Education and Training of the Workforce.* Conference Papers. Paris. OECD.

OECD (1992a) '1991–1992 Annual Review: France'. Economic and Development Review Committee. Paris. OECD. Mimeo.

OECD (1992b) *Education at a Glance. OECD indicators.* Paris. OECD/CERI.

OECD (1992c) *High-quality Education and Training for All.* Paris. OECD.

OECD (1992d) 'Labour market policies for the 1990s: Intergovernmental Conference on Further Education and Training of the Labour Force'. Item 4.

Meeting of the Employment, Labour and Social Affairs Committee at Ministerial Level. Paris. OECD. Mimeo.

OECD (1992e) 'Labour market policies for the 1990s: issues for discussion'. Item 4. Meeting of the Employment, Labour and Social Affairs Committee at Ministerial Level. Paris. OECD. Mimeo.

OECD (1992f) *New Directions in Work Organisation: The Industrial Relations Response.* Paris. OECD.

OECD (1992g) *Schools and Business: A New Partnership.* Paris. OECD/CERI.

OECD (1992h) *Science and Technology Policy: Review and Outlook 1991.* Paris. OECD.

OECD (1992i) *Technology and the Economy: The Key Relationships.* The Technology/ Economy Programme. Paris. OECD.

OECD (1993a) *Education at a Glance. OECD Indicators.* 2nd Edition. Paris. OECD.

OECD (1993b) *Higher Education and Employment: Synthesis Report.* Paris. OECD.

OECD (1994) *Employment/Unemployment Report to Ministers.* Paris. OECD, in press.

Oxenham, J. (1988), 'What do employers want from education?' in Lauglo, J. and Lillis, K. (eds) *Vocationalising Education: An International Perspective.* Oxford. Pergamon Press.

Papadopoulos, G. (1991) 'Linkages in vocational–technical education and training: synthesis of discussions'. Conference on The Changing Role of Vocational and Technical Education and Training, Phoenix, Arizona. OECD. Paris. Mimeo.

Passmore, J. (1970) *The Perfectibility of Man.* London. Duckworth.

Peters, R.S. (1966) *Ethics and Education.* London. George Allen & Unwin.

Pignatelli, F. (1987) 'The Technical and Vocational Education Initiative and Scottish educational developments' in Twining, J., Nisbet, S. and Megarry, J. (eds) *Vocational Education.* World Yearbook of Education 1987. London. Kogan Page.

Piore, M. and Sabel, C. (1984) *The Second Industrial Divide.* New York. Basic Books.

Pratzner, F.C. and Russell, J.F. (1984) *The Changing Workplace: Implications of Quality of Work Life Developments for Vocational Education.* Columbus, Ohio. National Center for Research in Vocational Education.

Pring, R., White, R. and Brockington, D. (1988) *14–18 Education and Training: Making Sense of the National Curriculum and the New Vocationalism? A Discussion Document.* Bristol. Youth Education Service.

Pritchard, R.M.O. (1992) 'The German dual system: educational utopia'. *Comparative Education* 28(2), p.131.

Public Law 101 (USA) (1990) *Carl D. Perkins Vocational and Applied Technology Education Act Amendments of 1990.* Public Law 101-392-Sept.25, 1990. Washington, DC.

Quick, R.H. (1895) *Essays on Educational Reformers,* Chapters VII, VIII, XII, XIII. London. Longmans, Green.

Raffe, D. (1991) 'Compulsory education and what then? Signals, choices, pathways'. Paper for conference on Linkages in Vocational–Technical Education, Phoenix, Arizona. Paris. OECD. Mimeo.

Raffe, D. (1992) *Participation of 16–18-year-olds in Education and Training.* NCE Briefing No. 3, May. London. National Commission on Education.

Raizen, S.A. (1991) 'Learning and work: the research base'. Discussion paper for OECD Conference on Vocational and Technical Education, March. Paris. OECD. Mimeo.

Rao, T.V., Wright, C. and Mukherjee, H. (1990) *Designing Entrepreneurial Skills Development Programmes: Resource Book for Technical and Vocational Institutions.* London. Commonwealth Secretariat.

Raup, R.B., Axtelle, G.E., Benne, K.D. and Smith, B.O. (1943) *The Improvement of Practical Intelligence.* New York. Harper.

Raven, J. (1984) *Competence in Modern Society: Its Identification, Development and*

Release. London. H.K. Lewis.

Raven, J. (1991) 'Developper les aptitudes et les compétences de tous les enfants'. Atelier de Recherche pédagogique sur les Enfants et Adolescents doués – Recherche et Education en Europe, Nijmegen. DESC/Rech (91)3. Strasbourg. Council of Europe. Mimeo.

Ravitch, D. (1983) *The Troubled Crusade: American Education 1945–1980.* New York. Basic Books.

Rawkins, P. (1993) *Human Resource Development in the Aid Process.* Ottawa. North–South Institute.

Reisse, W. (1992) 'Assessment, certification and recognition of occupational skills and competences: Germany'. Paper for conference on The Changing Role of Vocational and Technical Education and Training, Porto. Paris. OECD. Mimeo.

Rentznik, L, Spielmann, A., Brandenberg, J. and Stauffer, M. (1991) 'Co-ordinating learning in schools and enterprises: roles and responsibilities in view of techno- logical innovation'. Paper for conference on Technological Innovation and Eco- nomic Change: Pedagogical and Organisational Implications for Vocational and Technical Education and Training, Sainte-Croix. Paris. OECD. Mimeo.

Reutersward, A. (1992) 'Vocational training (Japan)'. Paper for OECD study on Public Employment Service in Japan, the UK, Spain and Norway. Paris. OECD. Mimeo.

Review Group on Further Education (1992) *Report to the Minister for Education on the Planning and Funding of Further Education Provision in Northern Ireland.* Bangor. DENI.

Roderick, G.Y. and Stephens, M. (1982) *The British Malaise: Industrial Performance, Education and Training in Britain Today.* Barcombe. Falmer Press.

Rojot, J. and Tergeist, P. (1992) 'Overview: industrial relations trends, internal labour market flexibility and work organisation' in *New Directions in Work Organ- isation.* Paris. OECD.

Romer, P.M. (1990) *Human Capital and Growth: Theory and Evidence.* Carnegie- Rochester Conference Series on Public Policy No. 32.

Royal Commission on Secondary Education (1895) *Report of the Commissioners.* Cmnd 7862. Bryce Report. 9 vols. London. Eyre & Spottiswoode for HMSO.

Rubber and Plastics Processing Industry Training Board (1982) *The Way Forward: A Practical Proposal for Introducing Change in School Curricula.* Fourth Report of the Study Group on the Education/Training of Young People. Brentford, Middx. Rubber and Plastics Processing Industry Training Board.

Rubinstein, W.D. (1977) 'Wealth, elites and the class structure of modern Britain'. *Past and Present* No. 76, August, p.99.

Ruby, A. (1992) '"If Freeman Butts calls tell him we might be changing course": a perspective on the competency movement and Australia's schools'. Paper for conference on Higher Education and the Competency Movement. Canberra. Centre for Continuing Education, Australian National University. Mimeo.

Rumberger, R.W. (1987) 'The potential impact of technology on the skill require- ments of future jobs in the United States' in Burke, G. and Rumberger, R.W. (eds) *The Future Impact of Technology on Work and Education.* London. Falmer Press.

Sadler, M.E. (ed.) (1902) *Education in Germany.* Board of Education, Special Reports on Educational Subjects Vol. 9. London. HMSO.

Sadler, P. (1989) 'Assessment and accreditation: TVEI, CPVE, and external examin- ations' in Warwick, D. (ed.) *Linking Schools and Industry.* Oxford. Blackwell.

Sako, M. (1991) 'The role of employers and unions in facilitating transition to employment and further learning'. Paper for conference on Linkages in Vocational-Technical Education and Training: Challenges – Responses – Actors, Phoenix, Arizona. Paris. OECD. Mimeo.

Samuelson Commission (1884) *Second Report of the Royal Commissioners on Technical Instruction.* 6 vols. London. Eyre & Spottiswoode for HMSO.

Saunders, L. (1992) 'The work-related curriculum: the new entitlement?' Annual Conference Paper. Slough, Berks. National Foundation for Educational Research. Mimeo.

SCANS (The Secretary's Commission on Achieving Necessary Skills) (1991) *What Work Requires of Schools.* A SCANS Report for America 2000. Washington, DC. US Department of Labor.

Schools Council for Curriculum and Examinations (1972) *16–19 Growth and Response. 1: Curricular Bases.* Working Paper No. 45. London. Evans/Methuen.

Schools Council (1983) *Planning One-year 16–17 Courses: A Follow-up to 'The Practical Curriculum' for LEAs, Schools and Colleges.* Schools Council Pamphlet No. 21. London. Schools Council.

Schools Inquiry (Taunton) Commission (1867) *Report Relative to Technical Education.* Cmnd 3898. Chairman Henry Labouchere, 1st Baron Taunton. London. Eyre & Spottiswoode for HMSO.

Schools Inquiry (Taunton) Commission (1868) *Report of the Commissioners.* Cmnd 3966. Chairman: Henry Labouchere, 1st Baron Taunton. 21 vols. London. Eyre and Spottiswoode for HMSO.

Schwartz, B. (1991) 'The accusations which are made against the schools are sometimes very violent'. *Workers in Education,* 20 August, IFTU/SPIE/IUFL, p.11.

Scott, M. (1989) *A New View of Economic Growth.* London. Oxford University Press.

Scottish Education Department (1977) *The Structure of the Curriculum in the Third and Fourth Years of the Scottish Secondary School.* Munn Report. Edinburgh. HMSO.

Scottish Enterprise (1992) *Strategies for the 1990s.* Glasgow. Scottish Enterprise.

Scottish Office (1991) *Access and Opportunity: A Strategy for Education and Training.* Cm 1530. Edinburgh. HMSO.

Scottish Office Education Department (1992) *Upper Secondary Education in Scotland.* Report of the Committee to Review Curriculum and Examinations in the Fifth and Sixth Years of Secondary Education in Scotland. Howie Report. Edinburgh. HMSO.

Sellin, B. (1983), 'The development of alternance training for young people in the European Community'. *Vocational Training Bulletin* No. 12, September, p.73.

Sellin, B. (1985) 'Alternance training for young people and adults'. *Vocational Training Bulletin* No. 18, September, 1985/II, p.21.

Shapin, S. and Barnes, B. (1976) 'Head and hand: rhetorical resources in British pedagogical writing, 1770–1850'. *Oxford Review of Education* 2(3), pp.231–253.

Shaw, G.B. (1907) *Major Barbara.* Edited by H.F. Brooks. Harlow. Longman.

Simon, B. (1960) *Studies in the History of Education 1780–1870.* London. Lawrence & Wishart.

Simons, D. (1966) *Georg Kerschensteiner.* London. Methuen.

Singh, R.R. (1991) *Education for the Twenty-First Century: Asia-Pacific Perspectives.* Bangkok. Unesco Principal Regional Office for Asia and the Pacific.

Skilbeck, M. (1984a) 'Curriculum development: from RDD to RED: Review, Evaluate, Develop' in Nisbet, M. (ed.) *World Yearbook of Education 1984/5.* London. Kogan Page.

Skilbeck, M. (1984b) *School-based Curriculum Development.* London. Harper & Row.

Skilbeck, M. (1985) *A Core Curriculum for the Common School.* London. Institute of Education, University of London.

Skilbeck, M. (1990) *Curriculum Reform: An Overview of Trends.* Paris. OECD.

Skilbeck, M., Lowe, N. and Tait, K. (eds) (1985) *A Question of Quality: The Core Skills Project of the Youth Training Scheme in International Perspective.* London. MSC/

London University, Institute of Education.

Smail, J.C. (1914) *Trade and Technical Education in Germany and France.* London. LCC.

Smith, B.O., Stanley, W.O. and Shores, H.J. (1957) *Fundamentals of Curriculum Development.* New York. Harcourt Brace & World.

Smith, K. (1984) *The British Economic Crisis.* Harmondsworth, Middx. Penguin.

Smithers, A. and Robinson, P. (1991) *Beyond Compulsory Schooling: A Numerical Picture.* London. Council for Industry and Higher Education.

Sorge, A. (1984) *Technological Change, Employment, Qualifications and Training.* Berlin. CEDEFOP.

Spens, W. (1938) *Board of Education Report of the Consultative Committee on Secondary Education with Special Reference to Grammar Schools and Technical High Schools.* The Spens Report. London. HMSO.

Stacey, N. (1988) 'Education and training of 16–19-year-olds after compulsory schooling in the United States'. Paris. OECD. Mimeo.

Stanton, G. (1992) 'Further education: choices and challenges for the 1990s'. Annual Conference Paper. Slough, Berks. National Foundation for Educational Research. Mimeo.

Statistics Sweden (1991) *Education in Sweden 1991: Facts and Figures.* Stockholm. Statistics Sweden.

Steedman, H. (1992) 'Assessment, certification and recognition of occupational skills and competences: issues and questions'. Paper for conference on The Changing Role of Vocational and Technical Education and Training, Porto. Paris. OECD. Mimeo.

Stern, D., Raby, M. and Dayton, C. (1992) *Career Academies: Partnerships for Reconstructing American High Schools.* San Francisco. Jossey-Bass.

Stradling, R. (1992) 'Pre-vocational education and training: lessons from Europe'. Annual Conference Paper. Slough, Berks. National Foundation for Educational Research. Mimeo.

Straw, J. (1992) *Modernising Post-16 Education and Training.* London. Labour Party.

Stronach, I. (1987), 'Ten years on'. *Forum* 29(3), p.64.

Sutherland, M. (1992) 'Germany' in Nisbet, J. (ed.) 'Assessment and curriculum reform'. Draft manuscript. Aberdeen. University of Aberdeen. Mimeo.

Sweet, R. (1987) 'Australian trends in skill requirements' in Burke, G. and Rumberger, R.W. (eds) *The Future Impact of Technology on Work and Education.* London. Falmer Press.

Sweet, R. (1988) 'What do developments in the labour market imply for post-compulsory education in Australia?'. *Australian Journal of Education* 32(3), p.331.

Taylor, R.E. (1981) 'The effects of vocational education on participants'. Paris. OECD. Mimeo.

Taylor, R.E., Kline, B., Ashmore, M.C., Ashley, W.M. and Lotto, L. (1985) 'Vocational education and economic development in the United States'. Paper for Joint Meeting of the National Association of State Directors of Vocational Education, the National Center for Research in Vocational Education and the OECD. Paris. OECD. Mimeo.

Taunton Report – see Schools Inquiry (Taunton) Commission (1867, 1868).

Tolley, G. (1986) 'Putting labels on people: the qualifications business'. *Journal of the Royal Society of Arts* No. 5363, Vol. CXXXIV, p.707–719.

Tomlins, B. and Miles, J. (1992) 'Reorganizing post-16 education: the tertiary option'. Annual Conference Paper. Slough, Berks. National Foundation for Educational Research. Mimeo.

Trades Union Congress (1989) *Skills 2000.* London. TUC.

Training and Employment Agency (1992) *Corporate Plan 1992–95.* Belfast. Training and Employment Agency.

Tuck, R. (1992) 'Assessment, Certification and Recognition of Occupational Skills and Competences. United Kingdom: Scotland'. Paper for conference on The Changing Role of Vocational and Technical Education and Training, Porto. Paris. OECD. Mimeo.

Twining, J., Nisbet, S. and Megarry, J. (eds) (1987) *Vocational Education*. World Yearbook of Education 1987. London. Kogan Page.

Unesco (1990) *Innovative Education for Promoting the Enterprise Competencies of Children and Youth*. Bangkok. Unesco Principal Office for Asia and the Pacific.

Unesco (1991) 'The role of technical and vocational education and its part in and contribution to the efforts undertaken towards basic education for all'. Paper for General Conference, Twenty-sixth Session, Paris. Paris. Unesco.

Unesco (1992) 'Unevoc in brief: international project on technical and vocational education'. Paris. Unesco. Mimeo.

van Rensburg, D.J.J. (1992) 'The changing needs and the correct mix of skills for a national manpower force'. Pretoria. Technikon Pretoria. Mimeo.

Vickers, M. (1991) *Building a National System for School-to-Work Transition: Lessons from Britain and Australia*. Somerville, Mass. Jobs for the Future.

Vorbeck, M. (1985) 'Council of Europe: education and training for young people aged 16 to 19: problems and tendencies'. *Vocational Training Bulletin* No. 17, July 1985/1, p.51.

Walker, D. (1993) 'A hybrid takes firm root'. *Times Educational Supplement*, 30 April, pp.10–11.

Walker, J. (1987) *School, Work and the Problems of Young People: A Cultural Approach to Curriculum Development*. Canberra. Curriculum Development Centre.

Ward, C. (1987) 'Qualifications and assessment of vocational education and training in the UK' in Twining, J., Nisbet, S. and Megarry, J. (eds) *Vocational Education*. World Yearbook of Education 1987. London. Kogan Page.

Warnat, W. (1992) 'Assessment, certification and recognition of occupational skills and competencies: the United States experience'. Paper for conference on The Changing Role of Vocational and Technical Education and Training, Porto. Paris. OECD. Mimeo.

Watson, J. (1991) 'The French Baccalauréat Professionel'. Working Paper No. 9. Post-16 Education Centre. London. Institute of Education, University of London.

Watts, A.G. (1980) *Work Experience Programs: The Views of British Youth*. Paris. CERI/OECD.

Webb, S. (1903) *London Education*. London. Longmans, Green.

Wellens, J. (1963) *The Training Revolution: From Shop-floor to Board-room*. London. Evans.

White, J. (1984) 'Learning to take it with you'. Draft manuscript, Institute of Education, University of London.

Whitehead, A.N. (1950) 'Technical education and its relation to science and literature' [1917] in *The Aims of Education and Other Essays*. London. Benn.

Wiener, M.J. (1981) *English Culture and the Decline of the Industrial Spirit 1850–1980*. Cambridge. Cambridge University Press.

Williams, R. (1975) *The Country and the City*. St. Albans, Herts. Paladin.

Williams, S. *et al.* (1981) *Youth Without Work: Three Countries Approach the Problem*. Paris. OECD.

Wilms, B. and Wilms, W.W. (1986) 'Captured by the American dream: vocational education in the United States'. Paper given at the Vocationalising Education Conference, Stockholm, 7–9 May, organised by the Institute of Education, University of London.

Wilms, W.W. and Hansell, S. (1982) 'The dubious promise of post-secondary vocational education: its pay-off to drop-outs and graduates in the USA'. *International Journal of Educational Development* 2(1), pp.43–59.

Wilson, D.N. (1990) 'Reform of technical–vocational education'. *La Educacion Revista InterAmericana de Desarrollo Educativo.* No. 107, pp.77–115.

Wilson, D.N. and Arce, J.F. (1991) 'Innovations in educational technology for vocational training' in Castro, C.M., Wilson, D.N., Oliveira, J.B. and Nettleton, G. (eds) *Innovations in Educational and Training Technologies.* Turin. ILO International Training Centre.

Woolhouse, J. (1985) 'The management of change in the curriculum'. Stanley Lecture. London. Royal Society of Arts.

Woolhouse, J. (1991) 'Vocational education and training in Britain and Europe'. Address delivered at NFER Member's Conference. Slough,Berks. National Foundation for Educational Research. Mimeo.

World Bank (1990) *The Dividend of Learning: World Bank Support for Learning.* Washington, DC. World Bank.

World Bank (1991) *Vocational and Technical Education and Training: A World Bank Policy Paper.* Washington, DC. World Bank.

Wray, M.J., Moor, C. and Hill, S. (1980) *Unified Vocational Preparation: An Evaluation of the Pilot Programme.* Windsor. NFER.

Wrench, J. (1987) 'The unfinished bridge: YTS and black youth' in Toyna, B. (ed.) *Racial Inequality in Education.* London. Tavistock.

Wright, C. (1992) 'What employers want from education'. Annual Conference Paper. Slough, Berks. National Foundation for Educational Research. Mimeo.

Yoshio, K. (1992) 'Higher education and employment: the changing relationship. The case of the humanities and social sciences. Country report: Japan'. Paris. OECD. Mimeo.

Young, D. (1982) 'Helping the young help themselves'. *Times Education Supplement,* 26 November.

Young, G.M. (1953) *Victorian England: Portrait of an Age.* London. Oxford University Press.

YTS (1984a) *Guide to the Revised Scheme Design and Content.* Sheffield. MSC.

YTS (1984b) *Guide to Scheme Design and Content.* March. Sheffield. MSC.

YTS (1985) *Guide to Scheme Design and Content.* Sheffield. MSC.

YTS (1987) 'Providers' briefing'. *Youth Training News* No. 38, June.

INDEX